The Americans Are Coming!

9/21/12

To Walker,

Hope to see you in class one day!

Best,
Robert Williams

NEW AFRICAN HISTORIES SERIES

Series editors: Jean Allman and Allen Isaacman

*Books in this series are published with support from
the Ohio University National Resource Center for African Studies.*

David William Cohen and E. S. Atieno Odhiambo, *The Risks of
Knowledge: Investigations into the Death of the Hon. Minister
John Robert Ouko in Kenya, 1990*

Belinda Bozzoli, *Theatres of Struggle and the End of Apartheid*

Gary Kynoch, *We Are Fighting the World: A History of Marashea
Gangs in South Africa, 1947–1999*

Stephanie Newell, *The Forger's Tale: The Search for Odeziaku*

Jacob A. Tropp, *Natures of Colonial Change: Environmental
Relations in the Making of the Transkei*

Jan Bender Shetler, *Imagining Serengeti: A History of Landscape
Memory in Tanzania from Earliest Times to the Present*

Cheikh Anta Babou, *Fighting the Greater Jihad: Amadu Bamba
and the Founding of the Muridiyya in Senegal, 1853–1913*

Marc Epprecht, *Heterosexual Africa? The History of an Idea from
the Age of Exploration to the Age of AIDS*

Marissa J. Moorman, *Intonations: A Social History of Music and
Nation in Luanda, Angola, from 1945 to Recent Times*

Karen E. Flint, *Healing Traditions: African Medicine, Cultural
Exchange, and Competition in South Africa, 1820–1948*

Derek R. Peterson and Giacomo Macola, editors, *Recasting the
Past: History Writing and Political Work in Modern Africa*

Moses Ochonu, *Colonial Meltdown: Northern Nigeria in the
Great Depression*

Emily Burrill, Richard Roberts, and Elizabeth Thornberry,
editors, *Domestic Violence and the Law in Colonial and
Postcolonial Africa*

Daniel R. Magaziner, *The Law and the Prophets: Black
Consciousness in South Africa, 1968–1977*

Emily Lynn Osborn, *Our New Husbands Are Here: Households,
Gender, and Politics in a West African State from the Slave
Trade to Colonial Rule*

Robert Trent Vinson, *The Americans Are Coming! Dreams of
African American Liberation in Segregationist South Africa*

The Americans Are Coming!

Dreams of African American Liberation
in Segregationist South Africa

෪

Robert Trent Vinson

OHIO UNIVERSITY PRESS ෪ ATHENS

Ohio University Press, Athens, Ohio 45701
ohioswallow.com
© 2012 by Ohio University Press
All rights reserved

Printed in the United States of America
Ohio University Press books are printed on acid-free paper ∞ ™

20 19 18 17 16 15 14 13 12   5 4 3 2

Portions of chapter 1 appeared in an earlier form in the author's article "Citizenship
over Race? African Americans in U.S.–South African Diplomacy, 1890–1925,"
Safundi: The Journal of South African and American Comparative Studies 5, nos. 1–2
(April 2004): 13–32. Used by permission of Taylor and Francis Group,
http://www.informaworld.com.

Some material also has appeared in a different form in the author's "'Sea Kaffirs':
American Negroes and the Gospel of Garveyism in Segregationist South Africa,"
Journal of African History 47, no. 2 (July 2006); and in "Providential Design:
American Negroes and Garveyism in South Africa," from *From Toussaint to Tupac:
The Black International since the Age of Revolution*, edited by
Michael O. West, William G. Martin, and Fanon Che Wilkins.
Copyright © 2009 by the University of North Carolina Press.
Used by permission of the publisher. www.uncpress.unc.edu

Library of Congress Cataloging-in-Publication Data

Vinson, Robert Trent.
The Americans are coming! : dreams of African American liberation in segregationist
South Africa / Robert Trent Vinson.
    p. cm. — (New African histories)
Includes bibliographical references and index.
ISBN 978-0-8214-1986-1 (pb : alk. paper)
1. Black nationalism—South Africa. 2. African Americans—Relations with Africans.
3. United States—Foreign public opinion, South African. 4. Blacks—South
Africa—Attitudes. 5. Garvey, Marcus, 1887–1940—Influence. 6. Universal Negro
Improvement Association. I. Title.
DT1756.V56 2011
320.54'60968—dc23

                                    2011040795

To my wife, Iyabo,
my daughter, Thandi,
and my mother, Roslyn,
all of whom hold up the sky

Contents

Illustrations

Preface

IN A sense, *The Americans Are Coming!* developed long before I entered academia. As a teenager in mid-1980s Los Angeles, like many young black males I had several unhappy experiences with police officers who responded to the crack epidemic and the more violent gang activity of that time by occupying our neighborhood with constantly circling helicopters equipped with spotlights, nicknamed "ghetto birds," and armored tanks, known as "batter rams," that demolished the homes of suspected drug dealers. Though the intensive after-school tennis lessons that led to a tennis scholarship to the University of Nevada–Las Vegas helped me steer clear of the gangs and drug dealers, more than once I was interrogated and beaten by white police officers for no apparent reason other than being young, black, and male.

At the same time, I saw television images of white police officers beating black people in apartheid South Africa and civil rights veterans Jesse Jackson, Rosa Parks, and Coretta Scott King protesting before the South African embassy in Washington, D.C. I read of African independence leaders such as Kwame Nkrumah and of black internationalists such as Malcolm X and Marcus Garvey, leader of an earlier incarnation of the global black politics of the antiapartheid movement (particularly his classic *Philosophy and Opinions of Marcus Garvey*). There were two South Africans—one black, one white—on my Nevada–Las Vegas tennis team, best friends bound together by their exiled status and their opposition to the apartheid regime. I became the top player on my college team and dreamed of pursuing a professional tennis career, but I wore T-shirts with images of a still jailed Nelson Mandela and sang antiapartheid lyrics of hip-hop groups like Public Enemy and reggae artists like Bob Marley, Black Uhuru, and Steel Pulse.

I soon discovered that a respectable college tennis career would be my ceiling in the sport, and in my last year in college, I joined with community organizers and other students to form a study group and tutorial service named after Garvey's School of African Philosophy. A professor suggested that I explore my interest in global black history in graduate school, and this led me, in turn, to Howard University to study with Joseph E. Harris, the dean of African diaspora studies. My doctoral dissertation was on Garveyism in the interwar years in South Africa. It was the first extended study on that topic.

Although I had known since graduate school that Africans had viewed "American Negroes" as role models since 1890, I realized more deeply the implications of that fact during my first years of teaching at Washington University in St. Louis, then at the College of William and Mary. Garvey was not the first. I understood Africans' deep despair and disillusionment with white rule and their high hopes that American Negroes would liberate them.

I began to conceive of a book that would be the first manuscript on Garveyism in South Africa and would also contextualize and explain the power of the long-standing African admiration for American Negro achievement despite centuries of slavery and Jim Crowism. Therefore, I have written *The Americans Are Coming!* to explore, track, and analyze a half century of the transatlantic movements of peoples, ideologies, and institutions that created and deepened the multifaceted relationships—political, economic, religious, and educational—that formed unbreakable bonds between South Africans and American Negroes.

Acknowledgments

MY NAME is on the cover of this book, but I could not have written it without the love, care, and support of countless people who sustained me as a person. The Vinson, McClendon, Olive, Osiapem, and Harvey families have been bedrocks. Of particular importance has been my mother, Roslyn Vinson-Henry, whose enthusiastic energy and moves to all five boroughs of New York and then to Los Angeles made inevitable my interest in people and ideas in motion. My grandmother, Josephine Vinson, has always been my greatest cheerleader. In Los Angeles, Richard Williams taught me, in a relatively short time, to play tennis at a level that earned me a tennis scholarship to the University of Nevada–Las Vegas. Over the past forty years, he and his brother Fred have trained hundreds of inner city kids to play well enough to earn college tennis scholarships. They are unsung heroes who touched my life in unimaginable ways. The Rancho Cienega Tennis Club members were my extended family who looked after me on and off the tennis court. In college, Larry Easley, Mack McLaurin, York Strother, and Craig Witcher were all important tennis coaches who guided my development, and Douglas Imig, Sharon McKeand, and Thomas Wright were particularly important professorial role models who opened my eyes to the wondrous possibilities of academia.

The faculty in the Departments of History and Africana Studies at Howard University were important mentors, particularly the Africanists and African-Americanists, Boubacar Barry, Aziz Batran, Eileen Boris, Robert Edgar, Joseph E. Harris, Linda Heywood, Elizabeth Clark-Lewis, Edna Medford, Adell Patton, Joseph Reidy, Ibrahim Sundiata, Arnold Taylor, Emory Tolbert, and Jeanne Toungara. I must also thank Deans Johnetta Davis, Joseph Reidy, and Orlando Taylor, the Kinnard family, Mary Ann Larkin, and Patric Pepper for crucial support during the Howard years. The research staffs at the Moorland-Spingarn Research Center at Howard University; the Schomburg Center for Research in Black Culture at the New York Public Library; the National Archives and Research Administration in College Park, Maryland, and Washington, D.C.; the Manuscript, Archives, and Rare Book Library at Emory University; and the Public Records Office in London were invaluable.

In South Africa, the research staffs at the National Archives of South Africa in Pretoria, Pietermaritzburg, and Cape Town; the University of Cape Town (particularly Allegra Louw); the University of the Western Cape; the University of the Witwatersrand; and the National Library of South Africa went the extra mile with typical South African courtesy and good humor. Support for the research and writing of this book came from the Sasakawa Foundation, the Carter G. Woodson Center at the University of Virginia, Washington University in St. Louis, and the College of William and Mary.

Rosanne Adderley, Mohamed Adhikari, Peter Alegi, David Anthony, Doug Anthony, Keletso Atkins, Theresa Barnes, Iris Berger, Iver Bernstein, Edda Fields-Black, Howard Brick, Leslie Brown, Tamara Brown, Judi Byfield, James Campbell, Rudolph Clay, Clifton Crais, Roger Davidson, Garrett Albert Duncan, Mary Ann Dzuback, Gerald Early, Holly Fisher, Andrea Friedman, Maggie Garb, Michael Gomez, Rick Halpern, Jerome Handler, Joseph Harris, Catherine Higgs, Sean Jacobs, Sheridan Johns, Ida Jones, Barbara Josiah, Robin D. G. Kelley, Amanda Kemp, Joyce Kirk, Peter Kastor, David Koenig, Paul Landau, Rebekah Lee, Alex Lichtenstein, Brown Bavusile Maaba, Anne Mager, Shula Marks, John Mason, Marya McQuirter, Rolland Murray, Bill Nasson, Sue Newton-King, Linda Nicholson, Kim Norwood, Shanti Parikh, Dylan Penningroth, Rendani Moses Ralinala, Marcus Rediker, Christopher Saunders, Emminette Sawyer, Lester Spence, Jill Stratton, Ben Talton, Joe Thompson, Annie Valk, Corey D. G. Walker, Yohuru Williams, Leslie Witz, and Carol Camp Yeakey are among the many persons who supported me on this long and winding road. In South Africa, the Brooks, King, Louw, Lyner, and Timm families were wonderful hosts, friends, and collaborators who tolerated the sudden appearances and disappearances of a wandering American. I cannot thank enough Bobby Hill, whose Marcus Garvey and UNIA papers are pioneering models of scholarship and powerful evidence of his dogged global pursuit of Garvey-related documents to which every Garvey scholar owes a very deep debt. Other Garvey scholars deserving of thanks include Ramla Bandele, Tshepo Masango Chery, Natanya Duncan, Adam Ewing, Steven Hahn, Claudrena Harold, Jahi Issa, Rupert Lewis, Mary Rolinson, Jarod Roll, James Spady, and Emory Tolbert.

The Department of History and the Program in African and African American Studies at Washington University in St. Louis were intellectually stimulating and personally warm spaces. The chairs of the Department of History, Derek Hirst and Hillel Kieval, were always very supportive, as were the chairs of African American Studies, Rafia Zafar and John Baugh. Raye Mahaney, Sheryl Peltz, Molly Shaikewitz, Adele Tuchler, and Margaret Williams were administrative wizards. Deans Edward Macias, Jim McLeod, and Justin Carroll generously allowed me leave to address pressing personal matters. As models of peerless scholarship, passionate teaching, and jovial collegiality, I must thank my wonderful colleagues at the College of William and Mary, particularly in the Lyon Gardiner Tyler Department of History and the Program of Africana Studies. Phil Daileader and Jim Whittenberg in History and Berhanu Abegaz, Jacqui McLendon, and Dee Royster in Africana Studies were supportive and empathetic chairs. Dean Carl Strikwerda facilitated my transition to William and Mary. Thanks, too, to Gail Conner and Roz Stearns for administrative assistance. Benedict Carton, Robert Edgar, Joe Miller, Tim Parsons, Kim Phillips, and Bill Tate mentored me with particularly wise counsel on life and academia, and always had my best interests at heart.

Jim Campbell, Benedict Carton, Robert Edgar, and Jeannette Hopkins read earlier versions of the entire manuscript and vastly improved it along the way. Edda Fields-Black, Mel Ely, Deborah Gaitskell, Cindy Hahamovitch, Steven Hahn, Anne Mager, Rolland Murray, Tim Parsons, Ron Schechter, Lester Spence, and Karin Wulf read parts of the manuscript and likewise offered useful suggestions. Of course, all remaining shortcomings rest on my shoulders.

New African Histories series editors Jean Allman and Allan Isaacman and Ohio University Press editorial director Gillian Berchowitz believed steadfastly in this book from start to finish, reading multiple versions of the manuscript and providing crucial support at critical moments along the scholarly journey. To them, to the anonymous readers who reviewed the manuscript, and to Nancy Basmajian, Joan Sherman, and other staff at the press, I express my deepest gratitude.

Finally, I thank my wife, Iyabo, for tolerating my divided attentions; my mother, Roslyn, for accepting my eccentricities; and my daughter, Thandile, for being the apple of my eye.

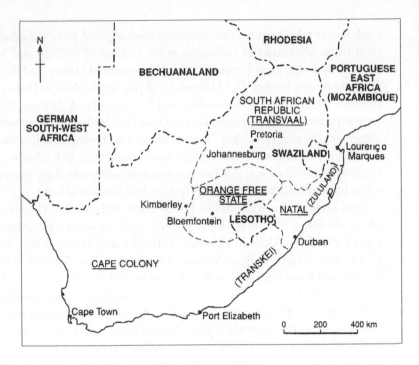

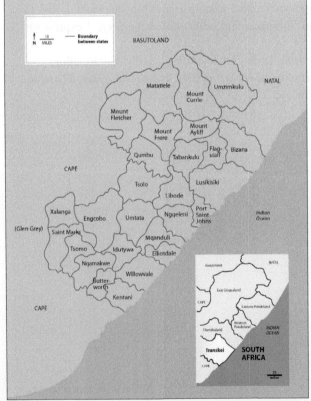

(*above*) The Union of South Africa in 1910 (provinces are underlined). Adapted from Kevin Shillington, *History of Southern Africa* (London: Longman, 1987), 137.

(*left*) Transkei, South Africa, the epicenter of the Garvey movement of Dr. Wellington. From Sean Redding, *Sorcery and Sovereignty: Tradition, Power, and Rebellion in South Africa, 1880–1963* (Athens: Ohio University Press, 2006), 37. Used by permission.

INTRODUCTION

The Americans Are Coming!

IN THE mid-1920s, the South African minister Daniel William Alexander, the son of a Cuban father and a shipbuilder who fought for the British in the South African War (1899–1902), complained that the segregationist laws of South African prime minister James Hertzog were "anti-native" and asserted that blacks worldwide had "long needed a leader like the Hon. Marcus Garvey."[1] The Jamaican-born, American-based Garvey had founded the Universal Negro Improvement Association (UNIA)—the largest black-led movement in world history, with over a thousand divisions in forty-three countries and more than a million followers across the globe. South Africans like Alexander devoured copies of Garvey's newspaper, the *Negro World*, and wrote hundreds of letters to the paper praising American Negroes and prophesying an "Africa for Africans," free from white colonial rule.[2]

Alexander led the South African branch of the African Orthodox Church, founded by the Antiguan-born George McGuire. McGuire was also the UNIA chaplain-general and the author of two critical UNIA texts—the *Universal Negro Catechism*, which claimed that God had ordained the UNIA to "redeem" Africa, and the *Universal Negro Ritual*, which contained nearly 150 hymns, prayers, and songs used during UNIA events. McGuire declared, "Garvey is a prophet," and he compared Garvey and oppressed blacks to Moses and the enslaved Israelites. Like Alexander, he believed Garvey was part of God's providential plan that had begun with the dispersal of millions of Africans from Africa and with slavery in the Western Hemisphere and would end with the triumphant return to Africa of diasporic blacks, sparking the regeneration of the continent.[3] Alexander and McGuire represent several themes that are discussed in this volume: the global nature of Garveyism, particularly

1

the indigenization and spread of Garveyism in South Africa; African disillusionment with white rule; Africans' admiration for—and hopes of achieving liberation through—American Negroes; and the role of religion and print culture in forging transnational identities and political linkages. Alexander and McGuire also demonstrate the nexus between Africans, West Indians, and African Americans; links between the UNIA and other organizations influenced deeply by Garveyism; and the persistent idea that the UNIA and American Negroes were divinely ordained to regenerate Africa.

In *The Americans Are Coming!* I argue that even though African Americans were subordinated in Jim Crow America, they were viewed by black South Africans as role models and potential liberators in their own battles against South African segregation. Africans were particularly attracted to an "up from slavery" narrative of African American success in the post–Civil War South, a narrative that was most closely associated with Booker T. Washington and African American singers and missionaries in South Africa. African American models of success disrupted a global color line constructed by whites worldwide, especially those in South Africa who claimed white rule was necessary to preserve modern civilization and usher blacks toward higher evolutionary development. The meteoric rise of Marcus Garvey and his Universal Negro Improvement Association caused some Africans to believe that African Americans were not just role models but also imminent liberators. The UNIA and Garveyism flourished in South Africa even as the movement declined in America, sparking ever-increasing transnational ties between Africans and diasporic blacks. As Garvey lost control of the floundering American UNIA and struggled unsuccessfully to regain his former prominence, Africans continued to utilize Garveyism, their travels to America, and their ties to American Negroes to further a liberationist course that would, decades later, finally be fulfilled in the global antiapartheid movement.

Focusing primarily on the period 1890 to 1940, this book explores the ways in which many Africans embraced and manipulated the idea that American Negroes, as role models and liberators, were essential to their goal of African independence. Though Africans disagreed among themselves about the efficacy of the political, educational, and socioeconomic ideals of Booker T. Washington, W. E. B. Du Bois, and Marcus Garvey, as well as the liberationist potential of American Negroes, they were in broad agreement that American Negroes were inspirational models of black success who proved blacks had the capacity to advance independent of white trusteeship. They admired their remarkable journey from slavery to freedom, their educational and socioeconomic advancement, their extraordinary cultural production, their urbane modernity, and their success in sport, which had the larger sociological implication of demonstrating what blacks could achieve if only given equal opportunities.

The book particularly demonstrates the kaleidoscopic nature of the Garvey movements in South Africa. There was no single South African Garvey movement. Garveyites in South Africa were the active agents, viewing Garveyism not as a fixed set of ideas but as a malleable ideology whose core ideals could be shaped and manipulated to advance different political, religious, educational, socioeconomic, cultural, and personal objectives. The result was many diffuse and decentralized South African Garveyisms, including many forms that would have been unknown and unrecognizable to Garvey himself. Metaphorically, the American Negro, like Marcus Garvey, became a modern-day Moses who would come to lead Africans out of a tyrannical Egypt and virtual slavery to the Promised Land of personal and political equality, education, and upward mobility. It was a dream that inspired and informed future leaders of South Africa, developed a global black consciousness, and spurred action that helped make the end of apartheid possible. But that dream also led to fantasy, despair, and disillusionment among black South Africans when Americans did not come to save them in the late nineteenth- and early twentieth-century Atlantic world.

African Americans and Africans had profound cultural, linguistic, educational, and other differences that often led to misunderstandings, misplaced expectations, and mutual disappointment. However, their similar histories of hope, despair, and disillusionment, along with their shared aspirations to be full citizens of their respective countries and for blacks to control nations and be fully respected on the world stage, often bridged the gaps between the two peoples.

African American travelers to South Africa discussed and sang about the Middle Passage; about the 244 years of American slavery; about their hopes for full citizenship and equal justice after Lincoln's Emancipation Proclamation; and about the Thirteenth, Fourteenth, and Fifteenth amendments that outlawed slavery, bestowed citizenship to African Americans, and extended the franchise to African American men in the aftermath of the Civil War. These hopes had given way to despair and disillusionment due to the determination of whites to transform African Americans from slaves to landless, economically exploited sharecroppers; to disenfranchise them through poll taxes, literacy tests, and grandfather clauses; and to terrorize them through racialized violence from white vigilante groups like the Ku Klux Klan, thousands of lynchings, and bloody coups such as that in Wilmington in 1898 that forced duly elected blacks and their allies from office. Blacks who served their country in the military during the Civil War, the Spanish-American War, and World War I were subjected to harsh segregated conditions, constant doubts about their character and fitness to serve, and vicious attacks by whites determined to show black veterans that their valiant service would not lead to full citizenship in postwar society.

Africans, too, had suffered from profound hardships, including nineteenth-century conquests by whites, the development of racial segregation during the mineral revolutions of the late 1800s, disenfranchisement, subordinate agricultural roles, and the denial of citizenship rights despite their military service during the South African War. African idealizations of American Negroes as role models and liberators peaked during particularly profound historical moments of disillusionment: the accelerated segregation during the mineral revolutions; the post–South African War British-Afrikaner pact that continued the disenfranchisement of most Africans; land dispossession and the lack of citizenship rights after the 1910 establishment of the Union of South Africa; and the 1929 "Black Peril" elections that proposed additional segregationist legislation, foreshadowing apartheid.

Although African diaspora studies have offered a more expansive framework for the study of continental Africa and the Americas, most works continue to center on diasporic blacks without attempting a substantial engagement with Africa and Africans.[4] By focusing on Africans as the active agents in the shaping and reshaping of the imagery of American Negroes and the diasporic ideology of Garveyism to resist segregation and white supremacy, this book demonstrates that blacks in South Africa were part of a two-way transatlantic traffic of peoples, institutions, and ideologies.[5] The book also goes beyond popular themes of migration, dispersal, and mobility to examine the intersection of politics, culture, education, sports, and religion in the ways that Africans indigenized the diasporic peoples, ideologies, and institutions in South Africa.[6]

I hope the book will be seen as groundbreaking in the recent renaissance in Garveyist studies that shifts the focus from Garvey and UNIA leadership to capture how blacks around the world shaped these ideologies of liberation in diffuse and differentiated forms to achieve local political objectives. Recent books by Mary Rolinson and Claudrena Harold examine Garveyism at local levels, particularly in the American South. And recent volumes of Robert A. Hill's *Marcus Garvey and UNIA Papers* reveal the depth of Garvey's impact in Africa. But virtually no scholarly monographs yet offer substantive accounts of Garveyism in Africa.[7]

By charting the hemispheric movement of black people, their ideas, and their institutions, *The Americans Are Coming!* moves South African historiography beyond its parochial borders. African peoples moved throughout South Africa, to the United States, and to Great Britain, and they engaged West Indian migrants to South Africa and the ideologies of the Jamaican Marcus Garvey, demonstrating clearly that they were not the passive, isolated tribal subjects that the South African government wished them to be. They made and unmade webs of power that included slavery and abolition, "civilizing" missions and "civilizing" imperialisms to fashion a dream of African liberation that resonated throughout the world. In this way, too, the transnational dimensions of the story, emphasizing linkages between Africans and American Negroes, move beyond comparative South African history, which often considers national histories in parallel dimensions.[8]

The Americans Are Coming! explores the concept of transnational white supremacy, or a global color line, and theories of providential design—notions that God enacted the Atlantic slave trade and slavery in America so that African-descended peoples could gain skills needed to liberate the African continent—to reframe South African and American studies in transnational, not comparative, contexts. In the international context of the 1900 Pan-African Conference in London, W. E. B. Du Bois called the problem of the new century "the problem of the color line." He referred most obviously to a global color line represented by European colonialism in Africa and Asia—but also by American military expansionism in the Philippines and Cuba and by white supremacist regimes in the United States, South Africa, and other countries.

As early as 1896, Jan Smuts, South Africa's future prime minister and an internationally respected statesman who helped to found both the League of Nations and the United Nations, exemplified the fearful white racist sentiments that undergirded the black peril paranoia that eventually included American Negroes:

> At the southern corner of a vast continent, peopled by over 10,000,000 barbarians, about half a million whites have taken up a position, with a view not only to working out their own destiny, but also of using that position as a basis for lifting up and opening up that vast dead-weight of immemorial barbarism and animal savagery to the light and blessing of ordered civilization. Unless the white race closes its ranks in this country, its position will soon become untenable in the face of that overwhelming majority of prolific barbarism.[9]

There were two sides of the global color line, as South African whites like the author Maurice Evans and the educator C. T. Loram saw as they traveled through the American South to learn how Jim Crowism could be more effectively applied in South Africa. The rise of segregation in South Africa was part and parcel of a larger system of white supremacy that included the emergence of Jim Crowism in the United States and the continued racism, landlessness, and economic deprivation that afflicted many black West Indians.

Whites, particularly British whites, believed that they had charted their own "up from barbarism" narrative in the Roman Empire, whose subjects they had been, to attain a global empire of their own that ruled over subject darker races. This social Darwinist European march toward civilization had taken several thousand years. To these new empire builders, the African journey toward civilization began with tutelage by European colonialism and would also take thousands of years. The white missionary and educator James Stewart, who visited Tuskegee to adapt its industrial education model in order to produce Africans who would not seek political rights, rhetorically asked Africans who were demanding citizenship rights: "Starting but as yesterday in the race of nations, do you soberly believe that in the two generations of the very imperfect civilization you have enjoyed and partially accepted, you can have overtaken those other nations who began that race two thousand years ago, and have been running hard at it for a thousand years at least?"[10]

Disillusioned with the white trustees of civilization, African Americans became alternate models of modernity. The stakes were high as blacks and whites debated the place of black people in the modern world. Could the Negro compete on the global stage? For Africans, the achievements of African Americans answered the question in the affirmative, then led to another: would blacks have the *opportunity* to compete on the global stage? Du Bois's evocation of a global color line exemplified the concerns of a transnational "talented tenth" that connected local struggles for racial equality with larger Pan-African consciousness and action. The linkages between American Negroes and black South Africans were part not only of an awareness of the parallels between American Jim Crowism and South African racial segregation but also of what white supremacist Lothrop Stoddard warned was a "rising tide of color," a growing identification with a global majority of people of color, including colonized and oppressed people in Africa, Ireland, India, and emerging nations like Japan.[11] Many black South Africans glimpsed their modern futures not in the faces of Europeans but in the faces of American Negroes. The pathway toward modernity was through African America, not a white Europe that wanted Africans to remain an unchanging, rural-based migrant labor force yoked to a segregationist system designed to procure cheap labor.

Expanding links between Africans and American Negroes heightened the South African state's determination to maintain control over Africans politically and in other ways. And ironically, they helped accelerate segregationist legislation in the interwar years, when more laws to restrain Africans were passed than in the preceding one hundred years.[12]

Notions of providential design also facilitated this black transnational relationship, demonstrating the little-recognized fact of the centrality of religion to political struggle. The comparative historiography of South Africa and America has pushed the study of South African history beyond its long parochial tendencies, but comparative studies continue to treat religion and politics in South Africa (and in Africa generally) as operating in parallel universes that relate only infrequently with each other. *The Americans Are*

Coming! uses archival sources, newspapers, and oral interviews from Africa, England, and the United States to show the centrality of religion as one of the earliest—and one of the few—areas in which Africans themselves regained much autonomy and control over their lives. On some level, although it has not been reported by historians, Africans, government officials, and white civil society did understand that independent black religious institutions, fostered by American blacks and their white allies, would be precursors to demands for African political independence.[13]

Unlike white supremacists who viewed blacks as a problem to be countered, blacks in South Africa and in the Americas often viewed themselves as potential saviors who could redeem a modern civilization corrupted by exclusivist racism. The future of black people—and of modern civilization itself—was at stake in the struggle to eliminate the global color line. As white supremacists argued that the history of blacks began with their contact with white civilization, many blacks offered a more optimistic historical narrative that began with the grandeur of early Egyptian and Ethiopian civilizations. They cast themselves as modern-day Israelites with a covenantal relationship with God, who had allowed the ancestors of American Negroes to be subjected to centuries of slavery so that they could relearn high civilization from ascendant Europeans and return to Africa with the skills needed for the regeneration of the continent. Many African Americans interested in Africa—either in Christian missions, educational institutions, or liberationist designs—viewed their work as the ultimate fulfillment of God's providential plan, a plan that had begun with enslavement and dispersal. African Americans in particular engaged black South Africa as part of a divinely ordained mission to forge a decolonized Africa for Africans. The claims of providential design, along with notions of black modernity, comprised a unifying ideal among African-descended peoples across a wide spectrum, including many African Americans, black West Indians, and black South Africans.

Education, too, became a transatlantic channel as Africans increasingly, if still in small numbers, gained financial and other support to attend African American–based and white-led schools and universities. These institutions were models for starting schools of their own in South Africa and also a means through which to witness personally the progress and achievements, as well as the failures and suffering, of African Americans recently emerged from slavery.

Chapter 1 begins with the story of the Virginia Jubilee Singers, an American Negro singing troupe from Hampton Institute in Virginia whose five years in South Africa in the 1890s offered South Africans the first sustained depiction of African Americans' history and life. The Jubilee Singers espoused an "up from slavery" narrative that envisioned African American progress out of slavery into freedom and overturned the earlier images of dull-witted, enslaved

African Americans that had been conveyed in traveling minstrel shows. Africans pointed to Jack Johnson, the world's first black heavyweight champion (1908–1916) whose domination of white challengers was recorded on films that circulated in South Africa, as proof of blacks' capacity to be equal and even superior to whites if given a level playing field. For many whites in South Africa, Johnson exemplified the black peril of African Americans who supposedly disrupted interracial harmony and gave "unreasonable" aspirations to Africans. By World War I, the South African government banned virtually all American Negroes from entering the country. In their attempts to enter and remain in South Africa, American Negro missionaries discovered the global nature of the color line, but they also deepened religious, educational, and cultural links with Africans and, in the use of the Hampton-Tuskegee model of industrial education, enhanced the powerful image of Booker T. Washington as the prototypical American Negro role model.

Chapter 2 details African disillusionment with white missionaries who claimed themselves and Christianity as "civilizing" liberators that would free society from supposed African pagan barbarism. But with the discovery of diamonds (in 1867) and gold (in 1886) in South Africa and the resultant rapid industrialization and urbanization, it was cheap, pliable African labor that was needed in order to exploit these minerals—not the Christianized, educated, enfranchised, propertied, and economically autonomous African citizenry that many missionaries had earlier claimed would be the desired outcome of their proselytizing. As white missionaries replicated white society's racially discriminatory practices in their own missions, African Christians turned to alternate models for advancement, particularly American Negroes like Washington and the industrial education model made famous by Washington's Tuskegee Institute. During the South African War between the British and Afrikaners, many Africans believed that the British, who had abolished slavery in 1838 to the chagrin of Afrikaner slaveholders and who reputedly believed in "equal rights for all civilized men," would allow them to be full citizens in a unified South African state. Yet British victory only meant the continued disenfranchisement of virtually all Africans; the creation of a unified "native policy" of segregation; and, with the Union of South Africa in 1910, British acquiescence to Afrikaner domestic political control that appropriated African lands and relegated Africans to being virtual aliens in their own country. More and more disillusioned with both the white missions of their upbringing and the British, two American-educated Africans, Pixley Seme and John Dube, founded and led the African National Congress (ANC). In its early years, this organization protested (among other unjust laws) the Natives Land Act of 1913, which restricted Africans, who made up 75 percent of the population, to only 6 percent of the total land. African petitions and deputations to Britain to override South African domestic laws failed; by 1919, the ANC and other Africans concluded that the British were not liberators and indeed were deeply complicit in their imprisonment under the rule of the Afrikaner-controlled national government. Liberation would have to come from elsewhere.

Chapter 3 describes the political maturation of Marcus Garvey and his founding of the Universal Negro Improvement Association and the African Communities (Imperial) League, which sought African independence from European colonialism; black politicoeconomic advancement; and black control of religious, educational, and cultural institutions. With more than three hundred thousand dues-paying members, a thousand chapters, and perhaps another million supporters around the world, the UNIA was not only the largest black-led movement in history but also one of the rare attempts by blacks to create a transnational state. Primarily because of South Africa's harsh racial conditions, the transmission of Garveyism to South African ports by American Negro sailors, and the dissemination of the UNIA newspaper *Negro World*, there were more UNIA chapters in South Africa than in any other African country. American Negroes in South Africa established local UNIA chapters, infusing them with a prophetic politics that spoke of divinely ordained deliverance from white rule, and the UNIA petitioned the League of Nations for control of South African–controlled Southwest Africa.

Chapter 4 addresses the spread and triumph of Garveyism in South Africa, particularly in non-UNIA organizations like the ANC and the Industrial and Commercial Workers Union (ICU)—despite Garvey's incarceration, his self-destructive battles with Du Bois and other black leaders in America, his peculiar links with white supremacist groups, the decline of the American UNIA, and anti-Garvey sentiment expressed by many Africans and some American Negroes in South Africa. Despite Garvey's troubles, Africans such as American-educated James Thaele continued to view American Negroes as models of success independent of white trusteeship. With his charismatic personality, his flamboyant leadership style, and his expert use of print media to advance Garveyism and advocate black separatist programs that often intersected with white segregationist programs, Thaele was the closest thing to Garvey himself in South Africa. He articulated the deep sense of disillusionment that blacks on both sides of the Atlantic felt when visions of post–World War I racial equality, justice, and self-determination failed to materialize. As a person with a theological degree, Thaele also represented African Christian tendencies to articulate a racially egalitarian Christianity that knew no color line and prophesied an imminent judgment day for ungodly racist whites.

Chapter 5 highlights the continued indigenization of Garvey's movement in Africa. Wellington Butelezi, a Zulu, was one of several Africans claiming to be American Negroes and part of an imminent liberationist invasion from

America. Building on past prophecies of deliverance from suffering that dated to the nineteenth century, Wellington expanded the view of American Negroes, portraying them not just as role models but also as liberators. Under Wellington, the UNIA became a vehicle to express popular discontent with white rule, to create and control black-led churches and schools, and to construct transnational racial identities connected to black American power rather than narrow ethnic identities subordinate to the South African state.

Chapter 6 details the ongoing decline in the stature of Garvey and the UNIA in the Northern Hemisphere as well as the continued ability of Africans to manipulate and shape Garveyism to address local politics and mobilize popular support for their chieftaincy claims. On the eve of World War II, there were final prophecies of American Negro liberation, but since Garvey and the Americans still did not come, a few Africans predicted liberation from an unlikely source that appeared to have the power to defeat both Britain and South Africa: Nazi Germany. Yet even as the dream of the American Negro liberator faded, students like Sibusisiwe Makhanya continued to view the United States as a promised land of highly valued education. After the death of Washington, South African students sought schooling in the liberal arts, the traditional education of the white elite, in contrast to the Booker T. Washington model of vocational/agricultural education that gave Africans less training for leadership in an eventually independent and modern Africa. Just before World War II broke out, the boxing victories of the second black world heavyweight champion, Joe Louis, and the cultural production of film and singing star Paul Robeson were inspirational success stories to Africans like American-educated ANC president Alfred Xuma. In the years ahead, Xuma's political ties with African American missionary Max Yergan and Robeson would inaugurate a new era of African–American Negro relationships that would unite their respective national struggles for racial equality in a global struggle for civil rights, human rights, and the end of apartheid.

PART I

~

PROVIDENTIAL DESIGN
The Alliance of American Negroes and Black South Africans

1 ↭ American Negroes as Racial Models

From "Honorary Whites" to "Black Perils"

IN OCTOBER 1890, the Virginia Jubilee Singers, ten graduates of Hampton Institute in Virginia, arrived in Cape Town, South Africa, for a tour that was scheduled to take several weeks but would last nearly five years.[1] Their performances fostered a powerful new era of black transnational relationships between the United States and South Africa and would transform the South African image of American blacks into models. A decade before the publication of Booker T. Washington's celebrated autobiography, *Up from Slavery*, which championed the progress that he and other African Americans had made in moving from slavery into freedom, the Virginia Jubilee Singers spread the "up from slavery" narrative of African American success around the world. Their five years in South Africa encouraged the growing idea among Africans and African Americans that they were of the same race, bound together in a program of transnational racial uplift. They did so even as whites attempted to subject the Jubilee Singers and other African Americans to racially restrictive laws aimed at Africans, declaring all blacks worldwide a subordinated people. The Virginia Jubilee Singers, along with other American Negroes in South Africa, also made visible a global color line more than a decade before W. E. B. Du Bois's landmark essay collection, *Souls of Black Folk*, advanced this important idea. This global color line highlighted the white supremacy ethic that undergirded European colonialism, American Jim Crowism, and imperialist empire building, as well as the developing political, religious, educational, and cultural bonds between American Negroes and Africans.

The Jubilee Singers were not the first American blacks to go to South Africa. Black American sailors had been part of America's whaling crews since the eighteenth century, and in 1862, a Confederate warship, the *Alabama*, docked in Cape Town and carried American slavery and racism to South Africa with African American slaves serving the crew and entertaining passengers. The slaves performed minstrel shows for white South Africans sympathetic to the Confederate cause and bitter about Britain's ending of slavery in the Cape Colony;[2] such shows had begun in the United States in the late 1820s, and they featured white performers in blackface caricaturing enslaved and free blacks. Crew members cheered on the "coons" and "niggers" who were their shipmates. During the American Civil War—the defining event that began the up from slavery narrative of black freedom and progress—blackface minstrelsy continued to circulate negative images of black Americans in South Africa. The renowned white Christy Minstrels of England also went to Cape Town in 1862. Among their stock characters, in blackface, were Jim Crow, a lazy and dull-witted plantation slave, and Zip Coon, a buffoon and dandy who mangled the English language and supposedly menaced white women.[3]

The Jubilee Singers, all of them Negroes (in the language of the time), were no cartoon figures but rather professionals with a serious purpose beyond sharing their glorious music. Their depictions of American Negro life and history contrasted sharply with the persistent and pervasive narrative of black inferiority in the American South as well as in South Africa. On tours of South Africa from 1890 to 1892 and from 1895 to 1898, the Jubilee Singers captured the imagination of the entire country with about a thousand wildly popular concerts featuring exultant and moving American Negro spirituals, dramatic and comedic skits, and minstrelsy.[4]

THE LIBERATION MESSAGE OF EMANCIPATION IN WORD AND SONG

As noted, the Virginia Jubilee Singers were from Hampton Institute, which was founded in 1868 as a teacher-training and industrial school for former slaves. Hampton was a paradox, representing both the emancipationist activities of black Americans *and* the post–Civil War restrictions on their freedom. The school stood in the shadow of Fort Monroe, whose commander, Benjamin Butler, had been the first Union general to allow African Americans, as a matter of policy, to escape from slavery behind Union lines. Fort Monroe was also the site of the first large-scale land redistribution for African Americans during the war, a model for Gen. William T. Sherman's Special Field Order 15 that famously mandated forty acres and a mule for African American freedpeople. Yet President Andrew Johnson's Amnesty Proclamation of 1865 required the Freedman's Bureau—a government agency designed to ease the freedman's transition from slavery to freedom and to help in the general reconstruction of the war-ravaged South—to remove freedpeople from the land they had settled during the war. The bureau's official for Hampton Roads, former Union general Samuel Chapman Armstrong, restored land to former slaveholders and provided them with ready labor by pressuring increasingly landless African American freedpeople to sign yearlong labor contracts, often with the very people who had held them in bondage. As the principal of Hampton Institute, Armstrong disregarded the liberal arts academic curriculum of white northern universities and black schools such as Fisk and Atlanta universities. He favored a simplified industrial education borrowed from British colonial officials in Asia and from his own missionary father's approach to education for Hawaiians, a model that redirected black educational aspirations toward an emphasis on personal morality and hygiene. It was a curriculum that would produce teachers, tradesmen, agriculturalists, and domestics who would not challenge the white-over-black political and economic status quo.

Yet out of this incubator of black subordination came the beginning of a black liberationist gospel for South Africa. The Virginia Jubilee Singers modeled themselves after the Fisk Jubilee Singers, whose successful tours of Europe in the 1870s had raised enough money to keep Fisk University, founded in 1868 by the American Missionary Association of New York, from going bankrupt. The Fisk singers electrified their audiences with powerful messages of despair, hope, and faith in divinely ordained deliverance from racial oppression. The biblical place-names in the spirituals they sang were coded language in the world of American slaves, who viewed themselves as modern-day Israelites in their spirituals. Egypt, Babylon, and hell were symbols of the American South; Pharaoh and his army were slave catchers; Egyptians and Satan were slave owners. Canaan, Heaven, and the Promised Land were territories of the U.S. North, Canada, and Africa. Songs of the Exodus from Egypt, Daniel's escape from the lion's den, Jonah's delivery from the belly of the whale, and the Hebrew children's escape from the fiery furnace all became God's acts of liberation—religious forms of Lincoln's Emancipation Proclamation.[5] The Fisk singers generated support for the Civil Rights Act of 1875, which sought to guarantee every person, regardless of race, color, or previous condition of servitude, equal treatment in public accommodations such as hotels, theaters, trains, and ships.[6]

Orpheus McAdoo had been with the Fisk singers in their tours of Europe, Australia, New Zealand, India, and the Far East.[7] In 1889, McAdoo created his own group, the Virginia Jubilee Singers, and a year later, he took his singers to South Africa in multiple tours that paved the way for the momentous transnational relationship that developed between black South Africans and the American Negroes from the United States and the Caribbean. McAdoo also had a message that was more than musical: music embodied the message and carried it where political orators could not go. McAdoo had been born into slavery in North Carolina, his mother the only literate slave on the plantation.

She taught her sons so well that they were able to graduate from Hampton Institute. Orpheus was a teacher there for nearly a decade before joining the Fisk singers and infusing his troupe with the Fisk liberationist gospel and civil rights ethos exemplified in the Thirteenth, Fourteenth, and Fifteenth amendments that had, respectively, abolished slavery, bestowed citizenship to African Americans, and enfranchised African American men.[8] In 1890, his Jubilee Singers performed in England, then sailed on to Cape Town. The charismatic entrepreneur McAdoo, with his immaculate suit, top hat, gloves, and cane, personified the up from slavery narrative made famous a decade later in the autobiography of his fellow ex-slave and former Hampton classmate Booker T. Washington. Before the music began, McAdoo's oration to both black and white audiences credited Christianity, education, and moral sobriety for the amazing progress of his race in America, rising from the depths of slavery to the Reconstruction era's election of blacks to national, state, and municipal offices.

Educated and worldly, the singers represented an African American elite, Du Bois's "talented tenth." Their liberation and their progress, seen as divinely ordained by Africans, placed American Negroes in the center of God's unfolding plan. "Go down Moses," the first published spiritual (1861), told a powerful story of God's commandment to Moses to order Pharaoh to release the Israelite slaves. In "Swing Low, Sweet Chariot," God's chariot of fire swept the prophet Elijah into heaven just as Underground Railroad conductors in the United States had seemed to descend from heaven to guide the enslaved to freedom.[9]

Whites, including such dignitaries as British governor-general Henry Locke and Transvaal president Paul Kruger, praised the brilliant music of the Jubilee Singers and marveled at McAdoo's tale of the rise of African American slaves to freedom. Kruger, perhaps thinking of encroaching British settlers who would soon instigate war against his Afrikaners and precipitate the South African War, shed tears when the troupe sang "Nobody Knows the Trouble I've Seen."[10] Another white proclaimed, "I do feel more hope for our coloured people in seeing what those of their own race have accomplished."[11] The Jubilee Singers soon became racial models for African elites, among them several future leaders of the South African Native National Congress (SANNC, which became the African National Congress, or ANC, in 1923), including Solomon Plaatje, Saul Msane, Patrick Lenkoane, Isaiah Bud M'belle, and Henry Ngcayiya. John Jabavu, in his *Imvo Zabantsundu*, the first black-owned South African newspaper, called the singers an "object lesson" for Africans, proof of "the superiority of the American colored people over the South African." The Jubilee Singers became a spiritual musical metaphor for an advanced civilization that "the Native here should try to attain."[12] American Negroes were inspirational evidence that access to Western education, Christian piety, and entrepreneurial capitalism could transform blacks into first-class citizens in a racially inclusive country. *Imvo* boasted of the Jubilee Singers as tangible confirmation of black civility and accomplishment: "As Africans, we are, of course, proud of the achievements of those of our race."[13]

The black newspaper *Kaffrarian Watchman* reported that Africans "could not quite understand what sort of people they [the singers] were. Some "hesitated to class them as kaffirs, as they seemed so smart and tidy in appearance, and moved about with all the ease and freedom among the white people that a high state of civilization and education alone can give."[14] Josiah Semouse, an African postal worker, exulted, "Hear! Today they have their own schools, primary, secondary and high schools, and also universities. They are run by them without the help of whites. They have magistrates, judges, lawyers, bishops, ministers and evangelists, and school masters." "When will the day come," he asked, "when the African people will be like the Americans? When will they stop being slaves and become nations with their own government?"[15]

McAdoo considered education central to black American progress and to future African progress, and apprehensive South African whites protested that his troupe was "singing to educate Negroes."[16] He told South African newspapers he had given £5,000 to schools for African Americans and lamented that no black South Africans were permitted to attend universities at home.[17] He also paid the tuition and transportation costs involved in enrolling one young African, Titus Mbongwe, in Hampton in 1890. Tragically, Mbongwe died in a train wreck in England en route to Virginia, but other Africans swamped Hampton Institute with letters inquiring about educational opportunities. Soon thereafter, Hampton educated about a dozen Africans in what became an educational pipeline; by 1924, about four hundred black South Africans had crossed the Atlantic to attend American colleges and universities.[18]

AMERICAN NEGROES IN SOUTH AFRICA: HONORARY WHITES OR AFRICAN "NATIVES"?

Orpheus McAdoo and his Virginia Jubilee Singers arrived in South Africa just as racial segregation accelerated there. The discovery of diamonds in Kimberley in 1867 and gold in Johannesburg in 1886, together with the exploitation of the cheap and plentiful labor of recently conquered Africans, soon made South Africa the world's leading producer of these minerals. Segregationist legislation designed to deny Africans citizenship rights in South Africa while at the same time exploiting their labor had begun in the mining towns and continued with the 1892 Franchise and Ballot Act, which used financial and educational qualifications to limit the African vote, and the 1894 Glen Grey Act, which assigned areas to segregate Africans from whites. Such legislation began a segregationist onslaught that denied Africans the right to vote; condemned them, by "color-bar" legislation, to the lowest-paying jobs; and provided them little judicial recourse to counter their systematic subordination. These laws culminated in the Natives Land Act of 1913 and the Natives (Urban Areas) Act of 1923, which mandated racial segregation in rural and urban areas, respectively.[19] In a long letter to the *Southern Workman*, a Hampton periodical, McAdoo protested, "There is no country in the world where prejudice is so strong as here in Africa . . . the native today is treated as badly as ever the slave was treated in Georgia." Particularly in the Orange Free State (OFS) and the Transvaal, Africans could not obtain business licenses, buy liquor, or use most public transportation and public facilities.[20]

Even favored American Negroes could not own businesses in their own names. In another long letter, McAdoo asked how a supposedly civilized and Christian white community could compel "every man of dark skin, even though he is a citizen of another country, to be in his house by 9 o'clock at night, or he is arrested." Jubilee Singers' performances were sometimes disrupted by rowdy whites, and whites, mistaking troupe members for Africans, sought to deny them access to bars and other public places.[21]

Yet despite continued affronts, the popular and celebrated Virginia Jubilee Singers were sometimes able to resist being restricted by segregationist laws and customs. They claimed that their American citizenship effectively made them exempt from racially discriminatory legislation in Afrikaner republics, the Transvaal and the Orange Free State, and in the two British possessions, the Cape Colony and Natal. As "honorary whites," they had unrestricted use of public transportation, could patronize hotels and bars, and were not required to carry passes or observe curfew restrictions, and they did not have to step off a sidewalk to let a white pass by. But they were subject to discrimination when some whites mistook them for Africans. In 1898, a Pietermaritzburg policeman spotted a Jubilee troupe member, Richard Collins, drinking in a whites-only bar, assumed he was an African, and promptly assaulted and arrested him. Collins persuaded the American consul to intervene on his behalf. The local court promptly dropped the charges, and the local newspaper, *Times of Natal*, chastised the trooper for his "blunder," expressing hope that no damage had been done to British-U.S. relations.[22] In the Transvaal, McAdoo won two court cases, one affirming his troupe's right to stay at a designated whites-only hotel, the other dismissing a different hotelier's false charge that he had failed to pay the troupe's lodging bill.

American citizenship had conveyed a similar status on blacks years before, since at least 1854 when the Transvaal issued an exemption pass to an American Negro.[23] In 1875 in Natal, "E. Page, a person of color" who had been arrested for violating a night curfew, argued that his American citizenship exempted him from discriminatory laws that applied to Africans. Although the local magistrate insisted the law applied to all black persons, he did not "press the charge."[24] In 1893, a white Transvaal policeman mistook a black American engineer, John

Ross, for an African and whipped him for "impudence." With Ross demanding redress, the U.S. Department of State brought a claim against the Transvaal government for $10,000 in damages. Ross felt his education, skills, and citizenship exempted him from this cruel treatment, and he fumed that submission to segregationist laws would place African Americans on the level of the "raw, savage, totally uneducated aborigine."[25] William Van Ness, the American consul at Johannesburg, demanded that the Transvaal government give the matter "immediate attention," since "the laws of the United States make no distinction in citizenship between white and colored." Several years later, Van Ness himself would protest incidents against African Americans whom white South Africans mistook for "natives."[26] In a visit to South Africa five years later, Henry McNeal Turner, a bishop in the African Methodist Episcopal (AME) Church, wrote to the AME journal, *Voice of Missions*, that "President Cleveland forced the Boers to pay twenty-five thousand dollars because they beat some black American." Presumably, he was referring to John Ross.[27]

The African American shipowner Harry Dean, in South Africa to foster African political and socioeconomic independence and to promote American-African cooperation, reported, "The American government, while not thoroughly honorable in all respects, will seldom endure ... insults to its citizens."[28] American consulates did require all American Negroes to carry an American passport, and most in South Africa procured their own, but at least one employer, the Langlaate Estate Gold Mining Company, arranged for a passport on behalf of an employee named J. Anderson.[29] McAdoo himself carried special exemption letters from the presidents of the Transvaal and the Orange Free State.[30] When he appealed to Paul Kruger, president of the Transvaal, for protection of the Jubilee Singers as "citizens of a Sister Republic," Kruger said that white South Africans, too, took America as their model: "We regard America as our pattern and are striving to imitate it."[31] McAdoo left South Africa in 1898 and died in Australia two years later. However, troupe member Will Thompson remained in Kimberley, where he joined future ANC leaders Isaiah Bud M'belle, Sol Plaatje, and Henry Ngcayiya in organizing a struggle against racial segregation in public transportation.[32]

The Jubilee Singers' American citizenship and star performances provided privileges unavailable to South African blacks. Their honorary white status was tacit acknowledgment by South African authorities that American blacks had acquired the hallmarks of civilization in *just one generation out of slavery*, not the two thousand years that whites claimed Africans would need to be "civilized" enough to regain their precolonial independence. Yet even as the singers exposed enraptured Africans to the gospel that liberationist Christianity and education were the keys to their inspirational up from slavery narrative, the counternarrative of white racial exclusivity would soon subject American

Negroes in South Africa to segregationist legislation that affected Africans, thereby further developing both sides of the global color line.

FEARS OF AFRICAN AMERICANS IN BRITISH SOUTH AFRICA

U.S. diplomats' successful assertion of the citizenship rights of black Americans coincided with the efforts of the Boer republics to court America as a potential ally against the British. In 1873, the Orange Free State, which had opened a consulate in Philadelphia the year before, signed a treaty of friendship and commerce with the United States. In 1899, the Transvaal was negotiating a similar treaty with Washington just as the South African War began. Three years later, the British defeated the Afrikaners and incorporated South Africa in the British Empire as a Crown Colony. Many British colonial authorities, missionaries, and others viewed black Americans as agitators who filled the heads of otherwise docile Africans with dangerous democratic notions of racial equality. Increasingly, whites began to associate black Americans with Ethiopianism, the religious movement of African Christians who broke with white missions in the late nineteenth century to establish churches of their own. These African Christians were known as Ethiopians largely because they viewed the biblical Ethiopia as a synonym for Africa and as a historical site of an ancient black Christian nation. Ethiopians interpreted Psalms 68:31, "Princes Shall Come Out of Egypt and Ethiopia Shall Stretch Forth Her Hands Unto God," as a prophecy that Africans would regain their independence. These ideas were amplified when, in 1896, Ethiopia defeated Italian whites and maintained its independence even as European powers colonized the rest of Africa.[33] In the 1890s, Ethiopianism's rejection of white authority had led several newspapers, a number of white missionaries, and South African government officials to refer to the movement as a threat. A *Cape Times* editorial called it "a patriotic movement, in that it seeks to enlist the sympathies and support of all natives qua natives." The editorial continued, "It is political in that one of the fundamental principles of the organization is to proceed much on the working lines of the Afrikaner Bond, though of course with directly opposite aspirations, and it is ecclesiastical, and for this reason exercises a disturbing effect upon the native mind."[34]

In 1896, the Ethiopian Church of South Africa became the fourteenth district of the African Methodist Episcopal Church, the most prominent black American link to Ethiopianism. To AME ministers, slavery provided a training ground for American blacks who would carry out God's "providential design," returning to Africa as saviors to "civilize" Africans. AME minister Absalom Jones had mused, nearly a century earlier, "Who knows but that a Joseph may rise up among them who shall be the instrument of feeding the African nations with the bread of life?"[35] According to providential design, black Americans had a divinely ordained role in history, and they joined Africans as members of a black transnational spiritual collective. Baptist missionary Charles Morris, in an address to a U.S. missionary conference in 1900, declared that "the American Negro had been marvelously preserved and Christianized for a purpose . . . destined to play a star part in the great drama of the world's development," the fulfillment of Psalms 68:31. The continent where Jesus lived his earliest years would rise again as a Christian world power.[36]

Many African Christians had come to believe that black Americans represented "the future of the black race of this continent," as central actors in God's plan. Mangena Mokone had established an Ethiopian church in Pretoria and joined forces with the AME. He likened black Americans to the prophet Nehemiah, who had reassembled dispersed Israelites from Babylonian captivity to forge a new Hebrew nation in Jerusalem. To African AME pastor Jacobus Xaba, black Americans were "born of God (as Moses in Egypt). Brothers consider that carefully."[37]

Although many American Negroes were no doubt willing to consider themselves worthy role models, as a practical matter most insisted that Africans would benefit more from British than from Afrikaner rule. Orpheus McAdoo complained that the Afrikaners "place every living creature before the native." The Jubilee Singers' Mamie Edwards added that God had invested divine power in the English as "chosen ones" destined to civilize Africa.[38] Horatio Scott, a native of Oakland, California, who had emigrated to South Africa in 1896, fought for the British against the Afrikaners "for the sake of my race" because the "Boers give the black man no rights save that of being flogged with a huge rhinoceros hide whip."[39] Fighting in several battles against Afrikaners, Scott championed England as a comparatively just nation and accused Afrikaners of forcing blacks to carry passes and of hauling them to prison pulled by horses with ropes around their necks. Afrikaners were, he said, guilty of multiple efforts to "humiliate the colored man."[40]

In 1903, the British organized the South African Native Affairs Commission (SANAC) to unify "native policy" among the four provinces. For the South African government and for white missionaries as well, the image of black Americans had begun to change: they were seen less as participants in a "civilizing mission" and more as primary instigators of the separatist Ethiopian movement. Whites were accusing African American journals, like the Colored American Magazine and the Voice of the Negro, and black-owned newspapers, such as the AME's Voice of Missions and the Indianapolis Freeman, of printing aggressively pro-African articles and employing the "Africa for Africans" slogan associated with the Ethiopian movement. The circulation of such periodicals in South Africa had created considerable concern among whites about the "subversiveness" of Ethiopianism.[41]

An alarmed missionary of the Free Church of Scotland warned, in the *Lagos Record*, of "a danger of a great deal of evil happening through these blacks from America coming in and mixing with the natives of South Africa. These men from America for generations suffered oppression, and they have naturally something to object to in the white man and a grievance against the white man. These men from America come in and make our natives imagine they have grievances when there are no grievances."[42] The 1905 final report of SANAC complained that black American missionaries provided financial support to African Christians, but it conceded that these missionaries were espousing no rebellious doctrines.[43] Yet many South African whites had come to regard American Negroes as agents of African resistance to white rule. Black Americans now became known in South Africa as the *Swaart Gevaar*, or Black Peril, reflecting white fears regarding possible black rebellion against white rule and sexual relations between black men and white women.[44]

David Hunter, editor of the *Christian Express*, expressed grave concern that the *Voice of Missions* embodied an Africa for the Africans ideal: "A man coming from America with any degree, which enhances his influence with the Native people," could lead Africans away from white rule. Racial animosity could exceed that of the American South, where Hunter mistakenly believed whites were a minority as they were in South Africa. He proposed that the government ban certain American Negroes to prevent "fresh impetus . . . from the United States." The most dangerous Ethiopian schools, he said, were those "ruled by the negroes in the Southern States of America," who were "so apt to bring in the spirit of race hatred which is so rife in the Southern States." Further, he contended that sending Africans to study in African American colleges and universities could expose them to dangerous ideas.[45]

In 1904, a prosegregationist author, Roderick Jones, maintained that the teachings of "American Negroes, . . . if not deliberately seditious, implant in the native mind crude ideas about the brotherhood of man, and foster a separatist spirit wholly incompatible with strict loyalty to . . . white rule." White South Africans were increasingly willing, he said, to "bundle the American Negro, bag and baggage, out of the country, under a law excluding undesirables."[46] Two years later, after rebellions erupted in Zululand against colonial taxation, land appropriation, and restrictive African patriarchy, some contemporary accounts attributed blame for the upheaval to American blacks.[47]

By then, it had become standard South African policy to deport black Americans who were already in the country and to refuse admittance to others. Despite international treaties and humanitarian rhetoric that frowned upon racial discrimination, imperial Britain allowed its self-governing dominions to enact racist legislation. Officials in the British government had already reassured South African authorities that they would not interfere with restrictive racial policies: "Your fate is in your own hands. . . . Do not anticipate any other meddling on the part of Downing Street, or of any section of the British people . . . the good sense of the British people will never tolerate any intermeddling in the purely domestic concerns of the people to whom it has conceded the fullest liberties of government."[48]

The postwar South African government now subjected black Americans to the same segregationist laws that restricted Africans. American Negroes, like their African brethren, could not use public transportation, walk on public sidewalks, or purchase liquor. In 1903, Harry Dean and another American Negro, James Brown, complained that they had to carry passes like "a native in his barbarous state"; they accused American consular officials of treating them "as though we were heathens, advancing the advice that we have no business in this country."[49] In 1904, a Transvaal court convicted a black American, Thomas Brown, of attempting to buy liquor. Brown had argued that "a man who is entitled to the vote in his own country is surely entitled to have a bottle of sherry in this country."[50] The presiding judge ruled that Brown's skin color overrode the rights and privileges of his American citizenship, and the American consulate, which had initially supported him, now refused to intervene.[51] In a 1906 case, William Henry Sampson, an American Negro, complained to the U.S. consul in Pretoria that he had been denied the right to buy liquor, whereupon the consul accepted the explanation of the secretary of native affairs that the local law "applied to all coloured persons without exception, and that no provision is made for the exception from its operation of any coloured citizens of America."[52] The government claimed eventually that African Americans and Africans were of the same race in permitting James Thompson, an American black working in the mines, to receive medical compensation for silicosis on the grounds that a 1911 Miner's Phthisis Act defined a *native* as "a member of the aboriginal races or tribes of Africa." American blacks, said one government official, "undoubtedly sprang from an aboriginal African race, the Negro race of Africa."[53]

The onset of Jim Crow legislation in the United States in the later years of the century, which reversed the gains of Reconstruction, had undermined black Americans' status in South Africa as well. Whites engaged freely in acts of racial terrorism, including lynchings and violent political coups; southern states disenfranchised blacks through the racially selective use of supposedly color-blind literacy tests and poll taxes; and the U.S. Supreme Court sanctioned state discrimination with the 1896 *Plessy v. Ferguson* decision that upheld a Louisiana law mandating racial segregation on railways. The advent of Jim Crowism in the American South also meant American diplomats were far less likely to contest South Africa's racially exclusive laws. In late 1903, Joseph Proffit, the American consul in Transvaal, told the U.S. Department of State,

"I am quite certain that the consular officers in this country have not brooked nor will they permit indignities to our citizens without protest to the proper authorities."[54] Yet by August 1904, he had shifted his ground. After more than a dozen black Americans complained to him that "our liberty once enjoyed under the late Government is abrogated and we are left without protection," he pronounced that "prevailing law relative to railway transportation does not differ in any essential respects from the laws obtaining in many of our Southern states. . . . I have sought to make the colored man content with his lot in South Africa since he is a guest of the British, he should abide by local laws."[55] His reversal no doubt reflected, in part, the declining economic influence of the United States as the British government, concerned about commercial competition in its colonies, imposed protective tariffs and limited the mobility of American businesspeople. To further lessen American economic influence, British colonial officials also encouraged the replacement of American mine managers, who operated more than half of South Africa's mines before 1900, with South African and British citizens. Such policies were in direct contrast to those of the prewar Afrikaner republics, which had openly sought closer relations with Americans and hence were more likely to yield to official American protests on behalf of black citizens.

The Virginia Jubilee Singers took to South Africa the up from slavery model later made famous by Booker T. Washington, thereby merging the history of African Americans with the freedom dreams of Africans. The acclaim and curiosity directed toward the singers bolstered the often successful attempts by American Negroes to have their American citizenship rights exempt them from South African segregation during the 1890s. However, by 1903, accelerated South African segregation and mounting suspicions among whites in South Africa that American Negroes' alliances with Africans threatened the status quo meant that black Americans were now labeled as black perils. As the deepening global color line incorporated the relentless binary logic of separating humans into white and "nonwhite" categories, citizenship, education, or levels of "civilization" were all trumped by the supposed racial fault line.

"THE NEGRO'S DELIVERER": JACK JOHNSON AS CINEMATIC BLACK PERIL

In 1910, another image of the American Negro as a model for South African blacks broke through local stereotypes of black inferiority. Two years earlier, a Texas-born boxer named Jack Johnson won a knockout victory over Canadian Tommy Burns in Sydney, Australia, to become the world's first black heavyweight champion. Fight films showcasing Johnson's powerful punches, his elusive defensive measures, and his amiable chatter with opponents and ringside spectators galvanized both black and white South Africans. In the fight with Burns, he had encouraged the Canadian to flail away at his stomach, which many whites considered the weak spot of all "yellow-bellied nigras." "Hit here Tah-my, now here Tah-my," Johnson tormented his opponent, "hit harder Tah-my, poor little Tah-my, who told you that you could fight?" As if determined to help Burns earn his record $30,000 purse (Johnson earned only $5,000), Johnson held up the sagging champion when Burns seemed on the verge of collapse. Australian police stopped the filming of the fight just as Burns was about to hit the canvas.[56] The black-owned *Richmond (Va.) Planet* crowed: "No event in forty years has given more genuine satisfaction to the colored people of this country than has the signal victory of Jack Johnson."[57]

Johnson's victory had given the lie to white claims that black boxers were inferior by nature to their white counterparts. Supposedly, white boxers exemplified a superior Anglo-Saxon courage, endurance, and resourcefulness that enabled Europeans and Americans to conquer the "darker races" of Asia, Africa, and the Pacific. Before the Johnson-Burns bout, white heavyweight champions, paradoxically, had drawn the color line in the ring. They refused to fight supposedly inferior, dull-witted black challengers, considering them unfit for combat and for the social Darwinian "survival of the fittest" competition among the world's races. Johnson's title shot would probably never have occurred had Japan not defeated the Russian navy in 1905 to become a world power and a source of pride for persons of color, including black South Africans who argued that the Japanese victory proved racial equality.[58] U.S. president Theodore Roosevelt, who saw an expansionist Japan as a "yellow peril" to America and its allies in the Pacific, dispatched a "great white fleet" featuring sixteen battleships to showcase American naval power and discourage Japanese ambitions in the Pacific. When Australia had become a self-governing British dominion in 1901, having previously pledged to assist its "brother Anglo-Saxons" in the Spanish-American War, Roosevelt had praised the country as an exemplary form of Anglo-Saxon expansion. He proclaimed that it was time to "substitute the big stick for politeness in dealing with Japan" in order to "maintain our rights" and declared that "the fleet had been sent round the Pacific for a purpose!"[59] As Australia welcomed the great white fleet with open arms, Hugh McIntosh, an Australian entrepreneur, predicted that boxing-mad American sailors and Australians with racist "white Australia" attitudes would pay top dollar to see a Johnson-Burns fight. With the promise of a record purse, McIntosh convinced Burns to cross the color line.[60]

The 1908 film of Johnson's one-punch knockout of middleweight champion Stanley Ketchel circulated widely, with advertisements featuring a handful of Ketchel's front teeth lodged in Johnson's glove.[61] In South Africa, films like *My Zulu's Heart* (1906), *The Voortrekkers: Birth of a Continent* (1916), and *King Solomon's Mines* (1918) perpetuated essential founding myths that ignored the white appropriation of African land and labor and portrayed whites taming violent and duplicitous African savages. Johnson's fight films bore a new script of prowess and intelligence, his blackness alone being revolutionary because almost all supposedly black males in film were actually white men in blackface.[62] Members of South Africa's small Indian population were allowed to see the films, but Africans themselves were forbidden to view the fight between Burns and Johnson, though some sneaked in anyway. Those who did not sneak in heard blow-by-blow accounts and could "gloat over the photographs and posters displayed in shop windows everywhere."[63]

On 4 July 1910, Johnson, alternately dubbed the "Negro's Deliverer" and the "Ethiopian Colossus," fought former heavyweight champion Jim Jeffries, the "Hope of the White Race," in Reno, Nevada, in what was billed as the battle of the century.[64] Jeffries had retired as champion to avoid facing Johnson, but Jack London, the famed sportswriter and novelist, issued a call to arms: "Jeff, it's up to you! The white man must be rescued!" Jeffries agreed to fight to prove "that a white man is better than a Negro."[65] William Jennings Bryan, the potent orator with presidential aspirations, assured Jeffries that "God is with you."[66] Booker T. Washington, proclaiming the fight the most significant event for the race since emancipation, installed a news ticker at Tuskegee so its black students could have running updates. Washington did so even though he disapproved of Johnson's relationships with white women (he married three white women in his lifetime) and his enthusiastic patronage of interracial gambling joints and houses of prostitution. A *Baltimore Afro-American Ledger* editorial, proclaiming that the fight would settle the question of racial supremacy, assured Johnson that "thousands of Negroes have nailed our name to your masthead. Nobody has so much to win or lose as you represent."[67]

A hostile crowd greeted Johnson's entrance into the ring with death threats and racial slurs as a band played the popular minstrel song "All Coons Look Alike to Me." Johnson knocked Jeffries down three times, and won by knockout in the fifteenth round.[68] Jeffries admitted that, even in his prime, "I couldn't have hit him in a thousand years."[69] In the days after the fight, angry whites around the country sparked racial rioting that left eighteen dead and hundreds injured.[70]

To black South Africans, Johnson's victory reaffirmed the special role of African Americans in refuting claims of black inferiority. A letter to the editor of the *Times of Natal* said, "The white races can do or say what they may, but the fact remains branded in the heavens that the Black man is wearing the laurels of the world, and may always be. A white man cannot do as he pleases. Man proposes but God disposes."[71] A letter to the editor of the *Bloemfontein Post* noted that "the white population of the world, especially in America and South Africa, are jealous because the champion of the world is a black man."[72]

The American-educated editor of *Ilanga lase Natal* (Sun of Natal), John Dube, in two pointed editorials, cited the "strange paradox" of "people who are held to be the most clever of nations, befooling themselves" by sanctioning barbarism. He called on the American and South African governments to ban boxing, since the sport could engender a racial hatred that "lies like a ravening tumor in the social body."[73] The *Times of Natal* wrote, "The fight will embitter existing race hatred in America, in [the] Philippines where it will be hailed with joy and will have a demoralizing effect upon the colored races . . . under British rule."[74]

White South Africans now demanded that the Johnson-Jeffries film be banned from the country. One editorial writer claimed the fight film "may do almost as much harm as if the actual fight itself had taken place in South Africa," spreading a "contagion" and "infection" that would destabilize colonialism.[75] White newspaper editorials engaged in circular logic—Jeffries's natural mental superiority, not Johnson's superior skills, had caused his defeat because "he possessed a higher nervous organism and was therefore more susceptible to pain and suffering. The only sphere in which the white is clearly and demonstrably the superior of the black is in the former's brain power manifested in a more ingenious and incessant mental activity."[76] Jeffries, wrote the *Bloemfontein Post*, "was doomed before he entered the ring, because he stripped himself of the mental advantage that the centuries had given him." Conversely, the *Post* claimed, Johnson "was already endowed by nature with the necessary physical qualities to ensure victory. The Negro was impregnably defended by a lower nervous organism and nothing save steel or bullet could disable him."[77] Two years later, in 1912, the South African government forbade further importation of Johnson's fight films. In the United States, theaters in the American South refused to show them, and Congress banned the interstate distribution of all fight films.[78]

AMERICAN NEGRO MISSIONARIES AS "UNDESIRABLE IMMIGRANTS"

Black South Africans exploited the physical and cinematic presence of American Negroes in South Africa to expose the lie of white supremacy and to exalt these Americans as worthy models for their own advancement. Largely because of this serious threat to white supremacy and the global color line, white segregationists viewed African Americans as black perils—individuals who were now subject to segregationist laws and who were to be banned from the country altogether. Into this deteriorating atmosphere sailed an enthusiastic, newly married American Negro couple, Herbert and Bessie Mae Payne. The Paynes had departed from New York in February 1917 under the auspices of the 2.5 million–member National Baptist Convention (NBC), the largest black religious organization in

America. They had come to relieve the Reverend James East while he took a sabbatical from the Middledrift, Eastern Cape, mission. The NBC presence in South Africa began in 1893 with a mission in Cape Town.[79] By 1897, the small church and school at Middledrift had grown to twenty satellites, with more than six hundred members and twenty-four African pastors and deacons. It became the pride of a black American Baptist mission that boasted more than eight thousand members among sixty mission stations.[80]

Payne's church, Metropolitan Baptist in New York City, had sent him to Virginia Theological Seminary and College to prepare for missionary work in Africa. His new wife, Bessie Mae Harden, was the granddaughter of a black Union soldier. The two sailed for South Africa via London and consulted there with the British Colonial Office and the British Home Office on South Africa's immigration policy. Reassured that there was no clause in South Africa's 1913 Immigration Act that would ban them as blacks, they sailed on to Cape Town. But there, the South African immigration authorities denied them admission and ordered them to take the next ship back to the United States. The authorities required them to provide a security deposit of £80 for a one-month temporary residence permit while they waited for the return voyage.[81] The Paynes received timely assistance from a fellow passenger, Solomon Plaatje, the first secretary-general of the African National Congress, who had gone to England to protest South Africa's discriminatory policies. Plaatje prevailed upon South African prime minister Louis Botha and minister of immigration Thomas Watt to reverse the Paynes deportation order and grant them time to appeal their status as "undesirable immigrants."[82]

Although Payne thanked George Murphy, the American consul-general at Cape Town, "in advance for the assistance you will give us as American citizens," the Department of the Interior in South Africa had other ideas. It confirmed that "under a Ministerial order, no coloured person is permitted to land in the Union of South Africa and it is in terms of this general order that the Reverend Payne and his wife were prohibited by the Minister."[83] The department had publicized this policy "for obvious reasons" but informed Murphy "so that in future, booking in regard to such people from America can be stopped."[84] (Two black American seamen, Timothy Johnson and Ewart Gibson, had been in jail almost two months awaiting an America-bound ship.) The Paynes protested that neither the British Colonial Office nor the Immigration Act banned black Americans. But the principal immigration officer replied that the Colonial Office had no authority over binding decisions on South African immigration policy. He cited a vaguely worded clause in the 1913 Immigration Act that referenced "any person or class of persons deemed by the Minister on economic grounds or on account of standard or habits of life to be unsuited to the requirements of the Union or any particular Province thereof."[85]

The Reverend James East, whom the Paynes were to replace, urged that their temporary permit be extended to six months. The Department of Interior, in turn, told East that the Paynes could stay if he renounced his domiciled rights, which he had earned after three years' residence and which prevented his deportation, and if he promised never to return to South Africa. East refused, but the department did grant the Paynes a six-month permit, after which either they or the Easts would have to leave. Meanwhile, the foreign missions secretary of the National Baptist Convention, L. G. Jordan, went to Washington, D.C., to appeal personally to Secretary of State Robert Lansing. Jordan lamented that the Paynes were to be "banished like some criminals and to go wandering the seas, subject to death at any time."[86] The U.S. Department of State instructed its Cape Town consulate to renew inquiries, but the authorities again rebuffed the overtures. Murphy, the American consul-general, declared the matter closed, concerned that repeated inquiries would further jeopardize U.S. relations with the South Africans: "The natives in the Union so far exceed in number the white population that the question of permitting the admission of other negroes is considered a serious one, requiring a strict enforcement of the law."[87]

Ironically, the Paynes dark skin color now made leaving impossible. The principal immigration officer informed them that "the Ellerman-Bucknall line, which has a good steamer going next month directly to the U.S., refuses to accept colored passengers either in the 1st or 2nd class." He extended their temporary permits by intervals, but the government, concerned about the supposedly subversive nature of American Negroes, again demanded that either the Easts or the Paynes leave the country.[88]

James East, more than any other African American Baptist missionary, transferred the Tuskegee model of industrial and agricultural education—and elements of Jim Crow race relations—to South Africa. East had been trained at the Nyack Missionary Training School in New York and at the Virginia Theological Seminary and College in Lynchburg. He considered the Buchanan Institute of his Middledrift mission a mini-Tuskegee, with industrial departments in blacksmithing, carpentry, and domestic science modeled after Booker T. Washington's vocational training program.[89] The institute's students were producing plows, horseshoes, wagons and carts, tables and chairs, cupboards, windows, and dressers that gave African homes a "civilized" veneer.[90] By 1920, the school, the largest of the Baptist Convention's eight schools, had nine teachers and one hundred students, from the first grade to the sixth. There was also a feeder school for leading secondary institutions like the nearby Lovedale Institute, the most prestigious school in South Africa for blacks. With English as the language of instruction, Buchanan had trained more than thirty teachers, and by 1920, a "large class" of young African men were in ministerial training. At least three Africans led their own churches, and several others worked with white Baptist mission stations.[91] East's wife, Lucinda, a domestic science teacher, had been teaching the girls of Buchanan household tasks such as how to sew and how to can and dry fruit. A trained physician's assistant, Lucinda also served as de facto doctor of the mission, particularly during the influenza pandemic.

James East, who had learned farming on his family's land in Alabama, employed Tuskegee agricultural methods in South Africa. Tuskegee used a traveling agricultural wagon for on-the-spot agricultural demonstrations throughout the South. East used a similar wagon to engage in similar practices in South Africa, as well as labor-intensive horses and mules instead of the customary cattle for plowing. His agricultural success attracted the attention of college administrators and government officials, who hired him as an agricultural demonstrator.[92] In late 1918, South Africa's Department of Agriculture hired East as the Ciskei's first agricultural demonstrator to teach African farmers.[93] He also lent his expertise to the agricultural program of the South African Native College, which was founded in 1916 partially to give Africans a college education in South Africa that would discourage them from attending American universities and associating with black Americans.[94]

Washington's Tuskegee had been the model for Buchanan on agricultural production and industrial skills, educating Africans in their "natural" rural environment and in ways that did not challenge white rule. But in America, Washington's model had, after his death in 1915, become increasingly passé, eclipsed both by the civil rights program of the National Association for the Advancement of Colored People (NAACP) and its editor and champion, W. E. B. Du Bois, and by the aggressive nationalism of Garveyism. Yet in South Africa, the Washington approach remained immensely popular.

For African leaders, Tuskegee, with its black principal and all-black staff, had become the ultimate model of self-determination and organizational development. After a visit to the school in 1922, Plaatje, secretary-general of the ANC, endorsed Washingtonian ideals in his newspaper, *Koranta ea Becoana*, and showed films of the school throughout South Africa.[95] D. D. T. Jabavu, son of *Imvo* editor Tengo Jabavu, had grown up reading his father's editorials praising Booker T. Washington, and in 1914, he sailed to the United States to prepare a government-commissioned report on Tuskegee-style industrial and agricultural programs for South Africa. Jabavu concluded, "We need a native Booker Washington to galvanize natives to action," and Washington, in turn, praised Jabavu as "a fine fellow, one of the best men we have ever had from Africa."[96] Jabavu and East became close friends and cofounded the Native Farmers Association (NFA) in 1918; by 1925, the NFA had more than forty chapters and several hundred African farmer members. Jabavu and East pressured the government to provide for African farmers the same amount of land, agricultural training, subsidies, and credit it gave to white farmers and to ease Africans' direct access to markets with the best prices.[97]

Despite the educational and agricultural success that came with the extension of the moderate Tuskegee ideal to South Africa, the government's fear of American Negro influence on the African majority ultimately prevailed. Lucinda East, concerned that her children had never been to the United States, left South Africa in 1920. Her husband, James, left six months later, never to return, fulfilling a pledge to leave in response to the government's stipulation. James East would become corresponding secretary of the National Baptist Convention's Foreign Mission Board and corresponding editor of its *Mission Herald.*[98]

The South African government had given the Easts' successors, Herbert and Bessie Payne, a one-year temporary residential permit, after which they were to leave (by 1 June 1921) or face imprisonment and a fine. The U.S. Department of State directed its new Cape Town consul-general to investigate the demand, but existing records show nothing further in that regard. While the Paynes waited for a ship, the government had forced Herbert to accept white Baptist oversight and to eliminate all liberal arts training from the Buchanan Institute. In 1923, plagued by persistent ill health, a lack of financial support from the National Baptist Convention, a virtual ban on black ownership of land (Payne had planned a farming school), and great personal tragedy (two of their children had died in infancy), the Paynes finally sailed home. They had managed to stay in South Africa for six years. The government refused to allow any other African American family to replace them, and John Sonjca, a wealthy African farmer and former pupil of East's, took up the management of Middledrift. The American missionaries themselves had hoped for eventual African leadership; it had come sooner than they anticipated.[99]

In some respects, certain African American missionaries believed they shared with whites a so-called civilizing mission in their interaction with Africans. Echoing Washington, James East himself believed that Africans benefited from the technological advances of European civilization and would "do well to take the white man as his example." If whites departed, he said, South Africa "would go at a rapid speed back to savagery." Despite his moderation, East believed South African whites feared that American Negroes would "teach the African native the principles of manhood and freedom, and so make impossible much of the injustice and forced labor of South Africa."[100] East reflected common African and black American thought in believing that "nobody can inspire a black man like another black man" to organize for "his own betterment."[101] East advised whites to "fling wide the gates" of opportunity—"otherwise the black man will go over the walls."[102]

In South Africa, as in Jim Crow America, American Negroes had discovered that the global color line was inescapable. Like whites in Jim Crow America, whites in South Africa subjected American Negroes to racial segregation not because of black failure but because of evidence of black success.[103] As the Virginia Jubilee Singers sang their gospels of liberation to great popular acclaim, as images of Jack Johnson's boxing exploits circulated around the world, and as the Paynes and Easts replicated African American religious and educational institutions in South Africa, self-governing South African whites strained to create a "white South Africa" that included the banning of African American peoples and images and the general subjugation of American Negro residents. As the cases of the Paynes and Easts demonstrate, South Africa, like other self-governing "white" British dominions Australia, New Zealand, and Canada, asserted its right to rule over blacks, trumping rhetorical imperial principles of racial equality for British subjects. The gradual exclusion and subordination of most American Negroes in South Africa and in the United States reflected the belief among whites that—as the supposed disaster of Reconstruction in the post–Civil War South proved—there could be no multiracial democracies that enshrined racial equality.

But though imperial Britain acquiesced to South African segregation, the local variant of transnational white supremacy, the "up from slavery" genie of black success was out of the bottle. Minstrelsy had circulated negative images of African Americans since the American Civil War, but subsequent American Negroes globalized a more optimistic, progressive narrative of black success in the post–Civil War American South. Africans regarded American Negroes as exemplary racial models for their own struggles for full citizenship rights in South Africa. The post–Civil War South had borne the triumphant "up from slavery" narrative, preparing the way for a transnational black liberationist movement that would be the foundation for Garveyism during the interwar years and, eventually, the global antiapartheid movement after World War II. White supremacist reactions to the Japanese victory over the Russians had created an opportunity for Jack Johnson to become the first heavyweight champion of the world, thereby furthering the "up from slavery" narrative. Similarly, black reactions to white supremacy would give rise to Marcus Garvey and his Africa for Africans ideal.

In their belief in a gradualist African upward mobility leading to eventual independence, the Payne and East families shared Booker T. Washington's moderate "up from slavery" narrative. As chapter 2 demonstrates, white American missionaries established mission stations for Africans in 1835, and by the late nineteenth century, several Africans trained at these stations traveled to the United States for university studies that would prepare them to become leaders of their people. In America, these Africans personally encountered

Washington and used his ideas as guiding principles in the founding of the African National Congress, organized to combat the segregationist practices of the South African government. ANC appeals to the British government, which had the power to nullify South African legislation, failed because Great Britain acquiesced to white South African demands for noninterference in domestic affairs. Nevertheless, Africans affiliated with white American missions and with Booker T. Washington deepened the connections between American Negroes and Africans, setting the stage for Garveyism, even as they realized that the British would not use their power to liberate them from South African segregation.

2 ◡ The Failed Dream of British Liberation and Christian Regeneration

IN THE late 1870s, a Zulu named John Nembula, who would become South Africa's first African physician, studied at schools of the American Board for Foreign Missions in Amanzimtoti, Natal. His grandmother and his father were the American Board's first converts.[1] Nembula went on to teach at Amanzimtoti Institute, later known as Adams College, in Natal, and then, in 1881, he sailed for America to help proofread and translate the American Board's Zulu Bible.[2] In the United States, he attended Oberlin College, the University of Michigan, and the Chicago Medical College of Northwestern University, planning to become a medical missionary to his people, the Zulus.[3] But when he was back in Africa, white residents of Umsinga district vehemently opposed his 1888 appointment as district surgeon and boycotted his practice. Nembula founded a "Native Cottage hospital," which closed three years later because of few patients, and then taught hygiene and physiology at Adams College with a medical missionary, at a facility that became McCord Hospital. He died in 1896, his potential and his dreams unfulfilled as a consequence of white determination that blacks not be allowed to succeed. Despite acquiring an education of impressive range and depth, he was denied the opportunity to become a leader of his people.[4]

Yet Nembula did find success through his influence on others. Among his students at Amanzimtoti was a youth named John Dube—an individual who would one day be dubbed the "Booker T. Washington of South Africa" and become the leading spokesperson for the African Christian elite and the first president of the African National Congress. The ANC, South Africa's oldest existing political party, led the fight against segregation and its successor, apartheid.

James Dube, John's father, was one of the American Board's earliest or-dained African ministers; he was pastor of the Inanda church and head of its day school. James Dube was also a founder of Inanda Seminary, the first south-ern African secondary school for African girls.[5] James's mother, Mayembe, had been the Inanda mission's first convert. At the American Board mission, established by Daniel Lindley (who had left his pulpit in North Carolina to go to Africa), Mayembe had sought refuge to avoid an arranged marriage to a brother of her deceased husband, a Qadi chief. She and other *amakholwa* (African Christians), in small, self-contained farming communities on the mission reserves, learned from the missionaries that to be Christian was to be civilized. American Board missionaries were training what they thought could be their future replacements—an educated class of farmers, artisans, ministers, teachers, and professionals who would spread Christianity across southern Africa. Few may have dreamed that they were planting seeds that would help to liberate South Africa.

John Dube entered Amanzimtoti, a preparatory school that offered educa-tion up to standard eight (tenth grade in the American educational system), along with agricultural and industrial training.[6] Amanzimtoti Theological School, later part of Adams College, and Inanda Seminary, a school for girls, were the most advanced schools for Africans in Natal. They adopted both the industrial Booker T. Washington education model, similar to that of the later Hampton Institute, and the Du Boisian liberal arts model, with classes in English, history, and mathematics.[7]

In 1887, an American Board missionary, William Cullen Wilcox, accompa-nied John Dube to America to help him enroll at Hampton. But Dube, who had funds from his father's commercial farming, preferred Oberlin, Wilcox's own alma mater. After two years in preparatory courses, Dube joined Wil-cox in lecturing on the Chautauqua circuit, informing eager audiences and stirring Christians to spread the gospel of salvation to benighted African idol worshippers.[8] A remarkable pamphlet written by Dube at the time, entitled "A Familiar Talk about My Native Land," glorified pioneering white missionaries in Africa like David Livingstone and Robert Moffat and suggested that he himself was an evangelist of God's chosen generation. He prophesied that Christianity would transform the "Dark Continent" into a modern Christian civilization: "Ethiopia shall stretch out her hands unto God," and Africa would take its place in the pantheon of higher civilizations.[9]

At twenty-one, Dube was back in Natal as one of an emerging amakholwa leadership group that envisioned greater African control of churches and schools and greater African involvement in Natal's political life. But whites in the area had other ideas. In 1893, Natal became a self-governing British colony, similar to Cape Colony, Canada, Newfoundland, New Zealand, and the Australian colonies. The 1893 Natal census listed 500,000 Africans, 43,742 whites, and 41,208 Indians. Some whites worried that Natal was "already not a white man's colony" and that it, supposedly like the American South during Reconstruction, would degenerate into a failed multiracial state unless they adopted American Jim Crow measures to entrench white rule. Borrowing from Mississippi's 1890 adoption of a literacy test to disenfranchise black Americans, the Natal Franchise Act of 1896 disenfranchised virtually all Africans. Pointing to the example of the "great Republic of America" and its attempts to limit immigration from eastern and central Europe in the U.S. Immigration Restriction Act of 1896, Natal enacted an immigration law in 1897 that granted colonial officials the right to exclude "undesirables," particularly persons of color.[10]

In this charged political environment, Dube clashed with a white American Board missionary, Stephen Pixley, who believed Africans would be incapable of running their own affairs for at least another hundred years.[11] Thereafter, Dube, who was a close relative of Mqhawe, the chief of the Qadi (an ethnic group subordinate to the Zulu), left Inanda to establish his own mission field. He soon had two churches and three schools in Qadi lands. In 1895, after Dube was elected pastor of the Inanda mission, Pixley protested that he was not ordained and thus unqualified.[12] But Pixley was even more concerned about the challenge to his own authority, and he considered Dube's leadership a precursor to wider African attempts to attain political independence.[13] Similarly, the Natal colonial government itself refused to fund any black-led school, lest Africans with skills compete with white farmers and skilled white laborers. By 1900, only three Africans in the whole of Natal could vote. Therefore, Dube, nicknamed "Mafukuzela," meaning "the one who struggles against obstacles," looked to America and specifically to Booker T. Washington for a path to liberation. In 1896, he returned to the United States to earn a theological degree from Brooklyn's Union Missionary Training Institute and to be ordained as a Congregational minister. He also raised funds for an industrial school modeled after Washington's Tuskegee Institute.[14] He had arrived in New York in time to hear Washington deliver a series of lectures on industrial education and Christianity as the keys to black advancement. At Tuskegee in May 1897, Dube met Washington and spoke at the graduation ceremony, delivering an address of "rare force" that made him the virtual "hero of the commencement."[15] Dube spoke, too, at the commencement of the Hampton Institute, declaring, "The kind of work done at Hampton is the kind of work my people need" to avoid sinking "into the vices of civilization instead of profiting from its virtues."[16]

Hampton, founded in 1868 by the Congregationalist American Missionary Association on land that was once a plantation, was among the eight teacher-training schools in the South for freedpeople.[17] Hampton's principal, Samuel

Chapman Armstrong, was the son of missionaries to Hawaii and had been a Union general in the Civil War, where he led black troops. But after the war, he had gone to Hampton as a Freedman's Bureau official and promptly restored land to former plantation owners and subjected landless freedpeople to onerous labor contracts. Believing that blacks needed, above all else, training in character and morality, Armstrong shaped Hampton to be a training ground for future black and Indian teachers who were schooled in Christianity, moral uplift, hygiene, and self-discipline. He also mandated a limited academic curriculum, including English and mathematics, and training in agricultural and industrial skills. Armstrong set up a work regime to instill moral values and a strong work ethic; first-year students had to earn two hours of instruction by performing ten hours of agricultural or industrial labor.[18]

Booker T. Washington, a freed slave born in Franklin County, Virginia, product of an unknown white man and his enslaved mistress, became Armstrong's most famous pupil. He subsequently taught school in the small town of Malden, then returned to Hampton to teach and later received an invitation to start a Hampton-like school in Tuskegee, Alabama.[19] There, without land or buildings but with a dedicated all-black staff, Washington raised funds to acquire land and buildings and recruited students to build the facilities and to cultivate and harvest the crops that fed them all. By 1900, Tuskegee's all-black faculty and staff of three hundred served an all-black student body of roughly fifteen hundred students. This number was twice as large as the combined student bodies of the University of Alabama and Auburn and one of the largest university enrollments in the country.[20] Tuskegee's strictures were rigorous; no dancing, liquor, tobacco, gambling, or unregulated dating was permitted. Washington considered the virtues of punctuality, individual responsibility, cleanliness, thrift, and self-discipline more important than academic learning. Still, Tuskegee's academic faculty held college degrees from Harvard, Michigan, Oberlin, Fisk, and comparable institutions, and a majority of its students trained to be teachers—not, as many had imagined, hewers of wood. Washington believed that the Hampton/Tuskegee educational model contributed to the rise of black literacy rates from less than 10 percent at emancipation to nearly 50 percent in 1900. He also believed that his methods had helped facilitate the increase in landownership among black farmers, from about 5 percent in 1880 to 25 percent in 1900.[21]

Many southern whites delighted in the idea of a black leader who seemed to accept the white-over-black political order of the Jim Crow South. Northern industrialists like Andrew Carnegie, John Rockefeller, and Robert Ogden donated hundreds of thousands of dollars to Tuskegee to develop a reliable pool of cheap but educated black workers. Carnegie declared Washington the second father of the country, and the black editor of the *New York*

Age, T. Thomas Fortune, called him the new Moses. Presidents William McKinley and Theodore Roosevelt funneled Republican patronage through Washington, who had become the most powerful black man in the world.[22] His famous autobiography, *Up from Slavery*, published in 1901, was a remarkably optimistic account of his rise from slavery to freedom and a metaphor for the progress of blacks. But Washington had detractors as well, among them Harvard graduates W. E. B. Du Bois and Monroe Trotter. Trotter, the editor of the *Boston Guardian* newspaper, complained that Washington ceded hard-fought constitutional rights for African Americans and offered an inferior—and limited—educational model that reflected acquiescence to Jim Crow.[23] But Washington continued to believe that his educational methods could solve the "native problem" in South Africa.

Black South Africans themselves revered Booker T. Washington and Tuskegee as tangible examples of what was possible for them. A wide array of Africans publicized and endorsed Tuskegee in their publications. These included the moderate editor of *Imvo Zabantsundu*, John Tengo Jabavu, as well as his more radical contemporary Allen K. Soga, editor of *Izwi Labantu*, and the Gold Coast–born editor of the *South African Spectator*, F. Z. S. Peregrino.[24] Sol Plaatje, the first secretary-general of the ANC, called Washington the "champion of the cause of the dark and backward races—a thankless job," and on his death in 1915, Plaatje lauded him as "the greatest black man of our time."[25] Washington shared a sense of interdependency between American Negroes and Africans:

> There is . . . a tie which few white men can understand, which binds the American Negro to the African Negro. . . . There is not only the tie of race, which is strong in any case, but there is the bond of color, which is especially important in the case of the black man. It is this common badge of color, for instance, which is responsible for the fact that whatever contributes, in any degree to the progress of the American Negro, contributes to the progress of the African Negro, and to the Negro in South America and the West Indies. When the African Negro succeeds, it helps the American Negro. When the African Negro fails, it hurts the reputation and the standing of the Negro in every part of the world.[26]

In 1900, John Dube wrote an extraordinary essay, "A Zulu's Message to Afro-Americans," imploring African Americans to go to Africa to regenerate the continent: "God has wonderfully prepared the Afro-Americans, through years of bondage by a civilized nation (even as were the Jews) for the task of civilizing their African brethren, a necessary first step to regain their independence."[27]

For Dube, Afro-Americans were important models in racial advancement and, as Christian missionaries, potential liberators of pagan Africans: "When they come, then we will talk a lot about our country. It will be well if at sometime, the first shall be last & the last shall be first."[28] Africans confronted with slavelike conditions understood from the American example that American Negroes could be precursors of their own future rebirth as modern global citizens.

Dube's growing belief that African Americans had a divinely ordained role in African liberation was mirrored by a touring partner on the American lecture circuit, Joseph Booth, a white Englishman famous for his mantra of "Africa for the Africans." Booth believed that "the white man can never bridge the gulf between himself and the native as the Negro can." African Americans were, he said, a "divinely prepared people for a work also prepared of God" and the "GREATEST HOPE" for Africans: "The Negro is the only one with these qualifications . . . the Negro therefore holds the key to Africa's future as no other people can. His position is unique."[29]

Joseph Booth was the fourth child of British Unitarian parents. Many Unitarians, American and English, had long been ardent abolitionists in the Atlantic world. Booth's pacifist inclinations as a fifteen-year-old led him to accuse his father of hypocrisy for ignoring the biblical injunction "Thou shalt not kill" in supporting family members who took up arms in the Crimean War. His father retorted that his son could choose his own religion when he was able to support himself. Booth promptly left home, married, and migrated to New Zealand and Australia in the early 1890s, where he made a name for himself in public debates. As many as a thousand gathered to hear him debate with atheists about religion, but when one such atheist called Booth a hypocrite for failing to take up missionary work in Africa and follow Christ's biblical command to sell all his worldly goods, Booth promptly left for Africa.

There, he preached on street corners in Cape Town, then migrated to the British colonial territory of Nyasaland.[30] He hoped to raise funds for the African Christian Union (ACU) to establish independent, black-led industrial and agricultural centers in southern Africa. John Nembula, Dube's former teacher, was an ACU secretary. African American officers included George White, of the Virginia Jubilee Singers; William Creditt, a prominent Baptist minister; Rudolph Rose, solicitor of the Morgan Negro Institute (later Morgan State University); and Alfred Lewis, solicitor of the prominent black newspaper the *Richmond Planet*.[31] Booth declared: "Let the African, sympathetically led by his more experienced Afro-American brother, develop his own country, establish his own manufacturers, work his own plantations, run his own ships, work his own mines, educate his own people, possess his own mission stations, conserve the wealth accruing from all sources, if possible, for the commonwealth and enlightenment of the people and the glory of God."[32]

Advocating the Africa for Africans goal, later made famous by Marcus Garvey, Booth joined seven different denominations over his missionary career, caring less about denominational loyalties than about his own objectives, which transcended religious conversion. In September 1895, 150 Africans in Durban debated for twenty-six hours on the ACU proposal for black-led centers. They rejected the proposal on the grounds that no living white man could be trusted, and a disappointed Booth left Natal for America. He later returned, but his fiery anticolonial politics led to deportation from South Africa and Nyasaland. On 8 August 1900, five years after Booth's ACU proposal, Dube opened Ohlange Institute at Inanda, the first South African school modeled explicitly after Tuskegee. Washington, Dube, and Booth all had similar beliefs that American Negroes were central to the advancement of Africans, but Africans rejected Booth's African Christian Union largely because the binary nature of the global color line made every white man untrustworthy in their eyes. As white leadership was increasingly called into question, African American leadership models like Booker T. Washington had enduring value for Africans like John Dube.

THE FAILURE OF THE BRITISH AS LIBERATORS AND LOOKING TO AMERICANS

For John Dube, industrial education was "our salvation, as a people."[33] Like Tuskegee, his Ohlange Institute was led by blacks, but it, too, relied heavily on white American philanthropy, in this case through an American-based Congregational committee. Dube encountered hostile whites who favored the minimum education required to produce pliant workers, lest more-advanced education produce "spoilt" Africans who would demand political and socioeconomic equality. Using Washington's tactics, he reassured them that Ohlange graduates would occupy unskilled positions on the bottom rung of the economic ladder. Yet Ohlange in fact trained thousands of Africans who rose well above the bottom rung, among them ANC cofounder Richard Msimang, accomplished writers B. W. Vilakazi and R. R. R. Dhlomo, and famed composer Reuben Caluza (who would later study at Hampton).[34]

Ohlange's nine-month school year offered the equivalent of a high school education for a few hundred boarding students and day scholars, most of them boys (school officials claimed there were no sufficiently separate accommodations for girls).[35] Its Tuskegee-like program emphasized self-help. Students paid their tuition, in part, by growing, eating, and selling their agricultural crops, tending animals, and constructing and maintaining buildings as part of their mandatory three hours of physical labor daily.[36] Ohlange's all-black staff included several American-educated teachers. One was a West Indian named Reynolds Scott, a Tuskegee graduate who left America with Dube in 1899 to help establish Ohlange and run the school's industrial department. John Dube's brother Charles, whom John had sent to Wilberforce University (an AME school in Ohio), served as "headmaster, principal and trustee" of Ohlange at various times between 1905 and 1926.[37] Charles's wife, Adelaide, who had also attended Wilberforce, taught standard seven students; Madikane Cele and his American wife, Julia, both Hampton graduates, also taught at Ohlange. A black American woman, Katherine Blackburn, taught biblical studies and business.[38]

The racial climate of South Africa did not allow Dube the luxury of being solely an educator. He began to play a public role as a journalist and, through journalism, as a leader in policy debate. He hoped for a British victory in the South African War, followed by African liberation from Afrikaners: "the lot of the native under the Boer," he said, was like "slavery, robbery and injustice."[39] Conveniently ignoring their own restrictive racial legislation, particularly in Natal, the British criticized the racial policies in the Boer republics and intimated that a British victory would herald greater African political rights in South Africa. The British high commissioner in South Africa, Lord Alfred Milner, declared: "It is not race or color but civilization which is the test of a man's capacity for political rights."[40] Joseph Chamberlain, secretary of state for the colonies, declared that Britain would not "consent to purchase peace by leaving the coloured population in the position in which they stood before the war, with not even the ordinary civil rights which the Government of the Cape Colony has long conceded to them."[41] Under British rule, Dube was convinced, Africans would expect equal rights as British citizens, including the franchise, landownership, and full economic and educational opportunities for individual and collective advancement.[42]

But the British victory in the South African War meant the expansion of the global color line. In the postwar negotiations, Milner proposed to defeated Afrikaner leaders that Africans would not be granted the franchise until Natal, Cape Colony, and the former Afrikaner republics, as a unified South Africa, became a self-governing dominion of the British Empire. Defeated Afrikaner general Jan Smuts—who would become an international statesman and help found the League of Nations and the United Nations and who served multiple terms as South African prime minister until 1948—objected to the presumption that Africans would eventually have the franchise. For Smuts, "the war between the white races will run its course and pass away . . . but the native question will never pass away; it will become more difficult as time goes on, and the day may come when the evils and horrors of this war will appear as nothing in comparison with its after effects produced on the native mind."[43]

He insisted that white South Africans maintain the right to deny Africans the franchise and, by extension, their aspirations for full citizenship.

Smuts prevailed, with article 8 of the postwar Treaty of Vereeniging affirming the stunning fact that the victorious British, who had the power to extend the franchise throughout South Africa, deferred to their vanquished Afrikaner enemies. With British-Boer reconciliation a higher priority than African political rights, Milner knew that "you only have to sacrifice the nigger absolutely and the game is easy. There is the whole crux of the South African position." He now proclaimed that "a political equality of white and black is impossible. The white man must rule, because he is elevated by many, many steps above the black man; steps which it will take the latter centuries to climb."[44]

Despite overwhelming African support for the British side in the war as well as the death of nearly fifteen thousand Africans, white nationalism had now unified the former combatants. The nonracial franchise was not extended beyond the Cape Colony. The pass laws in the former Afrikaner republics continued, and the British refused to transfer lands of rebellious Afrikaners to loyal Africans. Influential white segregationists maintained that Africans could exercise some tribal self-government on land reserves, but in reality, these reserves became a cheap labor pool, a means to rule indirectly through chiefs, and a place to send Africans who were unable to work. Segregation became a unifying ideology between Afrikaners and the English; it was an economic program that delivered inexpensive African labor to white employers and a political platform for whites' paternalistic control.[45] As he departed South Africa in 1905, Milner admitted that even he had underestimated the rabid antiblack sentiment among whites and regretted that he did not provide loopholes for educated Africans like Dube to have citizenship rights. He understood, too late, that the "white South Africa" that Smuts and others championed had no place for black citizens.[46]

Natal authorities had detained Dube during the South African War, supposedly for making seditious statements, for associating with American Negro missionaries, and for asserting that "justice would be done only when the African ruled the country." With printing skills learned in the United States and inspired by Tuskegee's *Southern Letter*, the *Tuskegee Student*, and Hampton's *Southern Workman*, Dube began to protest British colonial policies in a newspaper of his own. *Ilanga lase Natal*, established in 1903, was one of only a few African newspapers of that era to provide a rich forum for African protest and debate; the others included *Imvo Zabantsundu*, *Ipepa lo Hlanga*, *Izwi Labantu*, *Koranta ea Becoana*, and the *South African Spectator*. In the absence of parliamentary representation or other constitutional channels for Africans to communicate with the government, these newspapers served as a primary channel to colonial authorities.[47] When *Ilanga* adopted the slogan "*Vukani*

Bantu!" (Rise Up You People!), the Natal colonial governor reprimanded Dube. Detectives monitored him and Ohlange students and searched *Ilanga*, including its Zulu-language articles, for signs of rebellion.[48] Meanwhile, the paper continued to protest disenfranchisement, the job color bar, and limited education for Africans, citing the American Revolutionary protest against "taxation without representation" and Cecil Rhodes's call for "Equal Rights for All Civilized Men." It claimed, prophetically, that unjust measures would lead to greater African resistance.[49]

Dube continued to point to Britain's responsibility to safeguard African rights: "The Imperial Government, of which we are now all loyal citizens interested in, and sharing alike its responsibilities, is bound by both fundamental and specific obligations towards the natives and coloured races of South Africa to extend to them the same measure of equitable justice and consideration as is extended to those of European descent under the law."[50] Dube was vice president of the South African Native Convention (SANC), which had convened in 1909 to protest African disenfranchisement by the South Africa Act that sanctioned the Union of South Africa. He felt the act reflected "the apparent decline of British views in the treatment of the native question from those high standards which were once the pride and the crown and the glory of British statesmanship." Dube felt the "Imperial factor is the only moderating influence" on domestic white racism, and he advocated that Africans remain under Crown control.[51]

On 31 May 1910, exactly eight years after the Treaty of Vereeniging that ended the South African War, the four provinces became the Union of South Africa, a self-governing dominion within the British Empire that retained control of its domestic affairs. Africans were the sacrificial lambs to white reconciliation, and the British, aware that persons of color outnumbered whites five to one in the empire, claimed they had neither the desire nor the power to impose the claimed imperial tradition of equal rights under the law, irrespective of color, onto a "white South Africa." British parliamentarians noted that an extension of the Cape franchise to all of South Africa would inevitably lead to African majority rule. Citing the supposedly failed "Negro rule" of the multiracial American South during Reconstruction, the parliamentarians passed the South Africa Act the year before with a large majority.[52]

SEGREGATIONIST SOUTH AFRICA AND THE FOUNDING OF THE ANC

South African legislators quickly enacted segregationist laws, barring people of color from the Dutch Reformed Church (in 1911), restricting African freedom of movement and access to skilled jobs (in 1911), and passing the Immigration Restriction Act (in 1913) to limit black and Asian immigration. The Natives

Land Act of 1913 prohibited blacks, nearly 80 percent of South Africa's population, from purchasing or leasing land reserved for whites in 93 percent of the country's territory. It forbade Africans to buy land outside the 7 percent they owned and to rent or sharecrop on land owned by whites. Whites were allowed to evict from their land African sharecroppers who did not work directly for them. In the Orange Free State, where Africans did not have the legal right to own land, landless and homeless blacks wandered with their cattle around the province. Unable to buy or sharecrop land beyond their reserved areas, Africans were subjected by their new labor-tenant status to the Masters and Servants Act. This act allowed "masters" to bind "servants" to unfavorable, long-term contracts; to unilaterally punish and discipline; and to use child labor even against the parents' will.[53] Now the deputy prime minister, Smuts regarded this intentional, unified segregationist policy to be a great improvement over the more haphazard methods of individual provinces, but Africans like the lawyer and author Silas Molema felt these policies were "along the lines of the South of the United States."[54]

The influence of education that began with Africans such as John Nembula back in the 1870s and with John Dube in America in the late 1880s now began to spread to another generation but with continuity. Pixley Seme, the leading cofounder of the South African Native National Congress (renamed the African National Congress in 1923), was Dube's cousin. After attending the Methodist-sponsored Mount Hermon Preparatory School in western Massachusetts, Seme matriculated at Columbia University, becoming one of several Zulu students educated in American universities.[55] At Columbia, he took the school's top prize for oratory with an essay on "The Regeneration of Africa," echoing W. E. B. Du Bois's 1897 essay titled "Conservation of Races." Seme maintained that Africans had a distinctive racial genius, evident in the glories of ancient Egypt and Ethiopia. He and other African students exposed to Christianity by close contact with modern Western civilization would "return to their country," he said, "like arrows, to drive darkness from the land."[56] Seme would tell Washington, "We need your spirit in Africa."[57] In 1910, Seme earned a law degree at Oxford, opened a law practice in the Transvaal, and organized the African Farmers Association; the association was a landowning syndicate that purchased property, including four farms that adopted Tuskegee's progressive agricultural methods. He called for a national organization to apply the great lessons of Christianity—cooperation and unity among Africans and between blacks and whites, for the benefit of themselves and of the God all Christians served.[58]

Seme was the legal representative for members of the Swazi royal family, and he convinced them to provide moneys to fund and maintain the South African Native National Congress and support its newspaper, *Abantu-Batho,* which would later become the most widely read African newspaper. Like his cousin Dube, he epitomized Du Bois's "talented tenth," the cadre of future leaders of their people and their country. In 1912, at Bloemfontein, Seme presided over delegates representing organizations throughout South Africa and the British protectorates of Bechuanaland, Basutoland, and Swaziland. He explained the purpose of the gathering:

> We have discovered in the land of their birth, Africans are treated as hewers of wood and drawers of water. The white people of this country have formed what is known as the Union of South Africa—a union in which we have no voice in the making of laws and no part in their administration. We have called you therefore to this Conference so that we can together devise ways and means of forming our national union for the purpose of creating national unity and defending our rights and privileges.[59]

The formation of SANNC was a watershed in African regeneration, hastening the day when "Ethiopia would stretch forth her hands unto God, and when princes shall come out of Egypt."[60] Representing a greater consolidation of African opinion, SANNC would communicate to Africans their rights and responsibilities, both to the state and to themselves. SANNC would also review legislation, educate whites, and advise the government about African concerns. In 1909, on the eve of South African union, Dube had expected the Cape Colony's British liberalism to spread throughout a British-controlled South Africa.[61]

Seme was the SANNC's guiding spirit, and Dube was elected president of SANNC. Dube stressed a gradualist path toward political power, likening SANNC to a cow that grazed along the edges of the field and then moved to the center so gradually yet deliberately that other cows did not notice the progress from the periphery.[62] He explicitly modeled himself after Booker T. Washington and advised Africans to "hasten, slowly" and to elevate themselves through education:

> Booker T. Washington . . . is my guiding star (would that he were nigh to give us the help of his wise counsel!). I have chosen this great man, firstly because he is perhaps the most famous and the best living example of our Africa's sons; and, secondly because like him, I, too, have my heart centered mainly in the education of my race. Therein, methinks, lies the shortest and best way to their mental, moral, material and political betterment. . . . Onward! Upward! Into the higher places of civilization and Christianity.[63]

Dube protested that South Africa's restrictive laws violated African rights. He mocked South Africa's claim to represent Christian principles of justice and freedom: "Just government derived its rightful powers from the consent of the governed." South African politicians, he said, had impeded African progress in "the Gospel life and its accompanying Civilization." Dube argued that the exclusion of Africans from political citizenship made the state illegitimate and its laws nonbinding on Africans who proclaimed themselves British subjects protected by the Crown.[64]

Dube brought to the attention of the Natal Native Affairs Department eighty cases that demonstrated the adverse effects of the Natives Land Act; he appealed to the secretary of native affairs but to no avail. He denounced the act as "class legislation" that turned Africans into wage slaves. For Dube, the act proved Christianity itself could not "raise even the most enlightened race above the lowest levels of selfishness and greed and godless persecution." He chastised whites for their hypocrisy and their betrayal of Christian principles, declaring, "You tell us that . . . you are children of Christ guided solely by the eternal principle of blind justice regardless of colour or creed: What contemptible cant! What a blasphemous fraud."[65]

Would Great Britain liberate Africans from tyrannical South African rule? In 1914, Dube headed a SANNC delegation to London to lobby the British Parliament to veto the Natives Land Act. Alternatively, he argued, if territorial segregation were to be accepted, there had to be agreement on an equitable distribution of land to each race. The SANNC delegation declared that the act violated the 1843 proclamation from Queen Victoria after British annexation of Natal, vowing to treat all persons equally and stipulating "that there shall not be, in the eye of the law, any distinction or qualification whatever, founded on mere distinction of colour, origin, or language, or creed; but that the protection of the law, in letter and in substance, shall be extended impartially to all alike." If the British did not intervene, Dube cautioned, discriminatory polices would "inevitably lead to disaster."[66]

At the close of World War I, SANNC petitioned King George V again, reminding him that Africans had "closed ranks" in the war, temporarily putting aside their grievances to recruit twenty-four thousand Africans as a supportive labor force in German Southwest Africa. An additional ten thousand men joined the South African Native Labor Contingent to fight in France. King George had praised them for "fighting for the liberty and freedom of my subjects of all races and creeds throughout my Empire."[67] Africans had also raised funds to support the war effort. Yet Deputy Prime Minister Jan Smuts refused SANNC's offer to recruit African soldiers because he did not want black troops shooting at white troops, even if those white troops were the enemy. The British also relegated Africans to menial labor instead of allowing them to engage in combat. Further, Africans were offered only minimal compensation and were refused veterans' pensions.

Sir Richard Winfrey, British secretary for agriculture, had assured SANNC secretary Sol Plaatje, that "at the close of the war we shall do all in our power to help you regain that justice and freedom to which as loyal British subjects your people are justly entitled."[68] Africans had listened, too, with great interest to the speeches of British prime minister David Lloyd George and American president Woodrow Wilson as they proclaimed self-determination for small nations. Africans expected that the principle of self-determination would apply to them. They had fought, specifically, because they believed the professed war aims of the British—"to liberate oppressed nations; to grant every nation, great or small, the right to determine its sovereign destiny and the free choice . . . to make the world fit and safe for every man to live in freedom to choose his own destiny."[69]

Africans wanted England's lofty war aims to be applied to South Africa, and they demanded the franchise to protect themselves against a racist South African government. They had paid taxes despite their lack of political representation. They had embraced Victorian values of Christian morality, education, and commercial success as the path toward "civilization" and the supposedly color-blind rights of British subjects. They wanted the United States, with the assent of African peoples, to control the former German colonies in Africa and the Congo Free State, the site of Belgian misrule and mayhem, until, they acidly noted, Africans became "sufficiently advanced for their own civilized government."[70]

With the land question itself seemingly a lost cause, members of the 1919 SANNC delegation focused, again unsuccessfully, on demands for equal rights as British citizens within the British Empire. Particularly, they sought parliamentary representation as a protection against unjust laws. Getting nowhere with the Colonial Office, Plaatje and the SANNC delegation approached Lloyd George, who listened sympathetically to complaints about the pass laws and the Land Act as well as the lack of political representation. Lloyd George suggested to Smuts that he meet with the SANNC delegates on their return to South Africa. He also warned Smuts of the specter of bolshevism, spreading in the wake of the czar's downfall, and of black nationalist stirrings, particularly in the Garvey movement. But at the close of the war, British practices in neglecting Africans continued to be at odds with British ideals of equality. Disillusioned with the British, Africans began to look toward other sources of liberation from outside.

In 1917, John Dube had resigned as president of the South African Native National Congress and was replaced by Samuel Makgatho of the Transvaal and the antisegregation wing of the SANNC. The 1919 SANNC delegation, without Dube, was the last concerted attempt by Africans to secure British intervention in reversing discriminatory South African laws. Dube and Seme had disagreed about segregation, with Dube willing to consider an equitable territorial split and Seme opposed to segregation in principle. For some white liberals and black moderates in South Africa, Booker T. Washington and Tuskegee remained viable personal and institutional models of African American progress and leadership. In 1919, with the ascent of Garveyism, African Americans took the place of the British in the minds of many Africans as their potential liberators in South Africa.

The African protest tradition was an indirect product of mission education. In Natal, numerous prominent men had been educated under the mission system, including SANNC cofounders Seme, Mangena, and others; Dube; SANNC secretary Solomon Plaatje; and luminaries like Mark Radebe, Richard Msimang, H. Selby Msimang, R. V. Selope Thema, and Silas Molema of the founding conference. Yet these men did not choose the missionary model for themselves. They founded the SANNC to articulate the racially inclusive, egalitarian, and democratic values that were taught—but ultimately seldom practiced—in the Christian world that educated them.[71]

In his obituary for John Dube in 1946, *Ilanga lase Natal* editor Herbert Dhlomo recalled Dube's statement that he wanted to be judged not "by the heights that I have attained, but by the depths from which I have come." British-sanctioned segregation was a violation of all that African Christian elites respected in a progressive world order: "free labor, secure property rights linked to a free market in land and individual tenure, equality before the law and some notion of 'no taxation without representation.'" African students had left South Africa for American training hopeful that their beliefs in the so-called civilizing powers of Christianity, of education and commercial enterprise, and of the professional success and widespread landownership that were perceived to be logical outcomes would advance Africans, indirectly and collectively. The African Christian elite, of which John Dube was a primary spokesperson, felt a keen sense of betrayal by whites who saw Africans as too lazy, too pagan, and too inferior to compete in modern South Africa. These same whites pushed for restrictive legislation, complaining of increased African competition in landownership, in commercial farming, and in the labor market.[72]

The amakholwa—the mission-educated class of Africans—had believed that their adoption of missionary beliefs would yield tangible rewards for themselves and their African compatriots. The obvious success of American blacks, which they personally observed, reinforced this conviction. Their hopes were dashed in the aftermath of the diamond and gold mineral revolutions in South Africa that demanded cheap migrant labor, restricting the possibility of building a landowning, economically autonomous, and politically equal class of Africans. They concluded that even though Christianity and education were prerequisites for advancement, only politics would remove the barriers. Education could liberate them from heathen barbarism but not from the shackles of segregation and later, after another world war, of apartheid. The SANNC's moderate petition politics proved ineffective against the segregationist onslaught. The potential African leaders remained in limbo, unable and unwilling to return to traditional non-Christian African communities but at the same time incapable of gaining acceptance and making progress in a modern Western society.

The British had failed to liberate black South Africans from Afrikaner rule. And the SANNC failed, too, in its early political strategies of appealing to traditions of British liberalism through the use of petitions, deputations, and resolutions. But though there were limits to the Washingtonian model of gradualism and ultimate faith in white inclusiveness based on recognition of black advancement, African Americans remained enduring models of racial advancement. The long-standing South African dream of Booker T. Washington coming to South Africa died with the man known as the Wizard on 14 November 1915. One of Washington's admirers, Marcus Garvey — a British colonial subject in Jamaica with similar grievances against the British — soon became the most visible symbol of American Negro progress and of South African expectations for liberation by American Negroes. By 1920, black sailors were carrying the news of Garveyism to South African ports, adding to a more militant mood and producing new dreams of liberation. Would these new dreams bring real freedom and equality? Or would they, once again, prove to be mere chimeras?[73]

Africans understood clearly that their overwhelming numerical superiority would never allow South Africa to become a white country. Tyrannical racial segregation could only lead to destructive racial wars. Conversely, the application of supposedly color-blind British imperial policies to South Africa would mean equal political, civil, and socioeconomic rights for all South Africans — the only path to a lasting peace.

John Dube and Pixley Seme built on their American education, global travels, and admiration for the inspirational achievements of Booker T. Washington and other African Americans to help found the ANC, South Africa's oldest political party. Fighting against global white supremacy, Africans like Dube and Seme found less and less currency in the transnational identification of British subjects and drew closer to American Negroes, becoming representative examples of the wide circulation of people, ideologies, and institutions. In Washington (despite his moderation) and Tuskegee, Africans found a stirring *Up from Slavery* narrative of black advancement despite great hardships that had some parallel to their own struggles. They viewed Washington and

Tuskegee as exemplars of African American progress, the conveyers of potentially liberationist ideas and the vanguard for racial progress across national borders. African elites who developed a print culture in English facilitated transnational linkages with American Negroes, building bridges of communication across oceans and developing identities far beyond the ethnic identities that many South African whites sought to impose on Africans.

Enslaved African American man on Confederate ship *Alabama,* which spent several months in Cape Town during the Civil War; the ship's spectacular sinking of a Union vessel there was memorialized in the still popular song "Daar kom die Alabama." (Courtesy: South African Government Archives)

Orpheus McAdoo and the Alabama Cakewalkers, forerunners to the Virginia Jubilee Singers. (Courtesy: Hampton University Archives)

(*left*) Booker T. Washington, founder of Tuskegee Institute, widely admired as an example of black innovation, resourcefulness, and advancement. (Courtesy: Library of Congress)

(*below*) Jack Johnson knocking out Jim Jeffries in the fifteenth round of the "Fight of the Century" on 4 July 1910 in Reno, Nevada. The films of this fight circulated widely around the world, including in South Africa. (Courtesy: Nevada Historical Society)

The Reverend Herbert A. Payne in South Africa. (Author's private collection)

Delegation of the South African Native National Congress (later renamed the African National Congress) in London, England, in 1914 to seek repeal of the Natives Land Act of 1913. In the front row, (*left to right*) are Thomas Mapikela, John Dube, and Sol Plaatje. In the back row (*left to right*) are Walter Rubusana and Saul Msane. (Courtesy: National Library of South Africa)

(*above*) Henry Sylvester Williams, founder of the twentieth-century Pan-African movement, who lived and organized in South Africa from 1902 to 1906. (Courtesy: National Library of South Africa)

(*right*) Marcus Garvey in uniform, c. 1926. (Courtesy: Library of Congress)

(*left*) The Jamaican Arthur McKinley, a longtime resident of Cape Town, making a political speech in 1938. McKinley, a leading member of the Cape Town UNIA and the African National Congress, was well known in Cape Town for his fiery and satirical soapbox political speeches at the Grand Parade, near the Cape Town docks. (Courtesy: National Library of South Africa)

(*below*) Black Star Line stock certificate owned by the Antigua-born Cape Town resident James Lyner, whose four orphaned children were adopted by British Guyana–born Timothy Robertson, the first UNIA president in South Africa. (Author's private collection)

To the Beloved and Scattered Millions of the Negro Race

Greeting

This is to Certify that

Mr *Robert Gonsalves* of *16 Springfield St Capetown*

is a duly registered active member of the Universal Negro Improvement Association and African Communities (Imperial) League, an organization embracing the millions of men, women and children of Negro blood and of African descent of all countries of the world, striving for the FREEDOM, MANHOOD, and NATIONALISM of the Negro, and to hand down to posterity a FLAG OF EMPIRE—to restore to the world an Ethiopian Nation one and indivisible out of which shall come our princes and rulers—to bequeath to our children and our Grand Old Race the heritage of an Ancestry worthy of their time and thoughtful of the future.

Resting on the strength and mercy of Almighty God, and on the Effort and faith of our people all over the world, we the undersigned, as officers of the *Capetown* Division, append our names this *Twenty Ninth* day of *March* in the year of our Lord One Thousand Nine Hundred and *Twenty One*

William B. Jackson
President.

Ceasar Allen
General Secretary.

William B Chazwell
Treasurer.

President of Ladies' Division.

General Secretary Ladies' Division.

UNIA membership certificate of Antigua-born Robert Goncalves, who was a member of the Cape Town UNIA (Author's private collection)

The West Indian–American Association, which began in the World War I era as a fraternal organization for Cape Town residents who had been born in the Caribbean, North America, and South America. Many of these men went to Cape Town as sailors, found work on the city's docks, and established the earliest UNIA chapters in South Africa. (Courtesy: District Six Museum)

(*left*) Clements Kadalie (*seated, left*), titular head of the Industrial and Commercial Workers Union, was influenced greatly by American Negro leaders Marcus Garvey and Booker T. Washington and published essays on South African labor politics in African American periodicals. (Courtesy: National Library of South Africa)

(*below*) Cape ANC president James Thaele rallying black workers in Cape Town in 1930. (Courtesy: National Library of South Africa)

"Jolly" Jack Barnard, an American who owned a Johannesburg bookstore that sold books and newspapers by and about African Americans. Barnard attested to the great popularity of Marcus Garvey and UNIA books and newspapers among his South African clientele. (Courtesy: National Library of South Africa)

(*left*) Wellington Butelezi, a.k.a. Dr. Wellington, in academic regalia. (Courtesy: Robert R. Edgar collection)

(*below*) Paul Gulwa, a follower of Wellington Butelezi and a frequent correspondent with Marcus Garvey and other American UNIA officials. Gulwa founded the Umanyano Church, a Garveyite-influenced religious body that incorporated the UNIA colors of red, black, and green. (Courtesy: South African Government Archives)

Sibusisiwe Makhanya in America c. 1930. (Courtesy: Killie Campbell Africana Library, Durban, South Africa)

Leaders of the Council on African Affairs in San Francisco in 1946 at a UN meeting, protesting South Africa's proposal to incorporate Southwest Africa: Alpheus Hunton (*first from the left*), Max Yergan (*fourth from the left*), and W. E. B. Du Bois (*fifth from the left*), are shown with ANC president Alfred Xuma (*second from the right*). (Courtesy: National Library of South Africa)

Mural of Marcus Garvey, alongside antiapartheid activist Steve Biko, University of Cape Town, Cape Town, South Africa

Residents of Marcus Garvey settlement, a Rastafarian community outside Philippi,
South Africa

Marcus Garvey settlement

PART II

～

AMERICAN APOCALYPSE

Prophetic Garveyism and the Dream of American Negro Liberation

3 ↪ The Rise of Marcus Garvey and His Gospel of Garveyism in Southern Africa

In 1916, a virtually penniless, twenty-eight-year-old Marcus Garvey, the son of a stonemason and a domestic, arrived in Harlem from his home in Jamaica. His purpose was to raise funds for a school in Jamaica modeled after Booker T. Washington's Tuskegee Institute. No one would have predicted that he would not return home for eleven years, after presiding over the rise and the decline of the largest black-led movement in world history before or since.

At the peak of Garvey's Universal Negro Improvement Association (UNIA) in the early 1920s, the organization had about three hundred thousand dues-paying members in nearly twelve hundred divisions in forty-three countries, among them South Africa, where there were at least twenty-four.[1] In the immediate post–World War I era, Garvey channeled the anger and disillusionment of blacks worldwide to promote his goals of black economic and educational advancement, religious autonomy, African political independence, and racial unity. Skilled blacks, through strong race-based organizations, would be expected to lead the UNIA program of "African redemption," the resurrection of a glorious African past, in an independent Africa.

Garvey's record was one of stunning success and tragic failure. He was a master propagandist and organizer but an incompetent businessman whose most ambitious business, the Black Star Line of ships, collapsed in 1922. His ideas of racial purity and racial separatism led to controversial relationships with white supremacists, and in time, these dubious associations led black rivals like W. E. B. Du Bois and A. Philip Randolph to demand his deportation from the United States. He was imprisoned in Atlanta and deported back to Jamaica in 1927. And yet, Garveyism had wide influence, not only in the States but also in the Caribbean and throughout the world, including southern Africa. The movement became what one historian has called the first "global expression of black nationalism."[2] Garvey's ideas took on a life of their own in forms he had not imagined. Indirectly, he played a vital role in bringing about the end of white rule.

FROM EDUCATION TO RADICAL POLITICS

Marcus Garvey was born on 17 August 1887, a subject of the British Empire. He was the youngest child of Sarah Jane Richards, a domestic worker and petty trader, and Malchus Garvey, a stonemason, a bibliophile with a library of his own, and a respected arbiter of village disputes. (Even Malchus's wife called him Mr. Garvey.) Marcus played cricket and other games with the neighboring white children until his teens, when white parents forbade their offspring to consort with a "nigger."[3] A voracious reader, he consumed all of the books in the libraries of his father and godfather, Alfred Burrowes. He listened closely to the political discussions in his godfather's print shop, where he was an apprentice, and learned new words from his pocket dictionary.[4] He observed the rhetorical styles of preachers, street-corner politicians, and teachers, and he took part in debating societies and elocution contests. "All the time when I meet him," a friend said, "he wear jacket, and, every time, his two pockets full of paper, reading and telling us things that happen all over the world. How him know, I don't know, but him telling us."[5]

The editor of the *Jamaican Advocate*, Joseph Love, became young Garvey's mentor. The *Advocate* decried British colonialism and American Jim Crowism and glorified the Haitian Revolution. It also published news of Pan-Africanists like Du Bois; the back-to-Africa advocate Henry McNeal Turner, a bishop of the African Methodist Episcopal Church; and the Trinidadian Henry Sylvester Williams, whose 1900 Pan-African Conference in London initiated the Pan-African movement. Garvey began to express anti-colonial ideals in a short-lived newspaper of his own, *Garvey's Watchman*, and in pamphlets of public speeches, as well as when he served as secretary of the National Club, the first black nationalist organization in Jamaica to protest colonial abuses. Blackballed from local jobs when, as the only managerial foreman at a government printing plant, he sided with the workers in a labor strike, he left the island at age twenty-three. In Costa Rica, where he worked as a timekeeper, he saw "mutilated black bodies in the rivers and bushes," and he complained about working conditions through a daily paper he published, *La Nacion*, and in numerous petitions to unresponsive local British consuls. After traveling to Ecuador, Nicaragua, Venezuela, Colombia, and Panama, outraged at the treatment of blacks everywhere, he arrived in London, the heart of the British Empire and the center of the Pan-African world.[6]

Many black sailors, students, laborers, and other travelers from Africa, the Caribbean, and the Americas were in London at the time. As Garvey worked on the docks in London, Liverpool, and Cardiff, he listened to their stories of racial subjugation. From the balcony of the House of Commons, he heard debates on colonialism, and he made anticolonial speeches of his own in London's Hyde Park. He took university classes and wrote for the *Africa Times and Orient Review*, the preeminent Pan-African periodical, edited by a celebrated Egyptian-born author named Duse Mohamed Ali. Ali asserted that ancient Egypt had been a powerful black civilization when Europe's culture was still primitive. In an essay that would come to be regarded as a landmark, entitled "The British West Indies in the Mirror of Civilization: History Making by Colonial Negroes," Garvey detailed the history of racial abuses under British colonialism in the Caribbean. The essay predicted that West Indians would unite blacks from around the world to create a black empire as far-reaching as the British Empire itself.[7]

As Garvey sailed back to Jamaica, he learned of the dehumanizing effects of segregation in South Africa from a West Indian missionary and his mo-Sotho wife. He asked himself, as he wrote later: "Where is the black man's Government? Where is his King and his Kingdom? Where is his President, his country, and his ambassador, his army, his navy, his men of big affairs? I could not find them, and then I declared, 'I will help to make them.' . . . My brain was afire."[8] With the help of Amy Ashwood, who was to become his wife, Garvey founded the Universal Negro Improvement and Conservation Association (UNIA; "Conservation" was dropped from the official name in 1918) and African Communities (Imperial) League (ACL). The date was 1 August 1914, the eightieth anniversary of the abolition of slavery in British territories. Garvey was twenty-seven.

The UNIA began as a fraternal and benevolent society but with ambitious goals to establish an industrial school like Tuskegee, to develop black-owned businesses, and to improve the moral character of blacks in order to attain the "highest level of civilized culture." Garvey was, in many ways, middle class in style and in program—entrepreneurial, business-oriented, committed to free enterprise and the capitalist model, and focused on the improvement of Negro culture. Echoing Booker T. Washington, he believed "the bulk of our people are in darkness and are really unfit for good society."[9] For Garvey, blacks could not demand racial equality until they had made equal contributions to modern civilization.

Despite his initially moderate conception of the UNIA, the ease with which blacks could establish their own UNIA chapters would eventually create a decentralized movement that was united by broadly shared goals but shaped in manifestly different ways to address local conditions. By July 1918, with formal approval from Garvey and a commitment to contribute to the UNIA program, at least seven black, dues-paying individuals could start a chapter. Garvey stipulated that each chapter had to have officers, including a division chaplain, and an advisory board, and each member paid monthly dues of no more than 25¢ and an additional 10¢ per month for a life insurance premium to provide up to $75 for funeral expenses (only a few white-owned insurance companies issued policies to blacks).

The ACL was established as the corporate and propaganda wing of the UNIA for skilled blacks of the diaspora intent on creating independent and powerful African states. It offered membership to any black person in the world who shared its goals of African independence, racial unity, uplift, and advancement.[10]

Garvey appealed to Booker T. Washington to provide financial support for a Jamaican Tuskegee. Like Washington with his *Tuskegee Student*, he published his speeches on the front page of a newspaper of his own, the *Negro World*, which he established in 1918. He was convinced of the power of the printed word, especially its dissemination to literate blacks everywhere through newspapers. When Washington died in 1915, Garvey organized a UNIA memorial in Jamaica as a tribute to "the greatest hero sprung from the stock of scattered Ethiopia," a man who had raised "the dignity and manhood of his race . . . to the highest heights."[11]

By the year after Washington's death, Garvey had gone from Jamaica to Harlem to raise money for his Jamaican Tuskegee. But his plans for the school were never realized. The United States offered a larger platform for Garvey, and he stayed there. He invited Du Bois to chair his own first public lecture in the States (Du Bois declined). He met many black luminaries, including Tuskegee president Robert Moton and the bold antilynching crusader Ida B. Wells, and he revised his belief that West Indians would lead the race.[12] "The Negroes of both hemispheres," he now wrote, "have to defer to the American brother" who had advanced so rapidly up from slavery.[13] Yet the East St. Louis race riots of 1917 and outrages committed against black soldiers in Houston convinced him to join an increasingly radicalized Harlem.

Hubert Harrison of the Virgin Islands—"the father of Harlem radicalism," who was also known as the "Black Socrates"—became his mentor.[14] A. Philip Randolph, then a young socialist organizer, yielded his stepladder on Harlem street corners to Garvey so he could address the crowds. Claude McKay, himself a Jamaican, marveled, "Garvey shouted words, words spinning like bullets, words falling like bombs, sharp words like poisoned daggers, thundering words and phrases lit with all the hues of the rainbow to match the wild approving roar of his people."[15] After Harrison founded the Liberty League to demand black civil rights, Garvey, breaking with Booker T. Washington's apolitical model, joined the organization. In nightly speeches, he denounced the "savagery of a people who claim to be the dispensers of democracy."[16] He criticized Du Bois's controversial article "Close Ranks" in the NAACP's magazine the *Crisis*, of which Du Bois was the editor. Du Bois had urged blacks to "forget our special grievances and close our ranks shoulder to shoulder with our own white fellow citizens and the allied nations that are fighting for democracy," since "our second emancipation will be the outcome of this war."[17] Like Harrison, Garvey scored the NAACP as an elitist organization of "paper protest" politics reflecting the perspective of influential whites in its leadership, even though he himself was committed to paper protests.

By 1919, Garvey had established a UNIA branch in Harlem patterned after the Liberty League, and he was publishing the *Negro World*, modeled after Harrison's defunct *Voice*. In the paper, he announced plans for a black-owned shipping line, the Black Star Line. For it, he appropriated the tricolor flag of the Liberty League, changing its colors to black (for his people), red (for the blood spilled during slavery, Jim Crowism, and colonialism), and green (for the fertility of the African soil).[18] As Garvey told an audience in New York City, metaphorically addressing whites:

> The idea is this. You white folk have just finished a war for democracy. You have spread the doctrine that men, nations, races are equal. We negroes fought in that war. Now we want to reap some of the advantages you promised. Lots of our boys came back from the trenches determined never to tolerate the things you have done to negroes in this country. Then the negroes that stayed at home for the first time got decent jobs and pay such as they had never had before. Now we won't go back to pre-war conditions. We've grown out of them.[19]

In 1920, black delegates at the UNIA's annual convention compiled the Declaration of Rights of the Negro Peoples of the World. The UNIA Declaration of Rights employed language from the American Declaration of Independence to craft an early foundational document in an international human rights discursive framework that would be adopted decades later in the United Nations Declaration of Human Rights (1947) and the global antiapartheid movement. It declared "all men are created equal and entitled to the rights of life, liberty and the pursuit of happiness." It demanded an end to Jim Crowism and to European colonialism in Africa, with voting rights for blacks, equal access to good jobs, quality education, and health care. It also denounced the League of Nations as "null and void" for allowing European colonialism to continue in Africa. Countries engaged in lynching and other discriminatory practices were described as "outside the pale of civilization."[20]

With Booker T. Washington dead, Du Bois virtually cloistered in the NAACP offices in downtown Manhattan, and Harrison unable to translate his ideals into a strong mass organization, Garvey continued to transform his UNIA into an organization of race-first radicalism. His evolving message was centered on racial separatism and African redemption.[21] Liberia, the West African state founded by freed blacks in the early nineteenth century, was, said Garvey, the most propitious place for a UNIA presence in Africa. With the blessing of the Liberian government, UNIA engineers, land surveyors, and technicians made plans to build roads, railroads, factories, schools, and other infrastructure to modernize the country and settle five hundred families.[22] Garvey boasted that the UNIA—and a united black race—could modernize all of Africa in five years.[23]

In 1922, the UNIA protested to the League of Nations about its mandates to Britain, France, and Belgium in the former German colonies, on the grounds that blacks were "now sufficiently civilized to conduct the affairs of their homeland."[24] Africa was "the property of the Blacks," the UNIA declared, "and by God we are going to have them [European colonial possessions in Africa] now or some time later, even if all the world is itself in blood. Half the world can't be free and half slave."[25] Garvey appointed Ida B. Wells and A. Philip Randolph as UNIA delegates to the inaugural League of Nations meeting in Geneva, but the United States refused to grant them exit visas.[26] Nonetheless, the UNIA continued its intense focus on European colonialism in Africa.

To Garvey, South Africa was "the worst spot in the world for Negroes; worse than the Southern States of America." Still a British colonial subject him-self—he had not applied for U.S. citizenship—he protested Prime Minister Jan Smuts's goal of establishing a white South Africa, but he disliked the more overt white nationalism of Smuts's political rival James Hertzog even more.[27] By that time, Garvey knew black South Africans like the African National Congress leader Sol Plaatje, who had visited America in 1921,[28] and his paper, *Negro World*, would offer sophisticated news and analyses of African politics until it folded in 1933.[29] Garvey admired the anticolonial resistance move-ments of Mohandas Gandhi in India, Zaghul Pasha in Egypt, and the anti-English Irish Republican struggle led by Eamonn de Valera. He copied the Sinn Fein practice of naming central meeting sites Liberty Hall, and he called himself the provisional president of Africa, just as de Valera styled himself the provisional president of Ireland. Garvey also mimicked the postwar Irish Race Conventions by demanding freedom for the people of India and Ireland and all other colonized lands.[30]

Establishing the Black Star Line in 1919 was an important step toward Garvey's ultimate goal of developing a sustainable and interdependent black economic world, free from financial dependence on whites. He modeled his company on the White Star Line, the top British commercial shipping line (one of its ships was the doomed *Titanic*). The Black Star Line's central purpose, as Garvey saw it, was to conduct trade among West African countries and throughout the world, transporting diasporic blacks back to Africa, particularly to Liberia. The Black Star Line would also serve as the first set of ships in the navy of a coming black-controlled state.[31] The *Frederick Douglass*, a renamed cargo ship, made two commercial trips to American and Caribbean ports, where it was greeted by wildly cheering crowds.[32] Garvey ordered the ship to stop at many ports along the way so blacks could see the black-owned vessel in which large numbers of them had bought shares. The real commercial value of the line was not, however, its cargo runs but its ability to generate funds for the UNIA.[33] It became the most visible of several UNIA businesses, including the Phyllis Wheatley Hotel, the Universal Restaurant, and a clothing manufacturing and retail store. It helped swell UNIA ranks from an initial thirteen members in mid-1918 to a conservative 1920 estimate of three hundred thousand dues-paying members in twenty-five U.S. states, the Caribbean, Central America, and Africa.[34]

The UNIA's weekly newspaper, *Negro World*, under Garvey's editorial control, reached a circulation peak of nearly two hundred thousand copies by 1921. Featuring his speeches as front-page editorials, the paper served as Garvey's principal instrument for spreading the gospel of African independence, black political and socioeconomic uplift, racial pride, and unity. Garvey and the *Negro World* editors and columnists—Hubert Harrison, William Ferris, W. A. Domingo, T. Thomas Fortune, and John Bruce—were experienced newspapermen, learned scholars, and respected "race men." Articles were published in English, French, and Spanish.[35] Black sailors, Pullman porters, dockworkers, and others helped circulate the paper along their routes with such effectiveness that British and French colonial governments banned it from their colonies. The distinguished historian John Hope Franklin remembered that people in his own Oklahoma town had read the *Negro World* eagerly. Jomo Kenyatta, future president of Kenya, said Africans memorized its articles to share with other Africans "hungry for some doctrine which lifted them from the servile consciousness in which [they] lived."[36] The paper was distributed for free in impoverished locales.[37]

In years when negative images of blacks abounded in the form of would-be rapists in films like *Birth of a Nation*, caricatures in blackface minstrel shows, or happy-go-lucky mammy and uncle servants in advertising campaigns for pancake mixes and rice, Garvey was determined to project a strong image. In a quasi-military uniform and plumed hat, he presided over flamboyant UNIA parades through Harlem, marching with the African Legion, a paramilitary unit, and with the all-female Black Cross Nurses, UNIA juvenile divisions, and marching bands.[38] Garvey took his fiery speeches directly to the people, riding frequently through Harlem in an open-roofed car with a megaphone blasting his trademark slogan, "Africa for the Africans—those at home and those abroad."[39] At the UNIA Liberty Halls, followers waited in long lines to seek jobs and material assistance and to meet the "Negro Moses."[40]

Garvey had enemies, too. On 14 October 1919, he survived an assassination attempt, with two bullets in his legs and one that nicked his head. When he ascended a stage in Philadelphia five days later, followers were convinced that God had spared him to lead his people to the Promised Land. Garvey had promised, "We shall gather together our children, our treasures and our loved ones, and, as the children of Israel, by the command of God, faced the Promised Land, so in time we shall also."[41] The American liberators were coming. In sharp contrast to popular images of a white God, the UNIA announced that the deity had no color. Blacks should view God, Jesus Christ, and the Virgin Mary "through the spectacles of Ethiopia," as black, not white.[42]

The several hundred ministers who were UNIA members spread Garveyism in their churches, the most powerful black institutions in the country. The Reverend George Alexander McGuire, UNIA chaplain-general, wrote a UNIA liturgy, the *Universal Negro Ritual*, and the *Universal Negro Catechism*. UNIA Sunday meetings featured branch chaplains, sermons, prayers, religious hymns, biblical readings, and evocations of Garvey as a messiah or as Moses.[43] The masthead of the *Negro World* quoted Psalms 68:31—"Ethiopia must stretch forth her hands unto God and Princes shall come out of Egypt"—and Acts 17:26—"From one man he made every nation of men, that they should inhabit the whole earth; and he determined the times set for them and the exact places where they should live." Garvey proclaimed, "God Almighty brought the Negro out of slavery for a purpose. . . . We say every alien man must clear out of Africa that God Almighty gave us as our right and heritage. . . . God Almighty has a plan and a purpose for every race, and we have suffered long enough now to realize our purpose and enter into our plans."[44]

GARVEYISM AS A MOVEMENT

By 1922, even the NAACP field organizer William Pickens admitted that Garvey, through his "strength and personal magnetism, has founded so large a power in the English-speaking world as to add to the current vocabulary a new word, 'Garveyism.'"[45] The movement had spread like a brush fire, with more than 1,176 UNIA divisions throughout the black world (though nearly 80 percent were in the United States).[46] The twelve UNIA regions in America, led by high commissioners, initially maintained divisions in eastern seaboard cities like New York, Boston, and Philadelphia. Divisions then developed in the Midwest and in southern port cities such as Norfolk, Charleston, Mobile, and

New Orleans. Finally, divisions were established in the southern interior and in far West locales, among them Los Angeles. Between July 1919 and the 1921 UNIA annual convention, the organization chartered 480 new divisions, and the reported circulation of the *Negro World* went up from twenty-five thousand to seventy-five thousand in the six months preceding the convention.[47]

Only five years earlier, Marcus Garvey had arrived in Harlem from Jamaica with few contacts and meager resources. Trembling with nerves, he had collapsed and literally fallen on his face at his first public lecture there. Now, in 1921, at age thirty-four, he was the black Moses, poised to lead his people, blacks in southern Africa among them, to the Promised Land.

BLACK POSTWAR DISILLUSIONMENT, AMERICAN NEGRO SAILORS, AND THE TRANSMISSION OF GARVEYISM TO SOUTH AFRICA

The 1919 Paris Peace Conference gave birth to the League of Nations, an intergovernmental organization that had fifty-eight member states at its peak and was designed to prevent further war through collective security measures, the arbitration of international disputes, and the general protection of human rights. Japan, an acknowledged world power whose navies had cleared sea-lanes in the South Pacific and Indian Ocean for the Allied powers, proposed that a racial equality clause be added to the League of Nations Charter. Though a majority of nations supported the clause, the virulent opposition of U.S. president Woodrow Wilson, Australian prime minister Charles Hughes, and South African prime minister Jan Smuts, along with Great Britain, killed the proposal. They argued successfully that such a clause would give false hopes of equality to colonized and subordinated persons of color and thus interfere with white rule.

After the war, Africans continued to protest the British refusal to apply to them its theoretical principles of equality under the law. African political leader Mesach Pelem complained that the English equated the words *white* with *supremacy* and *black* with *slavery*. The medical doctor and author Silas Molema argued that the denial of the racial equality clause, after four years of Asian and African support for Britain, proved the hollowness of Western liberalism. Du Bois thought the time was ripe to update his 1910 "Souls of White Folk" essay for his essay collection *Darkwater* (1920). In it, he declared that "the white civil war in Europe was nothing to compare with the fight for freedom which the black and the brown and yellow men must make and will make unless their oppression and humiliation and insult at the hands of the White World ceases."[48] Smarting at the resurgence of white supremacy in the immediate postwar period, the black world, particularly South Africa, was primed for the Africa for Africans militancy of Garveyism.

In 1920 at a meeting in Durban at the Natal branch of the ANC, an American Negro sailor known only as Moses, a recent arrival from New York, made an unscheduled appearance. He told the audience that "Marcus Garvey was the man they relied upon . . . who would free Africa: that the first vessel of the fleet was named 'Frederick Douglass,' and this vessel had been sailing to different places . . . Africa would be freed . . . by Marcus Garvey."[49] Messengers of Garveyism like Moses had a significant advantage over resident Garveyites. Sailors could enter—and leave—before white authorities, openly hostile to Garveyism, became aware of their presence.

The UNIA message merged with the persistent dreams and prophecies of some Africans that God would send liberators to save them. In the port city of East London, rumors abounded that "Americans" would arrive in ships, with weapons, to help Africans kill whites.[50] Kenneth Spooner, a West Indian missionary who had emphasized Africa's centrality in the Bible to his students, joyously proclaimed, "His people were now on the seas coming to South Africa with a view to beating the European people here, and . . . in about six months time changes would be observed."[51] An African known as Mgoja, addressing a meeting of the Transvaal branch of the African National Congress, raised the cry that "America had a black fleet and it is coming."[52] That fleet was Garvey's Black Star Line. In neighboring Basutoland, an ardent nationalist, Josiel Lefela, said in an editorial in the Negro World, "Let us look forward to his Excellency Marcus Garvey the President of Africa, and the Americans, with anxious anticipation."[53] Gilbert Matshoba, a young African clerk in the Eastern Cape, reported to his uncle, Enoch Mgijima, leader of a religious group known as the Israelites, that Garvey had predicted the "blood of all wars is about to arrive." Matshoba seemed convinced that the UNIA would soon compel European colonizers to leave Africa.

Prime Minister Jan Smuts considered Garveyism a significant threat to the "security of the civilized order." Consequently, the government continued to ban virtually all American Negroes from South Africa.[54] Even Garvey's strongest critics, such as AME bishop William T. Vernon, came under government scrutiny. A Cape Town municipal official, responding to inquiries by the Portuguese government, had detained two Mozambicans who were in possession of Cape Town UNIA membership certificates. He warned that the UNIA "requires careful watching and may develop into a danger to the State." "A Black Republic and Socialism," said the official, "appear to be the bedrock of this Association. . . . This present 'negro movement' has a paper circulating here called the 'The Negro World' [and] the evolution, amalgamation of native black races and the various changes and movements are, in my opinion, rapidly arriving at a crisis."[55]

In 1923, the Cape Town newspaper, Cape Argus, proclaimed that about two hundred American Negroes were spreading Garveyism in the city.[56] The

West Indian Protective Society, an American-based anti-UNIA organization, warned the government of "colored persons coming into South Africa from the United States and the Panama Canal." It suggested the government ban all UNIA and Black Star Line stockholders. H. Selby Msimang—an anti-Garvey African trade unionist and an ANC leader, newspaper editor, and future Liberal Party cofounder—lamented on a visit to Cape Town that he had been "pestered with questions concerning the 'Back to Africa' movement by people who seemed to sleep in happy dreams of the coming of a Messiah in the person of Marcus Garvey and his army to restore the status quo of the Bantu in the land of their ancestors."[57] Again, it was thought, God was sending a liberator to rescue his people.

AMERICAN NEGROES IN SOUTH AFRICA

Black sailors enjoyed a mobility that made it difficult for authorities to apprehend them, but they were too transitory to lead any sustained political organization. In South Africa, the task of organizing was assumed, instead, by an American Negro community in Cape Town comprising roughly two hundred individuals. Most of these American Negroes were actually West Indians who, from the 1880s, had fled the economically depressed Caribbean for African port cities, especially Cape Town. There, a number of them had formed distinct communities. According to a 1904 Cape Colony census, 298 black West Indians lived there, many of them now workers in the dockyards. The West Indians had a reputation as "tough, hard back-boned Negroes . . . of the he-man type, aggressive and daring." They displayed Pan-African sentiments, fostering "notions of Combination and Co-operation among the disparate ethnic groups" in the Cape Town dockyards of Africans and mixed-race people called Coloureds.[58] They had tended to marry into the Coloured, not the African, community and hence were closer to the mixed-race, often more upwardly mobile class of Coloureds.

They were attracted to Cape Town, site of South Africa's earliest European settlement, because of its employment prospects, its large English-speaking population, and its reputation for racial liberalism. Further, Cape Town's nonracial franchise accorded voting rights to black males who met certain property requirements, unlike South Africa's other three provinces, which excluded all Africans from voting. By the early years of the twentieth century, Cape Town had become an industrial town of approximately eighty thousand people, most of them Africans and Coloureds. Africans generally lived in segregated townships outside the city, separated from most Coloureds, with most workers subjected to the industrial color bar and excluded from many other lines of work.

A Trinidadian by the name of Henry Sylvester Williams, founder in 1899 of the Pan-African movement, was the first black lawyer in the Cape Colony. He was a person young Garvey had admired, one of the many West Indians who resisted South African segregationist practices. Educated in Canada and England, Williams was in London in 1897 when he met Mary Kinloch, an African woman married to a Scottish mining engineer. Kinloch told a horrified Williams about the segregated and squalid compounds, the pass laws, the curfews, and the humiliating strip searches Africans endured in South Africa's gold and diamond mines. Thereafter, Williams and Kinloch barnstormed around England to rally public awareness of atrocities being committed against Africans.

Williams founded the African Association, with officers and members from Antigua, Trinidad, British Guyana, Barbados, South Africa, Sierra Leone, and the Gold Coast. In 1899, he coined the term *Pan-Africanism* to describe his transatlantic efforts. With a ringing endorsement from his friend Booker T. Washington, he organized the Pan-African Conference in London in June 1900. Blacks from around the globe convened to develop an international agenda for black political and civil rights, for racial unity and advancement, and for African self-government freed from European colonialism and imperialism. The conference report, entitled "To the Nations of the World," included Du Bois's memorable statement that "the problem of the twentieth century is the problem of the color line."[59]

Williams hoped that, after the South African War against the Afrikaners, British rule would bring blacks full political citizenship, economic prosperity, and social equality. However, the British effectively closed ranks with the defeated Afrikaners to maintain a white supremacist regime. Williams petitioned Queen Victoria to end the segregationist practices, but his and other black leaders' petitions were ignored. Leaving his white English wife and their infant child in London, he sailed for Cape Town, declaring that "if the Coloured people of South Africa were willing to be kept out of the higher walks of life . . . their brothers in the West Indies were not."[60] There, he established the South African Citizens Defense Committee of West Indians, Coloureds, Africans and Indians. He sought to end restrictions on black ownership of property and the de facto ban on black service on juries; his organization also protested segregationist practices in public facilities. The committee registered enough voters (black male property owners could still vote) to help elect to the Cape Town City Council Abdul Abdurahman, president of the African Political Organization (APO), the leading Coloured advocacy group in the country.[61]

Williams, formerly a schoolmaster in Trinidad, was convinced that "education was the only ladder by which the coloured races could rise."[62] He was a board member of the Wooding School, a preparatory school for children up to Standard Seven—well above the Standard Four levels of almost all schools for Africans. (The 1905 Education Act allocated more than £300,000 for the education of white children but only £5,000 for black children, and it imposed a Standard Four limit for blacks in state-sponsored schools, thus barring blacks from higher-paying jobs.)[63] In 1905, when Williams returned to England to join his family, he organized on behalf of black South Africans, as he would continue to do until his death in 1911.[64]

THE UNIA NETWORK IN SOUTH AFRICA

The black West Indians in southern Africa—almost five hundred as of 1905— had continued Pan-African work, primarily under the rubric of Marcus Garvey's UNIA. West Indians, particularly the dockworkers in the port city of Cape Town, established UNIA chapters. They also introduced UNIA ideology to the Industrial and Commercial Workers Union (ICU) and to the African National Congress, the two largest black South African organizations of the 1920s.[65] To West Indians and other blacks in South Africa, the UNIA had proved to be an effective conduit for publicizing local struggles on an international stage. It also became the principal bridge between Africans and American Negroes. Many Africans saw the UNIA and American Negroes as racial models *and* as their divinely ordained liberators from South African white supremacy. They proclaimed a prophetic Christianity, using an array of Judeo-Christian biblical texts, symbols, rituals, and metaphors to legitimate their claims for an independent Africa and for equal rights in the modern world. South African Garveyites and their many foes were aware of Garvey's own ideological battles in the United States with rivals like W. E. B. Du Bois, A. Philip Randolph, and Cyril Briggs, a black communist organizer. As we will see shortly, blacks in South Africa, like their American counterparts, engaged in a spirited debate about the competing models of racial advancement.

The UNIA, with its nationalist trappings—a constitutional bill of rights, a flag, a military, diplomats, industrial and commercial entities, and annual leg-islative conventions—was, in effect, a virtual symbol of a black government-in-exile. Garvey was elected provisional president of Africa. James Thaele, president of the ANC Western Province and its Cape Town branch, asserted that "just as the League of Nations is to European governments so are the UNIA . . . decrees or proclamations obligatory to us all."[66] H. L. Davids, president of a local Cape Town UNIA branch, called the UNIA charter as important to blacks worldwide as the British flag was to Commonwealth nations.[67] James Ghazu, a Cape Town–based sailor and later the general organizer of South African UNIA affairs, proclaimed in the *Negro World*: "Garveyism is a self-protecting system among the blacks to promote the race socially, eco-nomically and in the true form which God the creator of all races on this earth meant. The Negro desires to share in every possible thing that other races enjoy and . . . is just as fit to shape its own destiny as other races are."[68]

To Africans, Garvey's Black Star Line, along with the Negro Factories Corporation (a string of groceries, laundries, and other small businesses) of which it was a part, was a clear symbol of modernity and emergent nationhood. They saw the line as a more militant manifestation of Washington's self-reliance ideals: "We shall redeem Africa only by unity, diligent research and a resolve to build our own schools, colleges, universities, shops and building our own ships."[69]

Within South Africa, Cape Town had the earliest and the largest number of UNIA divisions—five. There were also branches in Pretoria, Johannesburg, and Vrede, more branches than in any other country. West Indian dockworkers were dominant in the first two UNIA divisions in the Cape Town area—the first, by 1920, in Goodwood and Parow, adjoining villages just outside the city. Little is known about this division, except that Timothy Robertson, a former ship's cook from British Guyana and a prominent shopkeeper in Parow, founded it. Robertson became the official UNIA organizer in Cape Town, distributing Garveyist literature, selling Black Star Line stock, and getting "every true African" to join the UNIA. He helped establish the Cape Town chapter by 1922.[70] West Indians dominated its leadership and took prominent roles in mass meetings, ceremonies, and socials of the West London, Woodstock, and Claremont divisions in Cape Town's southern suburbs.[71]

The Claremont division, which began in 1922 with thirty-three members, featured a predominantly Coloured officer corps.[72] The Woodstock division, also formed in 1922, included former Cape Town UNIA officers M. Emmanuel Johnson, a West Indian, as president and Richard Ndimande, an African, as secretary. (Johnson succeeded Robertson as the UNIA organizer.)[73] A later secretary, A. J. Maphike, who named his son Garvey Arend Maphike, would write a moving obituary at Garvey's death.[74] The West London (present-day Athlone) division was organized in 1924 with Coloured leadership, its affairs conducted in Afrikaans.[75] At its opening ceremony, the audience included Thaele; ICU head Clements Kadalie; and visiting American Negro sailors such as Peter Johnson, who "said many encouraging and inspiring things."[76]

Cape Town UNIA divisions held their Sunday afternoon meetings in accordance with the ritual order stipulated by the American UNIA headquarters.[77] Meetings opened with an elaborate procession and an officer's explanation of the organization's aims and objectives, as well as the latest news. Members reaffirmed their commitment to a providentially designed African independence through singing missionary hymns such as "From Greenland's Icy Mountains" and "Onward, Christian Soldiers" and reciting the UNIA Universal Prayer.[78] Then came readings from the *Negro World*, transcripts of Garvey's speeches, followed by stirring orations on Garveyite principles of self-help, unity, education, and racial uplift as the means to achieve "African redemption." The meetings concluded with the Ethiopian national anthem.

Inevitably, speakers could refer to Psalm 68:31's promise that "princes shall come out of Egypt and Ethiopia shall stretch forth her hands to God." Garvey was the prince and Ethiopia a black nation in communion with a God who had assigned it a providential role in world affairs.[79] William Jackson, the Cape Town UNIA president, declared: "Ethiopia will be taken naked from Egypt to a foreign country, there to be lynched, whipped, gimecrowed (jimcrowed), killed and finally, after experiencing many vicissitudes of torments and misery, will return to Africa and impart the civilization and knowledge obtained in the foreign country to his people."[80]

The "people," according to Jackson, were the "15,000,000 negroes of America who have to-day reached the highest scientific attainments in the world. Those Negroes are now preparing to come back to the land of their forefathers and impart the knowledge gained in foreign countries to their brethren in Africa. Your slogan must be One Aim, One God, and One Destiny."[81] Garvey was transmitting God's mandate, and Garveyite soldiers were "proselytizing for the UNIA orthodoxy," preaching "the doctrine of the UNIA, the first gospel of Garveyism." The *Negro World*, said Garveyite Nathaniel Ntengo, "must be a Bible to us."[82] Garveyism was the means whereby blacks could fulfill their racial potential "in the true form which God, the creator of all races on this earth meant."[83] Garveyites used quotes from the organizational *Universal Negro Catechism* to fortify their children against the false religion of white supremacy.[84]

To Timothy Robertson, the leading UNIA organizer, Garvey was a "true Moses" who would "emancipate the children of Ethiopia from the fetters of bondage."[85] Another Garveyite proclaimed, "Even the deaf, dumb and half dead have caught the vision of Mr. Garvey that Africa must be freed from the exploiters." Garveyism was the "Siloam Pool" (John 9:1–39) that granted sight to the blind and helpless who wandered in the wilderness. For blacks awaiting the coming of the Messiah and admission into God's kingdom, the Siloam Pool references were particularly suggestive. They linked the liberationist Old Testament prophecies of Isaiah 35:5 and 42:7 to Jesus's restoring of sight, both physical and spiritual.[86]

Religion was central to the family-friendly UNIA social events, which offered a private refuge from the hostile gaze of unfriendly whites.[87] In the Claremont division social, when the charter was unveiled, it was accompanied by readings from Genesis and declarations thanking God for delivering Garvey.[88] The UNIA band performed; there were musical cavalcades of piano, violin, and song, along with comic parodies and "tea cakes, fruit and minerals." At sacred concerts, there was singing of missionary hymns and ceremonial readings of the Universal Prayer and relevant biblical passages. These passages included Exodus 14:15, in which God chastises Moses and the Israelites not to depend solely on his divine favor—reinforcing the Garveyite theme of black self-help—and Genesis 1:26, in which God creates humans in his own image, whatever their race.

Members of the fraternal West Indian–American Association displayed framed portraits of Booker T. Washington, whom many West Indian and South African Garveyites likened to Garvey. Echoing Washington's up from slavery narrative, the *Black Man*, a Cape Town newspaper published by the ICU, praised the rise of "the brethren in America," shipped from Africa in "the fetters of bondage" to be made "hewers of wood and drawers of water." These American cousins, the *Black Man* continued, were now free and ready to return to Africa to end "the tyrannical rule of the selfish foreigners."[89] Several months earlier, Clements Kadalie, the ICU general secretary, told his comrades that his own "essential object is to be the great African Marcus Garvey and I don't mind of how much I shall pay for that education."[90] Kadalie had been inspired to enter public life by reading Washington's *Up from Slavery*. He and other ICU leaders, *Black Man* editor and World War I veteran Samuel Ncwana among them, believed that the best way to honor Washington's legacy of self-reliance was with strikes, boycotts, and other acts of civil disobedience. They issued ICU membership cards with the UNIA colors of red, black, and green and sold copies of the UNIA Declaration of Negro Rights.[91] They affected American Negro accents. To some black South Africans, "American Negro leaders had come to deliver them from slavery."[92]

Many present-day scholars are unaware that the leadership corps of the Industrial and Commercial Workers Union, South Africa's first mass black trade union, was imbued with Garveyite influence. Peter Wickins, for example, has stated, "There is no evidence that any of the leading figures of the ICU . . . was deeply influenced by Garvey."[93] Yet at least five West Indians served on the ICU National Executive and may have tried to transform it into an "auxiliary of the UNIA."[94] And in 1920, the ICU elected West Indians A. James King and James Gumbs, executive officer of Cape Town's UNIA, as president and vice president. In 1925, M. Emmanuel Johnson, UNIA organizer and Cape Town UNIA president, became a junior vice president on ICU's National Council and the local agent for the *Negro World*.[95]

Gumbs, a shipwright and former chemist, became ICU chairman in 1925 and had significant control of the organization's finances. ICU officers from Durban and Johannesburg once journeyed to Cape Town to convince him to release £400 of union funds for organizational expenses in Johannesburg. Gumbs was a member of the UNIA Advisory Board, the Ancient Order of the Free Gardeners, the Pick-Wick Cooperative Club, and the West Indian–American Association. H. D. Tyamzashe wrote of Gumbs that he was "a black gentleman in the true sense of the word, and conducted ICU Conferences with dignity, fairness, wisdom and cheerfulness. . . . He died at Cape Town in

1928 with the presidential colours flying over his grave. . . . HE WAS A MAN."[96] Kadalie recalled that Gumbs promised audiences that "we," meaning American Negroes, would soon reclaim Africa for the Africans.[97]

West Indians were represented in the ICU through a host of Cape Town organizations. James Lyner of the West Indian–American Association, the ICU, and the UNIA was a Black Star Line shareholder. James King, an early ICU president, was a UNIA member and secretary of the Pick-Wick Cooperative Club. Three other West Indians, J. Caesar Allen, Emile Wattlington, and William Jackson, belonged to both the UNIA and the West Indian–American Association.[98]

THE LEAGUE OF NATIONS AND THE PROPOSED UNIA SETTLEMENT IN SOUTHWEST AFRICA

Seen by Africans as potential liberators, Garvey and the American UNIA also sought assistance from an outside entity, the League of Nations, to achieve their Africa for the Africans goal. In addition to attempts to establish a colony in Liberia, the UNIA planned a colony for blacks in Southwest Africa, a League of Nations mandate territory occupied by South Africa. In 1920, the League had awarded to South Africa, on behalf of Great Britain, a mandate to administer and control Southwest Africa, after the Allies forced a defeated Germany to relinquish its African colonies. South Africa extended its segregationist laws to Southwest Africa, and soon thereafter, Garveyism emerged as a potent force in the territory. Fitzherbert Headly was a fiery West Indian stevedore who had lived in Luderitz, Southwest Africa, since 1909. He sent a letter to the editor of the *Negro World* in 1921, protesting that "we are segregated, discriminated, disfranchised, jim-crowed . . . and last, but not the least, butchered by the other fellow with rifle and machine gun bullets. But what we are dealing with mostly here is a level of segregation wholly in its aspects in the former regime of our oppressors the Germans."[99] Headly asked the *Negro World* to "kindly publish this broadcast so that the League of Nations can see and know what is going to become of their sacred mandate of this colony."[100]

At the 1919 Versailles Peace Conference, the UNIA had demanded complete African independence but to no avail. In 1922, it sent emissaries to the League's Geneva headquarters to lobby for UNIA development of former German colonies in Southwest Africa, Tanganyika, and Ruanda-Urundi as land bases for independent black states. At the 1919 Pan-African Congress at Versailles, NAACP leader W. E. B. Du Bois had suggested that the former German colonies, the Belgian Congo, and the Portuguese colonies, as well, be converted into a black-led territory. But since the NAACP had no chapters in Southwest Africa and since it lacked the UNIA's international renown, Du Bois's proposal carried little weight. Three years later, Garveyites in Southwest

Africa noted, "We have sent a delegation from the Parent Body in New York last month to the League of Nations, now sitting in Geneva, Switzerland, to ask that the Mandate of South West Africa be handed over to us to form a Government of our own."[101] The UNIA reminded the League that hundreds of thousands of blacks worldwide had bought war bonds, and many others had died in English, French, and American armies to defend the principles of freedom, democracy, and self-determination for independent black governments in Africa. Further, the UNIA told League representatives that despite nearly three hundred years of slavery, American blacks had produced scientists, engineers, educators, doctors, statesmen, and soldiers who were the equal of whites. UNIA colonies in Africa would fulfill God's providential design calling for once enslaved, highly skilled diasporic blacks to return to Africa to spread "culture and civilization."[102]

The League of Nations predictably ignored UNIA appeals. But Africans heeded Garvey's incendiary rhetoric. "The moment has come when the 40 million blacks must claim Africa as their own," he said. "There will be no question of asking England, Belgium, France and Italy why are you here but of ordering them to leave." Garvey declared that black soldiers who had enlisted to fight for white nations were denied liberty after the war even though without the contributions of black soldiers, "the Kaiser would be in Buckingham Palace today." He predicted that "the bloodiest war is yet to come," and he wondered ominously when black troops trained to kill for the Pax Britannica would "fight for our own cause?"[103]

UNIA members in Luderitz (a coastal diamond-mining town in Southwest Africa), most of them West Indians and West African workers, were exempt from segregationist laws. They established a school, maintained businesses, and disseminated the *Negro World* and other Garveyist literature among African contract workers on the local diamond mines. The UNIA chapter also provided sickness, death, and poverty benefits to their members. The UNIA president, Headly, spreading "the first gospel of Garveyism," also established UNIA chapters throughout Namibia, most notably in Windhoek. At its peak, the Windhoek UNIA boasted nearly 900 members, who eagerly read UNIA literature from Garvey, "the big black king in America," and warned whites that "this land is not yours, it is the property of America and the Herero."[104] By 1922, the Luderitz UNIA had 311 members (15 percent of all local blacks), among them West Indians, Liberians, South Africans, Herero, Nama, Ovambo, and Khoi-San peoples. Like the Cape Town UNIA, its branch meetings opened with the standard missionary hymn, "From Greenland's Icy Mountains," and opened and closed with prayers offered by the UNIA chaplain. The children's choir and the choir of the Black Cross Nurses sang songs such as "Garvey Is Calling" and "Ethiopia, Land of our Fathers."[105]

In Windhoek, Headly praised Garvey as a prophet who "with the vision of God . . . has brought new light among his people." He continued, "This our fatherland must be freed from the white man's rule, for this reign is simply stifling the talents and progressiveness of our people." Echoing the trope of Israelite slavery common among American Negroes, he pleaded, "Oh God, when will you hear our prayers and pleadings and relieve us of this state of bondage?"[106]

Marcus Garvey's travels in the Caribbean, South America, Europe, and the United States exposed him to the transnational nature of white supremacy but also to the up from slavery narrative of the Virginia Jubilee Singers and Booker T. Washington and the global Pan-Africanism of Du Bois and Henry Sylvester Williams. Like John Dube, Garvey was much influenced by Washington, but his politics moved far beyond the Wizard's. Garvey's appropriation of Washington's up from slavery model of racial self-help and economic self-sufficiency, combined with his own anticolonialism and racial nationalism, resulted in an increasingly successful American Negro model in interwar South Africa, where Africans drew parallels between colonial rule and slavery in the Americas. The UNIA channeled black despair and disillusionment with resurgent white supremacy in the postwar period into the largest black-led movement in world history. For millions of blacks around the globe, the UNIA was the means by which they could become dynamic historical agents who would reclaim Africa for Africans, control their own economies, build their own armies and navies, and be respected equals on the global stage.

But even Garvey and the UNIA could not overturn the white supremacist narrative that the sovereignty of (white) nations, not racial equality, was the fundamental principle of the British Empire, the United States, and the League of Nations. Garvey would soon suffer irreversible personal setbacks and witness the gradual disintegration of the American UNIA, yet his movement would have enduring strength in South Africa. For many South African blacks, Garvey became a Christ-like martyr figure, and Garveyist dreams of liberation swept across South Africa in prophetic and startling new dimensions.

4 ↩ Transnational Martyrdom and the Spread of Garveyism in South Africa

THE DOWNFALL OF GARVEY AND THE DECLINE OF THE AMERICAN UNIA

GARVEYISM TRIUMPHED in South Africa despite the successful attempts by the U.S. government and hostile black rivals to exploit Marcus Garvey's stubborn personality and poor money-management skills, which ultimately led to his jailing and deportation from America. Garveyism triumphed, too, despite the aggressive anti-Garvey and anti-UNIA attacks launched by the South African governments and antagonistic Africans who alternately looked to themselves, liberal whites, or other American Negroes as keys to their advancement.

This chapter argues that despite Garvey's prosecution by the U.S. Department of Justice, withering attacks by American and South African opponents, and the decline of the American UNIA, Garveyism in South Africa spread with new UNIA chapters and to non-UNIA organizations such as the ANC. Many of Garvey's opponents viewed him as a foolhardy and fraudulent latter-day Booker T. Washington, willing to surrender black American constitutional rights at the altar of white supremacy. South African Garveyites had very different perceptions. They believed the downfall of Garvey and the decline of the American UNIA proved the entrenched nature of the global color line and the civil religion of white supremacy. The U.S. government assumed the role of a modern-day Pontius Pilate prosecuting Garvey, the Negro Moses who was now also seen as a persecuted Christ-like figure. The ANC leader James Thaele, who had transcended the limited Hampton-Tuskegee model of industrial education in South Africa by earning two degrees at Lincoln University in the United States, became South Africa's foremost Garveyite, radicalizing the ANC in the process. After the 1924 elections in South Africa, which heralded the onset of additional segregationist legislation, Thaele and the ANC mirrored Garvey's attempts to use ideas of racial separation to find common ground with white segregationists. Disillusioned by the government's segregationist program, which offered no benefit to Africans, Thaele pointed to Garvey and American Negro achievement to prove that blacks could govern themselves and did not need white trusteeship.

As the UNIA and Garveyism spread around the world, Garvey made critical financial and strategic mistakes that led to the decline of his movement. He had ignored the pleas of his astute friend Ida B. Wells to postpone the launching of the Black Star Line until the UNIA had stronger financial backing. He pressed on toward his $2 million capitalization plan. However, overpayment for ships that, as retreads, needed constant repairs, coupled with slipshod business practices, imperiled the line. Despite Garvey's massive fund-raising tour of the Caribbean and Central America, raising tens of thousands of dollars from the sale of Black Star Line stock and from admission fees to his speeches, the shipping line failed.

Cuban president Mario Garcia Menocal had pledged to do business with his ships, but Garvey had to wait for five months in the Caribbean for a reentry visa to the United States after a barnstorming tour.[1] The State Department ignored the demands of the Department of Justice to refuse him reentry, fearing that banning him would make him a martyr among blacks at home and abroad. After one of Garvey's lawyers allegedly paid a $2,000 bribe, the State Department lifted the ban.[2]

Once back in the States, Garvey applied promptly for American citizenship in hopes of thwarting deportation, but hostile government officials and black rivals' exposés blocked his application. Du Bois had published, in the NAACP magazine *Crisis*, two carefully researched articles that praised Garvey's sincerity, boundless energy, and charismatic leadership but also exposed the UNIA's messy financial affairs. For example, the UNIA had paid $140,000 for the *Frederick Douglass*, more than twice its estimated worth, and constant repairs limited the ship to a mere three trips to the West Indies in three years; it was sold at auction for $1,625 to pay off part of its massive debts. The line's second ship, the *Antonio Maceo*, cost $60,000 but required another $45,000 for mechanical repairs, spent in vain because it had to be permanently consigned to dock. The *Shadyside*, the line's small yacht, was limited to excursions up and down the Hudson River. A UNIA ship captain complained that the line's vessels lost money because Garvey ordered stops in many ports as propaganda for the company, even as coconuts and other cargo perished and costs to feed and care for the detoured passengers climbed.[3]

On 12 January 1922, Garvey was indicted for mail fraud related to a charge of soliciting potential investors to buy stock in a ship called the *Orion* (which had already been renamed the *Phyllis Wheatley* in ads in the *Negro World*) before the line actually owned it. Checks bounced, and money was diverted from successful ventures, like the *Negro World*, to pay the line's bills. Garvey told Herbert Boulin, a confidant who turned out to be an informer for the U.S. Department of Justice, that he had twice contemplated suicide. On 1 April 1922, Garvey announced the suspension of operations of the line, and at the annual convention in August 1922, he, his officers, and assembled delegates traded bitter accusations and counteraccusations. In the aftermath, Garvey expelled his deputy James Eason, and salaried officials took a 50 percent pay cut.

Meanwhile, members of the African Blood Brotherhood, a rival organization, distributed anti-Garvey circulars to UNIA convention delegates in New York. The growth in the number of UNIA chapters slowed, and circulation figures for the *Negro World* declined. The $144,000 raised from bonds for the Liberian Construction Loan were diverted to pay other organizational expenses, and the Africa program collapsed when the Liberian government, eager to secure a U.S. government loan and to appease the British and French (who held adjoining colonies), charged that the UNIA threatened its sovereignty. At the same time, the UNIA demand that the League of Nations recognize blacks' claim to former German colonies, including South African–held Southwest Africa, had gone unanswered. There was also private trouble for Garvey. A bitterly contested divorce was complicated by his suspected romance with his secretary and future wife, Amy Jacques. Former employees filed lawsuits for back salary, and one opponent, the black communist leader Cyril Briggs of New York, successfully sued Garvey for libel for calling him a white man.[4]

By June 1922, Garvey was facing imprisonment and deportation to Jamaica. Increasingly desperate, he moderated his aggressive black nationalism to an accommodationist Booker T. Washington style that did not directly challenge white power, sought alliances with seemingly powerful whites, and included public statements that seemed to absolve whites and blame blacks for Jim Crow conditions. In a tour of the American South, Garvey met with Grand Wizard Edward Clarke of the Ku Klux Klan (KKK), a fateful decision that hastened his imprisonment, deportation, and the decline of his movement in the United States. Despite his earlier denunciations of the KKK, Garvey met with Clarke in the belief that shared themes of black emigration to Africa and racial separatism could lead the Klan to offer assistance to him and the back-to-Africa part of his program (interracial sex particularly violated the tenets of racial purity that Garvey and white southerners shared).[5] Citing Clarke's vow that the white majority would never treat blacks equally in America, Garvey advised blacks not to integrate into a "white man's country," and (unlike Washington) he argued that blacks should reclaim Africa instead. Astonishingly, Garvey described the Klan as a potential ally because, he said, unlike so-called liberal whites, Klan members were brutally honest about their racial feelings.[6]

His dalliance with the KKK began a series of curious alliances with the white supremacists who sought to ship blacks back to Africa. He urged followers to give "undivided and wholehearted support" to Mississippi senator Theodore Bilbo, who proposed federal legislation to finance African repatriation. Some Garveyites worked with Mississippi state senator T. S. McCallum and Maryland senator Joseph I. France on legislation to ask America's European allies to reserve African territory for emigrating African Americans.[7] Garvey himself allied with White America Society leader Earnest Sevier Cox and John Powell, head of the Anglo-Saxon Clubs of America, and he allowed Powell to lecture in Manhattan's sacred UNIA Liberty Hall.[8] Further, Garvey opposed antilynching legislation designed to make lynching a federal crime. This stance countered that of his archenemy, the NAACP, and he told one black audience, "If we had not been lynched and jim-crowed we would have never awakened and started a Republic of Africa."[9] He also congratulated President Warren G. Harding on a speech that reaffirmed Jim Crow. In New Orleans, where the landmark "separate but equal" *Plessy v. Ferguson* case began, he advised blacks to accept unequal railroad accommodations because they had not built the railroads.[10]

In earlier times, Du Bois had attacked Washington for seemingly acquiescing to white power, and now he and other blacks challenged Garvey's increased conservatism. A. Philip Randolph, leader of the Brotherhood of Sleeping Car Porters' black labor union and editor of the *Messenger*, a socialist paper, had introduced Garvey to many Harlemites, and he had served as a UNIA delegate to the Versailles Conference. He now broke completely with Garvey. The front pages of the *Messenger* blared, "Marcus Garvey! The Black Imperial Wizard Becomes Messenger Boy of the White Ku Klux Kleagle." Friends of Negro Freedom and the NAACP held weekly anti-Garvey rallies outside the 1922 UNIA convention, sparking violent confrontations that had to be broken up by police.[11] In nightly meetings, Harrison, Garvey's former mentor, scorned Garvey as a "bombastic, conceited and arrogant" man who had bankrupted the Black Star Line. Harrison lamented that hundreds of thousands of dollars collected from poor blacks for UNIA projects had been wasted on reckless spending, on exorbitant UNIA salaries, on gross overpayments, and on constant repairs for ships.[12]

Du Bois called Garvey "a lunatic or a traitor." He denounced Garvey's claim that America was a "white man's country" as a surrender of black civil rights. "This open ally of the Ku Klux Klan should be locked up or deported," he said. Like several opponents, Du Bois engaged in personal attacks against Garvey, calling him a "little, fat black man, ugly but with intelligent eyes."[13] Robert Bagnall, an NAACP organizer, described Garvey as a man of "unmixed stock . . . with protruding jaws, and heavy jowls, small bright pig-like eyes and rather bulldog face" and literally insane.[14] Randolph labeled him "a little half-wit Lilliputian."[15] The conservative journalist George Schuyler referred to Garvey as "America's greatest buffoon," a "sable Ponzi," and a "circus monkey . . . with his evolved tail, and with a little rouge on his long lips [that] would be sure to remind his audiences of this illustrious prototype that swung from the branches of trees in the dense African forest."[16]

Apparently, Garvey eagerly engaged his enemies, drawing strength from the fact that many supporters considered him a persecuted, Christ-like figure. His critics, he said, were promiscegenation, light-skinned mulattoes. Du Bois, a man of African, Dutch, and French ancestry, was a "lazy dependent mulatto," "a hater of black people" who "bewails every day the drop of Negro blood in his veins."[17] He accused Du Bois and the NAACP (which he referred to as the National Association for the Advancement of *Certain* People) of race suicide for their supposed advocacy of miscegenation. They were, he said, "the greatest enemies the black people have in the world" and would soon meet their Waterloo.[18] His rivals, well aware of the militarist character of the UNIA, took Garvey's enmity seriously. After all, Garvey had at his disposal armed bodyguards; the UNIA police and secret service; and the African Legion, a paramilitary group composed of black men in crisp military uniforms pledging allegiance to Garvey.[19] Someone sent Randolph the bloody, severed hand of a white man; he considered it a death threat from the UNIA and hired policemen for protection.[20]

In New Orleans on 1 January 1923, Garveyites were said to have killed James Eason, the former UNIA "head of American Negroes." Eason was an electrifying speaker who had established a rival organization, the Universal Negro Alliance. He denounced Garvey and the UNIA for sacrificing "New Negro" principles at the altar of white supremacy and for squandering "the nearly one million dollars collected from the members, with absolutely nothing to show for it."[21] Garvey had, in fact, dispatched Esau Ramus, a member of the UNIA's secret service, to New Orleans. There, a local UNIA police chief helped him organize a small band of UNIA members from the area to intimidate Eason. Ramus reportedly admitted Garvey had instructed that Eason "must not return to New York alive." After Eason's death, Garvey allegedly gave Ramus $60 to find sanctuary in Detroit.[22] NAACP officials and certain other prominent African Americans now petitioned the U.S. attorney general to bring Garvey's mail fraud case to trial and deport him if convicted.

In the 1920s, vigilant government investigations probed dissident activity in white political circles and radical black organizations for possible pro-German and pro-Bolshevist activities. Garvey and the UNIA drew close attention from the Military Investigative Bureau, the Bureau of Investigation, and the Department of State. J. Edgar Hoover, deputy head of the Bureau of Investigation (precursor of the FBI) and soon to be its director, considered Garvey and the UNIA the primary black threat to U.S. national security. Hoover, who had hired the bureau's first black agents, now recruited black informers to infiltrate the UNIA to collect evidence to justify Garvey's deportation. Among these informers were key legal advisers to Garvey, the circulation manager of the *Negro World*, and the leader of the African Legion, the UNIA's paramilitary group. When Garvey called such persons as witnesses to testify in his defense, he discovered their double identities.[23]

Garvey's federal trial began in May 1923 in New York City. The government charged that he and three other UNIA officials had used the mails fraudulently to induce nearly forty thousand blacks to contribute approximately $1 million to the now-bankrupt Black Star Line. At the trial, a parade of disgruntled former UNIA officials and investors testified that Garvey had overpaid for ships and had used the vessels as political propaganda pieces at the expense of possible profit. They claimed, too, that he had diverted moneys earmarked for the line to pay the expenses of the *Negro World* and other UNIA businesses, had failed to pay promised salaries, and had summarily dismissed accountants who protested his business practices.[24]

After Garvey was found guilty in June 1923, he denounced the judge and the district attorney as "damned dirty Jews" and promised revenge. He was sentenced to five years in prison and given a $1,000 fine. As federal marshals led him away to jail, a woman in the courtroom collapsed, wailing, "Dear God, Christ died on the cross for the same thing they are punishing Garvey for."[25] In the aftermath of the trial, mass rallies raised funds for an appeal. Petitions with hundreds of pages of signatures demanding his release were submitted to President Harding and the U.S. Justice Department.[26] Garvey spent three months in jail before being released on bail pending appeal. He then made a triumphant return to a cheering Harlem throng and toured southern and western states to raise funds and boost the morale of his followers. But he suffered additional setbacks with the Black Cross Navigation and Trading Company, the successor to the Black Star Line, and with the failing Liberian settlement scheme.[27] The following year, the UNIA announced the purchase of a large ship, the SS *Goethels*, renamed the SS *Booker T. Washington*, as a linchpin of the Black Cross Company. Garvey reopened negotiations with the government in Liberia to establish a UNIA colony there. The Americo-Liberian elite, under pressure from the British and French, sold the land the UNIA sought to the Firestone Company for more money than the UNIA alone could muster. UNIA officials in Liberia were hustled off to jail and sent back to America. A federal grand jury now indicted Garvey for perjury, for underreporting his income, and for falsely claiming a sister as his dependent.[28] The Black Cross Company sold off the *Booker T. Washington* for a quarter of the purchase price. In February 1925, Garvey lost the appeal of his sentence in the Black Star Line case, as well as a final appeal to the U.S. circuit court of appeals. He was arrested and confined at the Atlanta Federal Penitentiary to serve out his five-year sentence.[29]

Yet despite these damning events, American disciples continued to view Garvey as a persecuted Christ-like figure; as a Moses who led his people just short of the Promised Land; or as a modern-day Ezekiel, the long-suffering Old Testament prophet who prophesied divine redemption to the enslaved Israelites in Babylon. Garvey compared his plight to that of Jesus Christ, stating, "Christ died to make men free; I shall die to give courage and inspiration to the race."[30] Mournful supporters sang the Universal African National Anthem.[31] Tens of thousands (including the father of Malcolm X) who had already contributed thousands to Garvey's defense sent petitions for clemency to President Calvin Coolidge. Worried lest Garvey, in declining health, die in prison and become a martyr, the federal government released him on condition of deportation. On 2 December 1927, after more than two years in prison, Marcus Garvey sailed from New Orleans; he would not set foot in the United States again. His final words to the throngs of supporters who went to the pier were: "I leave America fully as happy as when I came . . . my entire life will be devoted to the support of the cause. I sincerely believe that it is only by nationalizing the Negro and awakening him to the possibilities of himself that his universal problem can be solved."[32]

By that time, the bankrupt UNIA owed more than $200,000 to creditors and had lost its ships, its publishing plant, and its Liberty Halls in New York and in Pittsburgh. But supporters continued to claim Garvey as a divinely ordained prophet destined "to lead his people out of political bondage and economic servitude." "We have a leader that a white man did not put before us, we have a leader that God sent to us."[33] Even his enemies acknowledged his power. NAACP field secretary and poet James Weldon Johnson said, "Garvey stirred the imagination of the masses as no Negro ever had. He raised more money in a few years than any other Negro organization had ever dreamed of. He had great power and great possibilities within his grasp."[34] The *Negro World* had predicted that Garvey's "continued confinement in jail will react disastrously against his oppressors and also quicken the realization of his vision of a free and redeemed Africa, while attacks at the unassailable spirit with which he has revolutionized the Negro will brand his persecutors as the enemies of freedom, liberty and fair play."[35]

ANTI-GARVEY ATTACKS IN SOUTH AFRICA

Garvey's conviction and jailing stalled the movement in the United States, and in South Africa, the situation intensified criticism as anti-Garveyites there were emboldened by the man's humiliating downfall in America. Ironically, Garvey's troubles also propelled Garveyism forward in South Africa, for his ideas became a mobilizing political force and sparked a national debate about which American Negroes were appropriate models for Africans. Eager to discredit Garveyism, the South African government had been disseminating news of Garvey's mail fraud conviction.[36] It circulated copies of the American daily the *World* that portrayed an imperious Garvey who represented himself after firing his lawyer. This Garvey bullied and berated the judge and the jury for participating in a witch hunt by the British government and U.S. law enforcement. Officials also circulated Garvey's apology, published in the *Negro World*, for calling Cyril Briggs a white man pretending to be a black nationalist leader.[37] Africans could read sensational accounts of the claims made by UNIA leaders that they owned four powerful ocean liners when in fact they possessed just one leaky vessel to account for the $1 million collected for the Black Star Line. The government subscribed to the *Negro World* to monitor news about UNIA affairs. Reading of a world tour by Garvey and two other UNIA officials that would include South Africa, they banned all UNIA officials from the country.[38]

Immigration laws also bedeviled moderate anti-Garveyite American Negro missionaries, including James East and Herbert Payne (see chapter 1). AME bishop William Vernon, a moderate former registrar of the U.S. Treasury, had to enlist distinguished whites, including former president William Howard Taft, to intervene on his behalf for entry into South Africa.[39] These African Americans were best positioned to undermine prophetic Garveyism. Payne, for example, asked Interior Minister Thomas Watt to ban Garveyist literature, since it had fueled unrealistic expectations of liberation. According to Payne, West Indians, not sober-minded African Americans, dominated the UNIA, and most intelligent blacks in America discounted Garvey and the UNIA. Payne's friend D. D. T. Jabavu told Watt that Payne had done much to "disabuse the Natives here of the Garvey Black Fleet illusion."[40] Vernon advised Africans to be loyal to the government, ignore politics, and press for citizenship rights only after they had raised their level of civilization. He considered slavery part of God's providential design but complained that Garveyism had made his own task of uplifting Africans more difficult.[41]

After an African mining strike in 1920, the Chamber of Mines established *Umteteli wa Bantu* (Mouthpiece of the People) as a moderate and apolitical counterpoint to the ANC's newspaper, *Abantu-Batho. Umteteli* warned Africans that Garvey's claim to the title of provisional president of Africa revealed dictatorial and imperialist intentions. Skin color and ancestral origin had created links between Africans and American Negroes, but Americans were "wholly dissimilar in character, thought and habit" to Africans. Their intervention in South Africa would lead to the absorption and ultimate extinction of Africans. *Umteteli* urged Africans to "go it alone" yet, paradoxically, "work in harmony with the Europeans in our midst as it is lunatic to be influenced by the impossible ideal of an All Black Africa."[42]

The first African-owned newspaper, *Imvo Zabantsundu*, had ignored Garveyism until 1921, when it compared it to Nongqawuse's cattle-killing prophecies of the 1850s.[43] These prophecies had effectively ended Xhosa resistance to British aggression as tens of thousands died and as starving Xhosa became menial laborers. *Imvo* dismissed Garvey as "off his head" and predicted disastrous consequences for his South African admirers, recalling Garvey's own conviction. Like *Umteteli*, it questioned linkages with American Negroes.[44] *Imvo* rejected the ideal of Garvey as American Negro liberator, though it praised American Negroes, Du Bois, and Booker T. Washington as useful exemplars for Africans. *Imvo* wrote that Du Bois was a "far-seeing thinker," and it published profiles of Tuskegee faculty like George Washington Carver. It also praised the pro-Washington, Gold Coast–born educator from America James Aggrey, who, in his 1921 and 1924 visits to South Africa, promoted interracial cooperation and called Garvey the worst enemy of black people.[45]

APO, the organ of the African Peoples Organization, the country's preeminent Coloured group, initially praised the Black Star Line and UNIA's plans to move its headquarters to Liberia. The paper's editors hoped that one of the ships would visit Cape Town soon.[46] But by late 1920, the sun had set on the APO-UNIA honeymoon. *APO* was now skeptical that black capitalism could benefit working-class people. It criticized Garvey's characterization of Du Bois's 1921 Pan African Congress as black beggars asking whites for an equal rights handout. *APO* also rejected Garvey's view that blacks, not whites, were ultimately responsible for racism. "The existing universal prejudice against negroes is not so much because they are black," Garvey had said to a Liberty Hall audience in New York in one of his Washingtonian moments, "but because they have done nothing praiseworthy on their own initiative in the last five hundred years to recommend them to the serious consideration of progressive races."[47] Garvey's reasoning, according to the editors at *APO*, had revived ideas of Booker T. Washington that Du Bois had challenged in *The Souls of Black Folk. APO* now attacked Garvey as a "Judas Iscariot" who sounded more like white South African segregationists than a Moses leading his people to the Promised Land.[48]

THE ENDURING FAITH OF SOUTH AFRICAN GARVEYITES

The decline of the American UNIA and the overt hostility of African and Coloured newspapers and African Americans in South Africa did not block the spread of Garveyism there. Pro-Garvey newspapers responded aggressively to their journalist peers. The *Black Man* fired back immediately, stating that God's providential design to emancipate blacks was being fulfilled by the UNIA. The UNIA was an "organization in which the hand of God has made itself felt for the return of His children, whom he thought fit should be hewers of wood and drawers of water until such times as now when He shall call them back to Africa whence they were taken."[49] The *Black Man* dismissed *Umteteli wa Bantu* as "an official organ of the Transvaal slave owners." It challenged attempts by AME minister Francis Gow to cast Garvey as a "useful instrument of the enemies of his race," claiming Gow was seeking "the favor of the white man at the expense of poor people."[50] Garveyites viewed Gow's remarks as unworthy of the AME, which they considered to be a "militant Negro religious organization" and the premier example of black religious institutional autonomy.[51]

Garveyites in Cape Town opened two new UNIA branches in Claremont and Woodstock, for, in their eyes, Garvey's arrest proved persecution by fearful whites.[52] After his conviction in June 1923, Cape Town chapters and individual supporters raised funds for his appeal.[53]

Garveyites sponsored "Marcus Garvey days," usually on the first Sunday of the month. Some sang hopefully of the death of white bosses, through the Negro spiritual "Massa's in the Cold, Cold Ground." Others said special prayers for Garvey and his wife and renewed loyalty pledges. UNIA divisions, including in Cape Town, sent a flood of petitions, letters, and resolutions to U.S. government officials, as well as money and letters of support to Garvey and UNIA headquarters. There were mass rallies.[54] J. C. Humble, the Cape Town division chaplain, evoked Jeremiah 23 to issue a stirring jeremiad against unjust whites, evoking providential design: "I will bestow punishment on you for the evil you have done declares the Lord. I myself will gather the remnant of my flock out of all the countries where I have driven them and will bring them back to their pasture where they will be fruitful and increase in number. The days are coming when I will raise up . . . a King who will reign wisely . . . then they will live in their own land."[55]

In prophetic warnings of the impending divine wrath of un-Christian whites, Fitz Headly offered this poetic jeremiad:

> There's a curse upon your union, fearful sounds are in the air; as if thunderbolts were framing answers to the natives' prayer; you may offer human victims, like the heathen priests of old; you have slaughtered many natives for their diamonds and gold; you can't stay the whirlwind when the storm begins to break; and our God in judgment calls for the natives' sake; and your sin-cursed union shall be shaken to its base; till you learn that justice is heritage of every race.[56]

Transnational Martyrdom and the Spread of Garveyism ⌐ 91

Garvey's conviction and imprisonment coincided with the formation of additional UNIA chapters on the Witswatersrand, including Johannesburg, Pretoria, Evaton, Sophiatown, and Waterpan. The Evaton branch reported seventy new members and nearly four hundred people present at a meeting in 1925. The Pretoria branch, formed in 1924, had a reported one hundred members five years later.[57] UNIA agents circulated the *Negro World*, Garvey's *Philosophy and Opinions*, and Garvey pictures, and a white American bookstore owner said his *Negro World* copies sold out quickly. A Garveyite declared that whites "can kill or imprison the body but they can do nothing with the spirit . . . we shall never quit the flag until Africa is free."[58] Garvey remained the "Great King"; Africans would "go through fire and water for and with him." "Britannica rules with the iron hand of brutality and enslavement," said Garveyite James Ghazu. But he predicted that only Garvey, "the messiah of the race," could free Africans as Moses had the Israelites.[59] As Abraham Lincoln ended slavery in America and Queen Victoria in the British territories, so Garvey would liberate Africans from the "shackles of slavery."[60]

Garveyite Symon Malinga cried, "Like Moses, let him have his brother Aaron to cross the Red Sea once more. God bless Africa! Long live America!"[61] UNIA members corresponded with American UNIA president E. B. Knox and Pittsburgh UNIA division president Samuel Haynes, a remarkable feat given that the South African government confiscated letters and literature from the United States. An ANC leader, T. D. Mweli Skota, said the seizure of mail was intended to "break our associations with America and other countries, which we will not allow."[62]

Joseph Masogha, the founder of the South African branch of the House of Athlyi, was the key disseminator of Garveyism in the diamond-mining town of Kimberley. Masogha distributed UNIA books and pictures, the *Negro World*, and other "American Negro" newspapers throughout South Africa and in his native Basutoland (now Lesotho). Educated up to standard four (fifth grade), Masogha's Garveyite activities earned him the enmity of government officials, who considered him a "notorious agitator." He was dismissed from his jobs as a postman and a constable for "drunkenness," presumably from the intoxicating ideology of Garveyism.[63] White postal workers regularly pummeled Masogha with "kicks, punches, sneers, [and] insults" as he collected *Negro World* shipments from the Kimberley post office, threatening ominously that he would soon be a "dead nigger."[64] Yet the indefatigable Masogha persevered, telling the UNIA headquarters in New York that he made professional and personal sacrifices to disseminate Garveyism in order to "spread this spirit of the New Negro. I have given my heart as an offering for this land of ours. I quite follow that there must be a sacrifice. I hope the UNIA will guide me."[65]

Masogha's efforts were instrumental in making Kimberley a Garveyite stronghold. South Africa's diamond center, Kimberley was an early model of urban segregation, with its townships, restrictive pass laws, closed compounds, migrant-labor system, and color-bar policies. De Beers Consolidated Mines, the world's largest diamond company, was headquartered in Kimberley, giving it the feel of a "company town." Correspondents to the *Negro World* attested to the paper's extensive circulation in Kimberley, and they railed against the town's segregationist practices; one writer asserted that "the time has arrived for the black races to assert themselves and throw off the white yoke."[66] James Charles Diraath, a Kimberley hospital worker and amateur photographer, noted of the *Negro World* that "every copy is carefully preserved and passed from hand to hand so that as many as possible may hear the truth." He concluded, "Thousands of our native people here. . . are greatly encouraged by the efforts of the Hon. Marcus Garvey and the splendid work of the UNIA."[67]

Such were the circumstances in which Masogha, in 1924, established a branch of the House of Athlyi.[68] Headquartered in Newark, New Jersey, the House of Athlyi was founded by Richard Athlyi Rogers, who hailed from the Caribbean island of Anguilla. Rogers articulated a version of the providential design ideal, and he assumed the title of shepherd, watching over his Ethiopian flock. God, he asserted, had commanded him to become a modern-day Moses to lead "Ethiopia's generations from the oppressive feet of the nations" and to transform them into a "nation among nations."[69]

In 1922, after they both addressed a UNIA meeting in Newark, Rogers "anointed" Marcus Garvey as his chief apostle. Impressed by Garvey's message, Rogers proclaimed him "an apostle of the Lord God for the redemption of Ethiopia and her suffering posterities." He commanded his congregation, estimated at five hundred, to join the UNIA, asserting further that he and Garvey "were anointed and sent forth by the Almighty God to lay the foundation of industry, liberty and justice unto the generations of Ethiopia that they prove themselves a power among the nations and in the glory of their God."[70] Defending Garvey against his detractors, Rogers commanded, "Raise not the weight of your finger on Marcus Garvey, neither speak ye against Him."[71]

Rogers and Garvey agreed on a number of issues, spiritual and material, including a belief that black people should conceive of God in their own image and seek economic empowerment. Garvey believed his program of economic self-reliance, which included the Black Star Line, the Negro Factories Corporation, and the Black Cross and Navigation Company, was a necessary complement to spiritual prophecies of African redemption. Rogers concurred: "For as much as the children of Ethiopia, God's favorite people of old, have turned away from his divine Majesty, neglecting *life economic*, believing they could on spiritual wings fly to the kingdom of God, consequently became a dependent for the welfare of others."[72]

Rogers wrote the *Holy Piby: The Black Man's Bible*, the preeminent sacred book of the House of Athlyi. The *Holy Piby* articulated an aggressive black liberationist theology, and it would later become a foundational text of Jamaica's Rastafarian movement.[73] Rogers's narrative included Twelve Commandments, otherwise known as the doctrine of Athlicanity. These commandments shared the Holy Bible's injunctions to observe thriftiness, cleanliness, and honesty but made several significant departures. The *Holy Piby* interpreted the Battle of Adwa, in which Ethiopia defeated Italy in 1896, as a sign of impending black liberation.[74] Rogers also claimed that blacks could only attain the "Kingdom of God" if they demanded social justice on earth, instead of passively waiting for heavenly rewards.[75] The *Holy Piby* advocated the establishment of a powerful black nationality through unity and self-reliance and forbade blacks from fighting one another. Rogers's text further refuted the "Hamitic Hypothesis," said to be a biblical curse on blacks as the supposed descendants of Ham, a claim long used by white Christians to justify the oppression of African peoples. Rogers warned black Christians to eschew such biblical interpretations: "Woe be unto a race of people who forsake their own and adhere to the doctrine of another. They shall be slaves to the people thereof."[76] Rather, blacks should use the *Holy Piby* as their guiding religious text, as it contained "all worthy prophecies and inspirations endowed by God upon the sons and daughters of Ethiopia."[77]

The House of Athlyi, according to Rogers, had been established to provide "a real religious and material brotherhood among the children of Ethiopia" and to combat the "confusion and hatred" practiced by white Christians. Resorting to the language of providential design, Rogers asserted that God would "tear down the walls" of oppression he had "permitted to hold Ethiopia in bondage, that she may know the devil and his unrighteousness." "Now I shall send forth an army of Athlyians who shall redeem my children and deliver them again to my arms."[78] "When the Lord God of Ethiopia is with us in battle for that to which we are entitled, show me the foe so powerful to set us down? Verily I say unto you there is none."[79]

In South Africa, such doctrines predictably met with strong official reproof. The local authorities in Kimberley denied Masogha land on which to build a church and school, while the national government refused to grant him and his ministers marriage licenses, denying them the right to marry congregants.[80] Considering the movement subversive, the authorities speculated that the term "Gaathly" was a contraction of Garvey and Athlyi, which "proved" that the "notorious Marcus Garvey" was a prime instigator of the House of Athlyi.

The African National Congress became increasingly attracted to the liberationist potential of Garveyism. Two successive national ANC presidents, the Reverend Zaccheus Mahabane and Josiah Gumede, expressed support for Garveyism, and the ANC letterhead featured the Garveyite slogan "One God, One Aim, One Destiny."[81] In 1925, the ANC sent a resolution to President Coolidge demanding a review of Garvey's conviction. The Johannesburg-based ANC newspaper *Abantu-Batho*, reporting favorably on the 1920 UNIA convention, adopted its "Africa for Africans" slogan and accepted Garvey's title of provisional president of Africa "[with authority to rule] on all things . . . African pertaining to a free and independent republic [which] shall be obeyed by all negroes." *Abantu-Batho* pointed to the Black Star Line as an example of UNIA black economic self-determination. In an article titled "Garveyism and What It Teaches," the paper said what Garveyism taught was that blacks could advance quickly if they could "own and operate steamship lines, build colleges and schools, build and own railways, own and operate gold, silver, coal iron and the diamond mines."[82] *Abantu-Batho* declared Garvey's Africa for Africans effort was as legitimate as the nationalist movements of the Irish, Egyptians, Indians, Jews, and others seeking self-determination. As late as 1930, three years after Garvey's deportation to Jamaica, *Abantu-Batho* stated that Garvey was "indeed a dangerous man for all the great powers that are exploiting Africa."[83]

James Thaele, the ANC national senior vice president, shadow minister of education, and leader of the Cape Town branch of the ANC, was the South African Marcus Garvey and the primary bridge between the ANC and the UNIA.[84] The son of a minor African chief and a Coloured mother in southwest Basutoland, Thaele had earned two BA degrees (one in liberal arts in 1917, the other in theology in 1921) from Lincoln University, the historically black Presbyterian liberal arts college near Philadelphia. Using the American educational channels opened by Rev. Pambani Mzimba, Thaele transcended the Tuskegee accommodationist model of his preparatory school, Lovedale Institute. Founded in 1841, Lovedale had once used a standard British liberal arts curriculum, complete with Greek and Latin, to train African ministers, teachers, agriculturalists, and tradespeople to fulfill the Cape liberal ideal—the assimilation of educated, enfranchised, propertied Africans into the Cape mercantile economy. But South Africa's mineral revolutions, rapid industrialization, and expanded commercial farming to feed growing populations could only develop with the use of cheap, plentiful, and minimally educated African labor. Lovedale principal James Stewart's visit to Tuskegee reinforced his view that industrial education was the means to prepare Africans for the menial occupations needed in the rapidly industrializing colonial economy and to effect greater control over black students. By the time Thaele matriculated at Lovedale, Stewart had dismantled the school's classical education model, arguing that it created Africans "apt to claim an equality, political and social, for which as a race, they are not yet prepared."[85]

Thaele entered Lincoln after a year of preparatory work at the nearby Downington Industrial and Agricultural School, and in 1909, at age twenty-one, he arrived at Lincoln to prepare for racial leadership. Founded in 1854 as Ashmun Institute and renamed in 1864 after Abraham Lincoln, the "Great Emancipator," Lincoln University trained African and African American students to be equal citizens and leaders of their respective countries. One Lincoln chaplain, the Reverend Courtlandt Van Rensselaer, declared, "African civilization is destined to demonstrate the EQUALITY OF THE RACES."[86] African students there said that Lincoln's classical liberal arts curriculum "trained young black men to stand on their own feet."[87] Thaele's fellow student Joseph Hill, who later became the first black professor at Lincoln, confirmed that African students understood the stark differences between a liberal arts education and an industrial education: "African students wanted a liberal arts college rather than an industrial education; so they came to Lincoln at a time when there was an educational rift in the United States between the liberal arts college for black men on the one hand, and the industrial college, like Tuskegee and Hampton. . . . They chose the liberal arts college, believing it was closer to their concept of freedom and equality."[88]

According to the Lincoln University catalog's course requirements for Thaele's degrees, his classical liberal arts education encompassed mathematics, science, literature, Greek, Latin, Hebrew, and French. At Lovedale, in its downgraded curriculum, he would have had none of these. Lincoln's cataloged curriculum included courses on the Old Testament and New Testament and elective classes in religious thought.[89] In Lincoln's popular Henry Highland Garnet Literary Society, Thaele joined in lively debates; literary pursuits; and nightly "bull sessions" on weighty international and national political, economic, and social issues.[90] He left Lincoln convinced that he was equipped to challenge South African white supremacy. He taught for a year at a Philadelphia high school, and since he returned to South Africa in 1922 a committed Garveyite, he likely participated in the Philadelphia UNIA or perhaps even attended a UNIA annual convention. Promoting the UNIA became central to his plan for racial leadership.

Thaele returned to a vastly different South Africa. When he left for Lincoln in 1909, there was no Union of South Africa, no African National Congress, no Natives Land Act. In 1922, all of these existed. He first appeared on the Cape Town political scene at UNIA meetings. There, he asserted repeatedly that black salvation "solely depends on the Negroes themselves" and that "Negroes will set up their own government in Africa, with rulers of their own race," because "the legions of Hell [white racists] cannot stay the onward march of the

Kushite race."[91] Thaele became editor of the *Workers Herald*, the newspaper of the Industrial and Commercial Workers Union, and later was the founding editor of the Garveyite *African World*, which a rival newspaper declared was devoted to American Negro interests.[92] In the *African World* and in open-air political speeches, Thaele declared a racial affinity with "American Negroes, our kith and kin." He looked upon the Garveyite UNIA as "the biggest thing today in Negro modern organizations . . . to be scrutinized, imbibed and assimilated" by Africans.[93] When ICU headquarters moved from Cape Town to Johannesburg, Thaele became president of the ANC in the Western Cape, challenging the government's segregationist policies.

The UNIA and ANC in Cape Town coordinated monthly "Marcus Garvey day" mass meetings throughout the two years of Garvey's incarceration.[94] To Thaele, the American government was a Pontius Pilate that would eventually succumb to Garvey's "adamant stand in championing the sacred cause of freedom for the Negro people."[95] ANC member A. J. Maphike declared, "The Almighty God will lead his people in the successful victory against the seemingly unbreakable odds of the present ruling powers of the world."[96] UNIA member Frank Mothiba asserted that "ultimately, God would open wide the gates of Africa and create a new Jerusalem for his children."[97]

The UNIA and ANC also joined in mass protest meetings, as happened during and after an infamous murder case in which a white Transvaal farmer had whipped and then killed a black female employee and had been sentenced to a mere six months of hard labor.[98] Other ANC personnel, Provincial Secretary Bransby Ndobe among them, attended Cape Town UNIA meetings and translated Garvey's classic exposition "African Fundamentalism" into his own native seSotho. The Jamaican ANC member Arthur McKinley was a fervent Garveyite. Other ANC members, including Frank Mothiba and Nathaniel Ntengo, affirmed their loyalty to the movement in letters to the *Negro World*.[99]

The rising global prestige of emerging nations of color was apparent in Cape Town: previously spurned Japanese ships, for example, could now dock there. ANC and UNIA members felt an affinity to anticolonial movements in India, Egypt, and Ireland. The UNIA, ANC, and Cape Indian Council jointly organized a political rally at which a visiting Indian nationalist and poet, Sarojina Naidoo, listened to a Garvey speech on a gramophone. She declared that "this program as laid down by your leader, Marcus Garvey, is the only solution to the emancipation of the Africans."[100] Garveyites, in turn, were inspired by Indian nationalism. Thaele noted that Indians had rallied when the British colonial government in India jailed Mohandas Gandhi, once a resident of South Africa. So, too, were Garveyites encouraged by the Egyptian nationalist movement of Mustapha Pasha and by the Irish nationalist movement under Eamon de Valera.[101]

Thaele's Garvey-like support for racial separation and black autonomy and his disdain for whites led him to a seemingly contradictory endorsement of the segregationist program of the white National Party's James Hertzog. Hertzog was an Afrikaner war hero, who in 1924 challenged the incumbent South African Party in national elections. At the national ANC meeting in May 1924, Africans voted for a "change in government" and for Hertzog as prime minister. They were disillusioned with the government's killing of 163 Israelites during the forced removal of this religious community from lands near Queenstown in 1921. They also pointed to the government's use of airplane bombs that contributed to the deaths of one hundred Bondelswaarts protesting against South African policies in Southwest Africa. Smuts openly stated that the South African political system reflected and reinforced inequality based on the "coloured line which is in existence today . . . it is a clearly marked line you can follow."[102]

ANC President Zaccheus Mahabane, like Thaele then and John Dube several years before, would accept segregation as long as the government divided land equally between blacks and whites.[103] Thaele was among other black leaders like Mahabane and ICU leader Clements Kadalie who supported Hertzog's candidacy, yet Hertzog's segregationist platform pledged loyalty to white workers and white farmers. With the black vote potentially decisive in twelve of the fifty-one Cape constituencies in a close election, Hertzog had promised to consult with Africans in shaping his segregation program, but his promises were vague. Thaele and other African supporters nonetheless were confident that they could influence the program in their own behalf.[104]

With Hertzog in office, Thaele and the ANC proposed that Hertzog's Native Bills provide for an equitable division of arable land between the races and the possibility for blacks to form their own nation. Thaele insisted in the *African World* that "in the black man's land, the black man must be supreme, free and untrammeled and with the same rights as British subjects to . . . secede from South Africa if they chose [to] develop along their own lines."[105] Europeans, including white missionaries and traders, would be banned from black territories to promote what ANC member Daniel Adams called the "natural and logical" idea of "independent parallel development."[106] Thaele's version of segregation was "separate but equal," and he had earlier welcomed parts of the Natives (Urban Areas) Act, which he thought could expand opportunities for rural African landownership. Following the model of Garvey's racial capitalism, Thaele, together with Samuel Ncwana, the founding editor of the *Black Man*, attempted unsuccessfully to buy large parcels of rural land, divide them into smaller plots, and sell them to Africans who, with territorial separation, could develop their own "latent genius."[107]

Thaele demanded that national ANC representatives be allowed to help shape the Native Bills to redress grievances, including the banning of Africans from parliamentary seats, from the Dutch Reformed Church, and from the Defense Union Force. They also protested the restrictions on African land and property ownership, the color bar in the industrial workplace, and the extension of pass laws to include African women.[108] Hertzog, in response, simply ignored his earlier ally Thaele and the ANC, declaring rural-based chiefs, not urbanized blacks, as the true representatives of African opinion. He invited men Thaele described as handpicked "chiefs and ministers of religion" to attend a "native conference" and represent African interests on the matter of segregation. Neither the ANC, which Thaele called the "only political mouthpiece of the African people," nor the ICU was invited to the conference. Thaele dismissed the African participants as "silly kaffirs" who represented "the backward past of our people."[109]

African support for Hertzog's National Party in the 1924 election yielded little tangible rewards. The Native Bills, as passed by Parliament in 1936, ultimately eliminated the franchise for qualified African males in the Cape in exchange for the reservation for African use of only 13 percent of South Africa's land.[110] Hertzog justified his use of segregation as an instrument to reinforce white supremacy by invoking the "racial time" arguments, contending that "it has taken the white man 2,000 years to become civilized and the black man cannot expect to reach the same standard in 200 years."[111] Even educated Africans were only "semi-civilized" and "still at heart barbarians."[112] Hertzog and other white segregationists viewed urban-based "detribalized" Africans like Thaele, who was demanding full political and civil rights, as evidence of the urgent need to accelerate segregation.

With the old Cape liberal ideal now abandoned, Thaele concluded that "the white man had failed to properly govern the subject races in the light of Christianity."[113] He looked instead to Garvey, to the UNIA, and to American Negroes as partners in the goal of achieving African independence. He expressed his dissatisfaction in his *African World*, financed partially from fees derived from tutoring African youth for matriculation examinations.[114] In the inaugural issue of the *African World*, Thaele had proclaimed that blacks were subject to the Garveyite UNIA much as whites were subject to the League of Nations. The UNIA would join blacks worldwide in a global struggle for black liberation. In an editorial, he wrote:

> I believe that it is essential to the early success of our cause that the Africans here at home should seek cooperation with the Africans

abroad. The Universal Negro Improvement Association and African Communities League is the biggest thing today in Negro modern organizations. Its programme must be scrutinized, imbibed, and assimilated by us. . . . The *Negro World* must be a bible to us in order to realize and bring to immediate fruition the inevitable practicality of the African Empire.[115]

The *African World* vowed to educate, civilize, and liberate whites as well. Thaele felt the white press had failed to enlighten the government and its readers about the "inevitable racial aspirations of the Kushite [African] race."[116] A "Caucasian somebody from the wilds of slum-ridden Europe" could teach whites nothing relevant. Even Great Britain's King George IV, the leader of the global British Empire, was a kaffir who had violated Christian principles by refusing to oppose South Africa's oppressive laws: "Since Queen Victoria's death, the white people make very bad laws and they call us arme skepsels [subhumans] and Kaffirs. . . . And King George himself is a Kaffir, because if he is not a Christian, he is a Kaffir."[117]

Thaele reprinted articles from the *Negro World* to counter white segregationist claims that Africans had no civilization before contact with whites. To the contrary, he argued, blacks from ancient African civilizations of Kush and Egypt had civilized whites. Whites now, to the extent that they were "civilizing" Africans, were merely repaying their centuries-old debt: white "modern improvements are but duplicates of a grander civilization that we reflected thousands of years ago . . . to be resurrected and reintroduced by the intelligence of our generation and our posterity."[118] Prosegregation whites were poor models of Western civilization. The so-called civilizing of blacks through Christianity and education could be achieved in a few years, not in generations and certainly not in the centuries whites claimed it would take, justifying their own continued dominance of Africans. Reversing the standard narrative of "the white man's burden," Thaele argued that black civilizations had lifted whites out of a barbarism so profound that it took, by their own admission, two thousand years to escape. Surely, American Negroes, who had emerged from the degrading effects of the Atlantic slave trade and hundreds of years of slavery to equal and surpass white levels of civilization, were more appropriate models for Africans now engaged in a similar climb. Thaele concluded that Garvey had led the "New Negro" renaissance: "The UNIA created the New Negro. . . . The New Negro is a problem to those who do not understand him. They do not know what to do with him. But he knows what to do with himself. He is going to blast his way to complete independence and nationhood."[119]

In the late 1920s, Thaele and the Cape ANC organized oppressed rural farmworkers in the Western Cape to end the "degrading, superficial and artificial" laws that enslaved the "manhood and womanhood" of blacks. These efforts were among the few attempts made at that time to organize the rural black population and encourage cooperation between Africans and Coloureds.[120] Thaele lauded, too, Communists as members of the party that was "destined to bring forward in the near future a far-reaching change in social conditions."[121] With the demise of the *African World* in 1926, the Cape ANC used the Communist Party organ, *Umsebenzi* (The Worker), to publicize its own organization of rural farmworkers. Thaele remained president of the Cape ANC until 1938 and died ten years later.

Despite seeming white dominance in the post–World War I environment, whites continued to experience anxiety about their self-preservation. Elaborating on Charles Pearson's prophecies of whites soon to be overrun by numerically superior persons of color, Lothrop Stoddard's *The Rising Tide of Color against White World Supremacy* (1920) and Madison Grant's *Passing of the Great Race* (1918) gave intellectual ballast to whites who legislated and enforced segregation as a means to preserve the white race and white rule in South Africa and around the world. Garvey's increased conservatism was evident not only in his curious interactions with the Ku Klux Klan but also in his engagement with the League of Nations; after all, he wanted to replace one group of outside trustees—whites—with another—American Negroes—and thus he, like Washington, East, Payne, and other American Negroes, did not fully believe that Africans could progress without outside intervention. But African supporters of Garvey took little notice of his more moderate position. They appropriated his ideas to fit local contexts, pointed to his jailing as motivation to organize against white supremacy, and debated the utility of American Negro models to advance their own political strategies and build transatlantic intellectual ties with American Negroes in their print culture. Such ties helped Africans construct national and transnational identities beyond the narrow ethnic identities the state sought to impose on them.

Africans like James Thaele continued to attend American schools to transcend the limited South African mission school education that whites hoped would produce pliable Africans who would not challenge state power, To the contrary, American-educated Africans continued to be at the forefront of anti-colonial resistance. "Black Englishmen" such as Thaele, with their clothing, language, newspapers, and nationalist politics, threatened white rule because they suggested that the supposed superior properties of whiteness were not exclusive to whites but were skills and attributes that could be attained by anyone afforded the opportunity. Africans like Thaele threatened the rationale behind the presumed civilizing mission of Africans that would necessitate white rule for centuries. Thaele's engagement with Communists and Indians foreshadowed the multiracial politics that defined the ANC during the apartheid era.

The competing narratives of white supremacy and the up from slavery narrative of American Negro progress continued into the 1930s. The desperation of Africans subjected to accelerated segregation in South Africa facilitated the millennial idea that American Negroes were not only role models but also potential liberators. Though Africans like James Thaele had trumpeted their American Negro connections and affected American Negro accents to legitimate their political leadership, the Zulu Wellington Butelezi actually claimed to *be* an American Negro named Dr. Butler Wellington. "Dr. Wellington," supposedly sent to South Africa by Marcus Garvey, prophesied that American Negroes would liberate all Africans who joined the UNIA, thereby sparking a new round of UNIA chapters and renewing Garveyist fervor in South Africa.

5 ↬ "Charlatan or Savior?"

Dr. Wellington's Prophecies and Program of Deliverance

A PROPHECY OF SOUTH AFRICAN LIBERATION

In 1926, an American Negro known as Dr. Butler Hansford Wellington told transfixed Africans in South Africa a fascinating tale. He said that he had left his medical practice in Chicago to tell them that the United States, the most powerful nation on earth, was led by a "mighty race of black people overseas, dreaded by all European nations," who made "locomotives, ships, motor cars, airplanes and mighty weapons of war."[1] Wellington said he was one of forty American Negroes sent to initiate a takeover of South Africa, which Britain's King George V had promised to them as compensation for American intervention in World War I. Jan Smuts, so Wellington said, had resigned as prime minister, but Gen. James Hertzog, who assumed his title, had refused to cede the country to the Americans. Wellington announced that "Gen." Marcus Garvey would lead a fleet of airplanes carrying African American troops to establish an independent South Africa as a modern black state. They would strike with flaming balls of charcoal against whites and Africans alike who did not belong to Garvey's Universal Negro Improvement Association. Armies "[are] coming from America to drive the white people from Africa."[2]

A ZULU POSING AS AN AMERICAN NEGRO PROPHET

Dr. Wellington, in fact, was neither a doctor nor an American Negro. He was a Zulu named Wellington Elias Butelezi. He claimed an American medical degree he did not have and alternated between ministerial robes and an academic cap and gown. He spoke only English at meetings in Africa. He also identified himself falsely as a minister of the African Methodist Episcopal Church and toured the Transkei in a Dodge sedan driven by a personal chauffeur.[3] He urged Africans to "gaze into the glass" of his magic mirror—a type of camera obscura—to watch the skies and spot the American planes arriving to drop the flaming balls of charcoal and dump the infidels into the sea. To bolster his millennial claims, Wellington waved pictures of Garvey and UNIA official Henrietta Vinton Davis as American Negro leaders determined to free Africans from white domination.

What were the origins and purpose of this fake American doctor-preacher named Wellington? Was he simply a fraud or a con artist? Or was he a man of pathos whose psychology was disturbed by racial self-hatred? He remains, in many ways, a puzzle today, but not altogether so.

Wellington accelerated the indigenization of global Garveyism, which was central to his independent American churches and schools and African demands for more land and freedom of movement that challenged the power of the state, missionaries, and white civil society. Africans adopted transnational "American" identities that disrupted attempts by the state to enforce the narrow tribalism that became a hallmark of the later apartheid period. Africans like James Thaele affected accents associated with the American Negro and boasted about their American degrees and connections to boost their political legitimacy; Africans like Wellington went even further, fueling their movements by actually impersonating American Negroes. Wellington's prophecies that American Negroes would liberate Africans continued the evolution of Garveyism far beyond what Garvey himself imagined and condoned. The Wellington movement also advanced the imagery of American Negroes from up from slavery racial models, returning to Africa in God's providential design, to imminent liberators poised to restore African independence.

Wellington Elias Butelezi was born on 26 January 1899 in the Melmoth district of Natal, the eldest of five children.[4] He was baptized in the Church of Sweden a month after birth and became a member of the African Christian, or *kholwa*, community. At the Lutheran-affiliated Mpumulo Training College, he passed Standard Six and then took jobs as a salesman, a clerk, a teacher, and an herbalist. The Church of Sweden excommunicated him for unknown reasons.[5] At twenty, Butelezi petitioned for and was granted exemption from Native Law. He said he did so "in order to raise my status and that [of] my children and [to ensure that my] property may be preserved after death and that they may obtain higher opportunities."[6] He could now travel freely throughout the country without restrictive passes, and he had a right to possess property. He planned to go to the United States to inform Marcus Garvey's UNIA delegates of the perilous state of African education and to raise funds for church buildings, but instead, in 1921 he enrolled at Lovedale, the training ground for aspiring African elites.[7] To the amusement of classmates, he adopted multiple identities. He dressed in a flamboyant style and was nicknamed "Bootlaces" for the riding breeches he wore. Though he completed only a single term, he somehow managed to persuade Natal authorities to grant him an *inyanga* (African herbalist) license permitting him to practice as an herbalist. Yet Butelezi claimed to be a medical practitioner qualified to practice Western-based medicine, which is what his license mistakenly indicated.[8]

In August 1923, Wellington Butelezi was arrested on eight counts of practicing as a doctor in New Hanover, Natal.[9] He then made plans to enroll at Oxford to become a real physician, and the American-educated Garveyite James Thaele wrote in support of his passport application. However, the Criminal Investigation Division of South Africa's Department of the Interior denied it on the grounds that he lacked the necessary academic prerequisites. He appeared next in Johannesburg, where the black-owned newspaper *Umteteli wa Bantu* wrote that he was posing as an American Negro medical doctor with several American degrees. A police investigation hastened his departure from the area.[10] By 1925, a Dr. Butler Hansford Wellington was practicing in Qachas Nek, Basutoland, as a "Homeopathic Medical Practitioner and Specialist in Pediatric Diseases." He promised to diagnose tuberculosis and other diseases by running battery-powered currents through his patients' bodies.[11] In 1926, Wellington Butelezi petitioned the Department of Native Affairs to officially change his name to Dr. Butler Hansford Wellington.

Soon, he was an organizer in the African Garvey movement, holding "several seditious meetings," as a magistrate wrote to the secretary for native affairs. He worked with a West Indian, Ernest Wallace, and with American Negroes who had established branches of the Universal Negro Improvement Association in Qachas Nek and Matatiele, Basutoland, and in the nearby Transkeian district of Mount Fletcher. He would later claim that he had known Wallace in the United States and that they had crossed paths in Cambridge, England.[12] (Wallace may have been the "Ennis" who promoted American Negroes as a liberationist vanguard at a Durban meeting of the African National Congress that year.) Wallace had not been sent to South Africa, so he said, "to tell the negroes in America what to do" but to ask Africans to "work out their own salvation." Africans were to prepare for the time "when the Son of Man shall come out on His Chariot of Fire to redeem his people," when the God of Israel will "stretch out his hands over the Ethiopian race."[13]

By that point, Butelezi had cast himself as a leader of a transnational political organization prepared to topple the South African state. His supporters followed his example, calling themselves Americans; they waved American flags and prepared for the Apocalypse.[14] They demanded equal treatment with whites, including basic citizenship rights, decent jobs, housing, health care, and enough land to sustain themselves and their families.[15] They assumed cosmopolitan transnational identities within the international black world while continuing the Ethiopianist tradition of maintaining independent African churches and schools. Many were products of Christian missions themselves, but they condemned the hypocrisy of self-professed white Christians who denied them Christian principles of equality and justice in order to sustain a white supremacist South Africa.[16]

PAST APOCALYPTIC PROPHECIES
AND WELLINGTON'S NEW PROPHECIES

Wellington's American Negro prophecies had tapped into similar "outside liberator" mythologies that had circulated in central and southern Africa since the nineteenth century. In the 1850s, Nongqawuse, a fifteen-year-old Xhosa girl, proclaimed that Xhosa ancestors would arise from the dead to liberate her people from the encroaching British as soon as the Xhosa killed their cattle and destroyed their granaries.[17] Other prophecies of liberation were circulated in the 1890s during British partition and a devastating rinderpest epidemic that killed about 90 percent of the cattle in the country. In the early twentieth century, various African prophets in the Rhodesias, the Belgian Congo, Nyasaland, and Southwest Africa predicted that African American liberators would arrive via airplanes, ships, and motorcycles, even coming from under ground, to expel colonial whites and reinstate African independence. During World War I, rumors spread in South Africa that German liberators, in conjunction with Afrikaner rebels, would help Africans by halting raids on their cattle by South African soldiers and rescuing them from colonial oppression.[18]

In 1920, a young African clerk named Gilbert Matshoba, reporting on the UNIA convention to his uncle, Enoch Mgijima, leader of the Israelites, said Marcus Garvey had announced that the "blood of all wars is about to arrive." The UNIA would drive European colonizers out of Africa. "Father, that is the news of our black countrymen," Gilbert stated. "It is published in the newspaper."[19] At Bulhoek, a settlement outside Queenstown, on land they had commandeered to wait for the world's end and Judgment Day, Israelites had built homes and harvested crops; they claimed this terrain as God's, not the government's, and hence their own since blacks were God's people. Expecting imminent liberation, they celebrated Passover and the Exodus from Egyptian slavery, but no Americans came. Government troops arrived instead, and South Africa's first modern political massacre left 163 Israelites dead and 92 wounded.[20]

In 1923, Nonteta, a female herbalist and prophet in the Eastern Cape, told her church members that she had died but had seen visions of a coming apocalypse as she passed away. She had been resurrected by God to convert Africans to Christ. She prophesied that "the American Negroes are coming who will cut the throats of the Europeans and converted natives who are converted under the existing churches."[21] Nonteta had experienced prophetic visions in the wake of the devastating influenza pandemic of late 1918, in which two hundred and fifty thousand people had died in southern Africa. She preached black unity to overthrow white supremacy, ordered African children out of government churches and schools, and prepared followers for a Judgment Day heralded by the arrival of the Americans. Children in government-sanctioned schools sang passages from Revelation 19, which they understood as a promise of impending judgment: "Hallelujah! Salvation and glory and power belong to our God for true and just are his judgments. He has condemned the great prostitute who corrupted the earth by her adulteries. He has avenged on her the blood of his servants."[22]

Nonteta quoted Exodus 10:1–20, Joel 1:2–2:11, and Revelation 9:1–11 as proof that locust plagues and the droughts that followed were divine punishment of humans who oppressed God's people. Government officials responded by confining her in a psychiatric hospital in Pretoria, where she died of stomach and liver cancer on 20 May 1935. A follower remembered: "We used to dream in the hope that the Americans were coming to release us. It was just a rumor, but what you hear as a rumor, you always dream about. I can't tell you who told us these rumors but there was always hope throughout that the Americans would free us. As oppressed people, we always had hope that we would be released."[23]

At African National Congress meetings in Johannesburg around this time, another prophet, named Josephina, announced that God's word had appeared to her through lightning bolts and visions. Paraphrasing Revelation 9, Josephina warned Africans to prepare for twelve days of darkness.[24] She cited Deuteronomy 28 to predict that 1923 "would be the year for a plague of locusts [with] the heads of human beings and tails like scorpions."[25]

Wellington Butelezi's assumed American persona lent him more status than earlier prophets of liberation had had and helped give him legitimacy before his African audiences. He also benefited from the fact that many in these rather remote regions had never seen an American Negro and could not readily have exposed his fraudulent identity. His (fake) American medical degree increased his allure, since African Americans were considered to possess the educational, technological, and military capacity required to overthrow colonial rule.[26] W. D. Cingo, a Garvey opponent in the Transkei, observed in 1927 that many Africans believed "the mad dreams and literature of Marcus Garvey," whose movement made the word *America* synonymous with "Bantu national freedom and liberty."[27] Eager Africans had "waited everyday for those Americans to come to free South Africa."[28]

American bishop William T. Vernon of the African Methodist Episcopal Church, who traveled throughout South Africa between 1920 and 1924, had also observed that Africans tended to place American Negroes on a pedestal:

"The African is prone to think that the white people can do certain things because they are white; that the American Negro can do other things because
he is an American but that the African cannot do these things because he is
handicapped educationally)."[29] Wellington Butelezi was soon organizing in
South Africa under his own UNIA banner, though his multiple convictions
for impersonation and for violating local pass laws encouraged him to seek
new audiences in new places. He petitioned the government to "alter or con-
ceal my name as Elias Butelezi and put it for Butler Hansford Wellington."[30]

DR. WELLINGTON AND THE TRANSKEI

Dr. Wellington's Garveyist message of an apocalyptic end "in the near distant
future" found an audience in the Transkei. There, Africans were agitating
against landlessness, taxation, poverty, and government intrusion in their lives.[31]
In Herschel, Wellington—appearing "dignified in expensive clothing" and
"always accompanied by people with cars and people of means"—abetted
government school boycotts led by a female political group known as the
Amafelandawonye. Twenty-seven women were jailed for closing white-run
schools. The Amafelandawonye-Wellington alliance would go on to form eighteen separatist schools.[32]

Wellington galvanized followers because he framed his prophecies in ways
that resonated with African religious conceptions of the colonial state. Thus,
Africans believed Europeans "possessed of powerful materials for sorcery . . .
all *ubuthi* [magical substances]": "They are the real *amagqwira* [witches]."[33]
Wellington, a respected herbalist with reputed magical powers, promised that
the *impundulu* (supernatural power) of African Americans would overwhelm
the Europeans. Wellington urged followers to look into what must have been a
camera obscura to see Americans preparing for attack. American ships loaded
with Indian corn arrived to supplement the harvests and ease the hunger made
severe through droughts.[34] Local Garveyite UNIA organizers claimed to have
seen Americans with military fortifications, and they provided dates of liberation.[35] UNIA children's choirs began to sing "Nkosi' Sikeleli Afrika" and other
freedom songs, instead of the usual "God Save the King."[36]

Wellingtonites were refusing to submit to mandated vaccinations, informing magistrates they would pay their UNIA membership dues instead of state
taxes.[37] Wellington himself complained of onerous taxation without parliamentary representation and pointed out the government's dependence on
the taxes paid by Africans. By 1927, several magistrates were reporting lower
tax revenues despite good harvests.[38] The Tsolo magistrate, Edgar Lonsdale,
exclaimed, "I have never known any man to get such an influence over the natives in such a short time."[39] An interpreter in a Tsolo court said of Wellington's
popularity: "The natives who to some extent resent the increased taxation,

firmly believe this man's saying and look to a happy time of release from European rule which the American Government will bring."[40]

Wellingtonites identified themselves to each other with red, black, and green membership badges pledging to "pull down the British Empire"; they painted their houses black and slaughtered pigs, white goats, and white fowl.[41] Wellington's biblical references likened his people to the enslaved Israelites in Egypt. He referenced particularly those Israelites who killed lambs to identify themselves as God's followers to avoid the locust plague and keep their fields intact, even as the fields of the Egyptians were decimated. He cited scripture from Luke as anticipating the Apocalypse: "Now when these things begin to take place, look up and raise your heads, because your redemption is drawing near." Supporters echoed Revelation 16:6 in saying that the blood of enemies would be given to Dr. Wellington to drink as Wellington announced plans for a black airplane fleet to free Africans. As some non-UNIA Africans hid in the forests to avoid encountering the coming Americans, he urged the people to prepare for liberation.[42]

"AMERICAN" SCHOOLS AS AGENTS OF LIBERATION

UNIA members did not wait for the Americans to arrive. Many had already cast themselves as "Americans," just as Butelezi had. Wellington had told them that black people should control churches and schools. His followers established 200 or so independent churches and over 180 schools as alternatives to white-controlled religious and educational institutions.[43] Wellington's own African Christian Church preached a liberationist Christianity. Members who held marriage ceremonies in his churches avoided the burdensome fees, documentation, and other requirements demanded by the state and European ministers.[44] Most UNIA church and school members pledged allegiance to Marcus Garvey, not to the South African government.[45] By 1928, Wellington had also organized two "universities" — St. Welford Universal Industrial College, in Mount Fletcher district, and St. Booker Washington Liberty Industrial College, in Edendale, Natal — to prepare an African leadership.[46] Numerous complaints by government officials and others throughout the Transkei, Cape Province, Natal, and Basutoland suggest that similar churches and schools existed there. Black-led churches and schools linked Wellington to a longer tradition of so-called Ethiopian churches that had broken off from white denominations in the 1890s.

UNIA members believed, with good cause, that white institutions reaffirmed white supremacy by conditioning Africans for subservience. "In schools you are taught to say Boss to any white man young or big all the same," Wellington said. "Your names are Jim, John, George, Jack, etc. You go to Church but they won't mix with you."[47] UNIA institutions reaffirmed both Garveyist principles and an overt Africanism. Former ANC secretary-general Walter Sisulu, Nelson

Mandela's political mentor, attended a Wellingtonite school; his mother was a UNIA teacher. Sisulu remembered that African cultural values had infused the curriculum. The "Americans" prayed to "the God of Mtirara, or Langalibalele," not to "the God of Abraham, Isaac and Jacob, because they were white."[48]

The African Communities League, the business arm of the UNIA, included an education department charged with overseeing school operations. All UNIA members were expected to subsidize the cost of schools with a specified portion of their membership dues. They also were supposed to contribute to a quarterly collection to subsidize the building of new schools and the anticipated American teachers and textbooks. Parents had to make additional payments. Most teachers had only the equivalent of an eighth-grade education. They had insufficient facilities and equipment, and they had to scribble lessons on the walls of huts. Moreover, they endured frequent harassment both from the state and from mission societies.[49]

Wellington's promises of teachers and textbooks from America were unfulfilled; still, many UNIA churches and schools persisted during the late 1920s and throughout the 1930s. With white mission schools that served Africans suffering drastic declines in enrollment because of the UNIA's competing learning centers, government officials sought to close the UNIA schools. UNIA supporters confronted the officials with "assegais and sticks as though the enemy had approached" and turned the tables by closing several white-run schools with boycotts and intimidation. In Nqamakwe district, a UNIA leader, Sam Nyembezi, assaulted a local headman who attempted to shut a Wellington school, dividing families in intradistrict factionalism. In Nqamakwe, there were reports of spouses separating. Two pro-UNIA members assaulted a nephew who opposed the movement and expelled him and his wife from the homestead after he refused to allow a visiting UNIA leader to use his blankets for the night. In Tsolo district, members were said to have burned the houses of several opponents.[50]

STATE AND AFRICAN ATTEMPTS TO STOP THE WELLINGTON UNIA

When jailing or expelling dissenters from central areas did not work, government officials tried to end radical African political activity with legislation and edicts. They also gave greater powers to African chiefs allied with the government, denying political space to troublemakers like Wellington.

Headmen, local magistrates, and anti-Wellingtonites asked officials to close UNIA institutions and eject Wellington from the Transkei.[51] A state intelligence network of policemen, detectives, informants, and infiltrators provided information on UNIA meetings but seldom discovered the postmeeting gatherings that were closed to nonmembers. The state did convert two of Wellington's personal drivers into government informants.[52] In one of several violent confrontations, Wellingtonites killed an African constable in Qumbu district during a failed police attempt to arrest a UNIA organizer.[53]

As trained lawyers, magistrates were painfully aware that the antidissident legislation could not defeat the UNIA. They did, on a regular basis, arrest and convict Wellington for contravening minor laws, but he would simply pay the fines and continue to organize. UNIA schools could not be closed legally unless they were set up within a two-mile radius of an existing school. One frustrated magistrate expressed his urge to bring in "a squadron of police to knock sense into them [UNIA members]."[54] In 1926, the magistrate in Herschel evicted Wellington from his district. When Wellington's attorneys demanded to know what law validated this action, the magistrate, in panicked correspondence to his superiors, acknowledged that the action was illegal.[55]

Edward Chalmers Bam, an African court interpreter in Tsolo district, wrote in an affidavit that Wellingtonites "firmly believe in all Dr. Wellington says and no argument will convince them that he is not an American negro but a Zulu. They believe he has great magic powers and that the white men fear him and they say that is why he has not been arrested and sentenced to a long term of imprisonment."[56] An African detective, Peter Dicks, warned the government to take decisive action or face unspeakable consequences.[57] Lionel Harris, a white trader reporting that UNIA members were "laughing at authority," demanded that the government use military force to prove it was not afraid of Wellington.[58] Harris quoted Wellingtonites as saying they had little to lose: "Even if we are killed it matters little as we may as well be dead as live under the present white man's rule with heavy taxation, dipping etc."[59]

In the first of several targeted dates, Wellington announced that the Americans would arrive on March 12, 1927. Panicked white civilians demanded weapons from the government. The South African Police (SAP), in a show of force, displayed machine guns near habitable areas and deployed government airplanes to fly menacingly over Wellingtonite strongholds in Qumbu, Mount Fletcher, and Tsolo districts. The plan was to fly low over the kraals of known UNIA leaders and drop warning notes identifying the aircraft and ridiculing the prospect of American liberation. The notes would announce that Wellington was to be permanently banned from the Transkei and that any armed insurrection would be crushed. Mobile squadrons patrolled Wellington strongholds. One UNIA organizer retained legal counsel to protect himself against disciplinary state action. Other Wellingtonites, white police officer Ernest Woon said, were "sullen, hostile and insolent," convinced that the planes they saw were American, not the government's. One loyalist chief nearly killed the pilot of a government plane that had crashed near Umtata, certain that the aircraft belonged to the Americans.[60]

The transnational nature of the so-called Americans was a significant challenge to a South African government that sought to "retribalize" Africans as native subjects with no political or economic rights. Former prime minister Jan Smuts lamented that "urbanized and detribalized natives" were the source of the "color problem."[61] The Native Administration Act of 1927 would formally establish two-tiered political, judicial, and administrative systems that divided whites and Africans. One set of systems was for modern, "civilized," white citizens and was based on civil law and parliamentary procedures. The other set of systems was for a premodern, "semicivilized" community of native subjects outside the South African body politic, and it was based on customary law and rule by decree. The effect of the law would be to balkanize the African racial majority into smaller ethnic groups whose chiefs, employed by the government to administer and enforce colonial laws, would be the supposed representatives of African political opinion. By locating African political opinion within ethnic-based tribes, the act was part of an ongoing attempt by government to marginalize educated and "de-tribalized" Africans like Butelezi. It was also designed to marginalize organizations such as the ANC and the Industrial and Commercial Workers Union (ICU), which claimed to represent African national opinion.

The Native Administration Act would be particularly relevant for the Transkei, an area controlled by the British since 1894 and home to southern Nguni polities. Government power flowed downward from the secretary of native affairs, based in Pretoria, through the chief magistrate residing in the Transkeian capital of Umtata. The chief magistrate oversaw twenty-seven individual magistrates, each of whom was a trained lawyer and presided over an administrative district. Magistrates administered and enforced civil law, distributed land, and monitored the appointed African headmen who collected taxes and oversaw the approximately forty locations within each district. In 1924, there were only 242 white policemen and 176 African constables to police 1 million Africans stretched across 16,000 square miles, divided into twenty-seven districts. The scarcity of police power meant that the enforcement and administration of government laws, directives, and desires depended largely on the administrative and judicial talents of headmen, clerks, and interpreters. Government officials also relied on the missionaries, traders, teachers, and others in civil society who supported and upheld state rule. Magistrates reinforced their power in their daily interactions with Africans, requiring them to take off headgear, for example, and to receive objects with two hands. Verbal challenges to their authority were prohibited.[62] Looking without seeing, magistrates compiled encyclopedic facts about their districts, filing detailed reports about the deepening poverty of Africans while dismissing African claims that growing landlessness was the root of the problem. Magistrates insisted, instead, that Africans were inefficient farmers.[63]

In 1925, with the passage of the Native Taxation and Development Act, magistrates solicited additional payments from overtaxed Africans. Married men were now required to pay thirty shillings per wife annually to satisfy the "hut" tax, and livestock owners had to pay a tax of between six pence and one shilling per cow. All unmarried and/or landless men paid an annual poll tax (or general rate) of one pound, ten shillings. In Mpondoland, the poll tax alone equaled a month's pay for a worker in the sugarcane fields. Yet there was no parallel increase in government services. The government said it had no money to fund and staff African schools or to maintain arsenic-laced dipping tanks to stave off tick-borne diseases. High commodity prices and drought conditions contributed to widespread starvation and malnutrition. Africans were able to express grievances only through the "toy telephone," as they called it, referring to their tax-supported Transkeian General Council, known as the Bunga, which had no substantive power. It is no wonder that many Africans began to spend their scarce moneys on possible liberation.[64]

The most effective measure to control Wellington and, to a lesser extent, the UNIA movement was the Native Administration Act of 1927. The act allowed the minister of native affairs to eject "undesirables" from certain districts and the governor-general to create laws for the Transkei by simple proclamation instead of through prescribed parliamentary measures. On 12 March, the day Wellington had prophesied the Americans would arrive, the governor-general banned him from the Transkeian territories.[65] Magistrates, each acting as judge and jury, jailed organizers and revoked the landholdings of individuals who hosted UNIA meetings and of schools on their property.[66] Public oratory that "incited hostility between natives and Europeans" was declared criminal, and the government convicted several UNIA leaders for violating the decree.[67]

Nonetheless, Wellington's followers continued to organize churches and schools, protest government policies, and intimidate non-UNIA Africans. African chiefs told government officials they could stop the Wellingtonites only if they were granted real, rather than symbolic, power to police their districts and influence state policies. They would require an expansion of their powers as chiefs, since they no longer had the authority to crush such movements as they had had in the time of African independence.[68] Now, as government employees, they did not have the respect of their people.

In the 1927 session of the Transkei General Council, one councilor blamed "the influence of certain Americans" in Matatiele for Wellington's excesses. The government had done little to stop the movement, encouraging Africans to believe it was powerless to do so. He reported rumors that the magistrate in

Mount Fletcher, epicenter of the movement, had fled in terror after viewing American airplanes in Wellington's camera obscura.[69]

In the 1928 Bunga, Transkei's chiefs and magistrates once again pointed fingers at each other. Despite Wellington's banishment from the Transkei under the powers of the Native Administration Act, UNIA activity continued. Chiefs insisted that only a restoration of their former powers would give them the authority they needed to stop the dissident movement. Their responsibility ended when they informed the government. They told magistrates that even allies agreed that many Africans "had lost confidence in the white man." The magistrates insisted that Africans had a duty not only to report but also to stop the movement. Should a man notify his headman of a burning hut and then stand aside waiting for the headman to arrive while the hut burned down?[70]

Missionaries, for their part, criticized the government for ignoring Africans' legitimate grievances. The Reverend Harold Hills cited "the repressive legislation of the present government, particularly raised taxes, and the generally rough treatment posed to Africans by Europeans," as "watering fertile soil in which the seed has grown quickly." More prosperous Africans resented the Color Bar Act, which excluded Africans from railway employment. They also railed against Prime Minister Hertzog's native bills, especially a provision to disenfranchise the few Africans in the Cape Colony who met the educational and property qualifications for voting.[71] Rev. J. G. Locke said the poll tax "united the so-called Red Native and the School Native as nothing has done hitherto in the history of South Africa."[72] The Anglican bishop of St. John's suggested that the government withdraw the native bills and called on "politicians to give the so-called native question a rest for 15 or 20 years."[73] Rev. T. L. Kobus, who considered Africans ignorant children, was nonetheless convinced that they were right in asserting that higher taxes provided no real benefit, especially when the government claimed it lacked money to staff and fund their schools.[74]

By April 1929, Chief Magistrate Robert Welsh was declaring the UNIA movement either nonexistent, dormant, or weakening in twenty-five of the twenty-seven Transkei districts. The outlawing of schools not recognized by the government and the prosecution of those who participated in UNIA schools was responsible for this turn of events. Welsh had imposed fines of up to £50 per week for continued defiance.[75]

Banned from the Transkei, Wellington could address his followers only when they crossed the border and entered the Cape Colony. He was under increasing fire for his constant demands for money to pay American liberators and buy textbooks, neither of which had arrived. UNIA membership was stagnant because, one African said, "the Americans were said to be coming to Africa and people will not join the movement as they don't see the Americans."[76]

AN AMERICAN PERSONA: WHO WAS THIS FALSE PROPHET?

By the late 1920s, Wellington's opponents had effectively disproved his American citizenship and his UNIA ties as well. Marcus Garvey himself, in 1927, had warned *Negro World* readers that Wellington was not a UNIA officer and had no authorization to collect money or establish chapters.[77] A former Garveyite, Samuel Ncwana, had published an article attesting to personal knowledge of Wellington's Zulu birth, and the newspaper *Ilanga lase Natal*, edited by John Dube, derided Wellington as a "common Zulu with a predilection to leadership and fame."[78] A Qumbu headman had noted Wellington's "Zulu tribal mark, a cut in the right ear, which he has sewn up."[79] Hecklers were calling out to Wellington as "Butelezi." His refusals to reveal his origins to several aggressive questioners had led one meeting to descend into disorder.[80] A government official in Natal said Wellington could not provide the technical names of human bones.[81] A Wesleyan minister, Allen Lea, in an extensive essay, reported that Natalian Africans considered Wellington an unscrupulous man who feigned ignorance of the Zulu language. An African informant had told him that Wellington acknowledged his American persona was a means of making money to acquire valuable land at Edendale.[82] Some hostile Africans who journeyed to Edendale reported that Zulus held "Wellington Butelezi" in extremely low regard and considered his followers in the Transkei "very foolish to follow such a man."[83]

In 1927 and 1928, in the face of the mounting hostility, Wellington summoned about five hundred supporters from the Transkei to his conferences at Edendale, his Natal headquarters.[84] He displayed Garvey's picture, read messages from UNIA officials, and announced plans to attend the UNIA's annual conferences.[85] He denied that he was really Elias Butelezi, the Natal-born, Lovedale-educated African, stating, "I am sure nobody knows me in this country."[86] But then, at one of his many trials for breaking pass laws, his own father testified that he was Zulu.[87] Wellington declared his father's testimony false and refused to answer queries about his place of birth. Several persons said they had remained silent despite personally knowing of Wellington's fluency in SeSotho, the lingua franca of his Basutoland and northern Transkei strongholds, and hearing him acknowledge, albeit privately, his Zulu birth.[88] The newspaper *Imvo Zabantsundu* reported gleefully that Africans in Queenstown had rejected Wellington, along with "the doctrine of Africa being redeemed from slavery by forces from America." *Imvo* advised the government to let the whole matter die a natural death.

Then suddenly, Wellington ended his American charade and no longer claimed to be a top Garveyite. He continued to espouse familiar themes of white injustice, black institution building, and a liberationist Pan-African Christianity. However, he focused more on a Booker T. Washington–style of defensive segregation, emphasizing land acquisition, business entrepreneur-ship, self-reliance, industrial education, and moral uplift. His speeches in East London in 1929 offered a complete denial of his earlier prophecies. Respond-ing to Clements Kadalie's Independent ICU (IICU),[89] he denied he had ever stated that "the Americans are at sea and will soon drive away the Europeans." He ridiculed Africans who had waited for "the Americans to come to Africa, they will never come and do not expect flying machines from America, I will teach you how to make a flying machine."[90] At the same time, he denounced as blatant liars those who called him Butelezi "and other nicknames." He continued to claim degrees from several American universities, telling audi-ences he was a professor of medicine in Chicago, a "philosopher, a Master of Ethnology, a Master of Arts, a Bachelor of Science, a Theologian. I passed through several other branches of higher education."[91]

THE POSTPROPHECY CAREER OF WELLINGTON

The Wellington movement survived for a number of years in the 1930s in the Transkei and the Cape Colony. In the 1929 Black Peril elections, Prime Minister James Hertzog renewed efforts to disenfranchise all Africans and enact more seg-regationist legislation. Wellington shifted the meaning of separate black devel-opment as a means to support and benefit from liberation by American Negroes to a concept that could coexist within the government's segregationist objec-tives. He applauded the state's proposals for "separate institutions for Natives" to "develop along their own lines," a principle that "finds a very warm reception in the programme of the African Communities League." He argued that Africans, "in their present stage of development," had to realize their full potential "under the tutelage of the white man."[92] His avowed support of traditional African prac-tices, like the marriage practice of *lobola*,[93] coincided with state efforts to bolster "tribes" as a brake on supposed African degeneration. To UNIA members and even to the prophet Nonteta, whom he visited at the Pretoria mental hospital in a failed bid to win over her supporters, he now interpreted African traditionalism and self-sufficiency as the means to African nationhood.[94]

Describing his own efforts at self-development, Wellington cited his use of the African Communities League as an umbrella organization for his busi-ness and educational endeavors. These included applications for a general agent and broker's license to establish the Herschel and Transkei Trading Company, as well as a "Native Eating House," described as a "coffee house establishment." He noted, too, his building of a church and the St. Booker Washington Liberty Industrial College. Africans wanted to "be left alone, to make our own arrangements."[95]

Throughout the 1930s, Wellington continued to appeal for permission to reenter the Transkei and other areas from which he had been banned, for "educational and spiritual purposes only" and to provide support for his wife and child there. The vehement opposition to him on the part of white (and some black) churchmen was, he said, due solely to the loss of African parishioners and schoolchildren to his own churches and schools.[96]

Wellington's flagging popularity was briefly revived by his stirring defense of the sovereignty of Ethiopia, one of only two independent African countries (Liberia was the other) after Italy's invasion of 1935.[97] His meetings began to attract around two hundred persons, in contrast to the thirty or fewer who had attended recent gatherings. declared that he and a stable of two hundred horses would soon embark for "East Africa to defend your own people." But when the "doctor" failed to provide satisfactory answers to questions from audience members, they dismissed his requests for funds.[98]

The Abyssinian campaign was Wellington's last hurrah. The government jailed him several times between 1937 and 1944, on charges of entering the Transkei without a pass, nonpayment of taxes, and theft. He was also arrested for possession of alcohol and other unspecified offenses.[99] Seeing no end to the government pursuit, Wellington tried to leave the country, but officials refused to issue him a passport. In 1942, he resurfaced in Johannesburg, and he later appeared in Melmoth, Natal, in 1947. A sister told a researcher he had visited her in Natal in the early 1950s, but she had no knowledge of his subsequent whereabouts. Thereafter, Wellington disappeared from the public record. No clue remains of his last days or of his death.[100]

At least two of Wellington's officers, Elias Mfaxa and Enoch Mbijana, also offered liberationist prophecies about American Negroes. Mfaxa embellished Wellington's own claims by declaring that African Americans had originated in South Africa.[101] Enoch Mbijana contended that he himself was an American named John Mackey, a "colonel in Wellington's forces." An observer pointed out that Mackey understood Xhosa, though he feigned incomprehension. Mbijana/Mackey continued to preach the coming of American liberators.[102] During World War II, some UNIA members told followers that the alleged Americans *and* Germans led by Adolph Hitler would join to overthrow the South African state.[103]

Wellington Butelezi had exploited those he claimed to help, persuading impoverished Africans to surrender their sparse and hard-earned money to his own well-lined pockets. Sad facts suggest that he was nothing more than an unscrupulous charlatan preying on the gullibility and desperation of ever more marginalized Africans. Yet fraud or not, Wellington did endure repeated imprisonments and harassment for his refusal to bow to authority. Would he have braved a life so precarious if he were wholly insincere? Or was he a tragic figure of pathos or even psychosis, pretending, out of self-contempt or a sense of inferiority, to be someone who had an equal right to pride and self-respect? Or perhaps, in some respect, was he all of these—con man and fraud, exploiter of the gullible, a serious and sacrificial crusader, and a tragic figure? Was the fantasy of pride and liberation better than the reality he lived?

The only clear picture that emerges from Wellington's multiple mythologies is that his myth of self sparked a myth of liberation from America that never came. And yet it led to a political movement that reverberated throughout the Transkei for several decades. He employed legends and past prophecies of African American liberators to construct a millennial solution to the suffering of Africans. He mobilized rural Africans, a group, as Helen Bradford notes, that was particularly difficult to organize, countering state efforts to promote the narrow ethnic tribalism that became a hallmark of the looming apartheid period. From this perspective, Butelezi's delusional claims could be seen as a masterwork of political genius. As Wellington appropriated and adopted Garvey's ideas in the absence of Garvey himself, so too did his lieutenants— several of whom were government-employed chiefs—use his ideas to advance their own agendas. As Garvey lost control of the floundering American UNIA and struggled unsuccessfully to regain his former prominence, Africans continued to utilize Garveyism, their travels to the United States, and their ties to American Negroes to further a liberationist course that would, decades later, finally be fulfilled in the global antiapartheid movement.

6 ⤚ A Dream Deferred

The End of the Dream of American Negro
Liberation and the Beginnings of the
Global Antiapartheid Movement

BY 1930, Garveyism was so pervasive in South Africa that even chiefs and headmen (government employees charged with administering and enforcing colonial law) became Garveyites to further their objectives. Garvey lost control of his organization and the idea of Garveyism, yet Africans continued to evoke the dream of American Negro liberation until World War II. But even as hopes of imminent deliverance faded, the continued vitality of the up from slavery narrative of American Negro progress, which had begun with the Virginia Jubilee Singers and had facilitated the explosion of Garveyism in South Africa, cemented the partnership of Africans and American Negroes in the goal of transnational black liberation.

The defeat of Nazi Germany did not solve the problem of transnational whiteness, as the onset of South African apartheid (and the continuance of American Jim Crow) demonstrated. Even as Garvey declined further politically and ultimately died a lonely death, his Africa for Africans message inspired Africans in their successful bids for political independence in the second half of the twentieth century. But because of the onset of apartheid in South Africa, his Africa for Africans prophecy would not prevail there for decades. The close cooperation between the resurgent African National Congress and the Council on African Affairs, the first antiapartheid organization in America, halted South Africa's attempts to incorporate neighboring territories and states in southern Africa. The alliance between these two organizations, borne from the long-standing relationship between African Americans and Africans, began the global movement that finally toppled the apartheid regime in 1994.

The influence of Garveyism in the chieftainship politics in the former Transkei support the noted historian Shula Marks's observation that "chieftaincy and the position of the headmanship continued to be, perhaps increasingly became, the political arena within which local political struggles were fought."[1] While Garvey was imprisoned, deported from the United States, and struggling to reinvigorate the UNIA, African chiefs and headmen, appointed by the government to administer and enforce colonial laws among fellow Africans, helped spread Garveyism to remote rural regions of South Africa. In the northern Transkei region of Mount Fletcher, for instance, headman Edward Zibi not only served as vice president of Wellington's Basutoland and Eastern Cape UNIA division but also led both the UNIA's African Christian Church and St. Welford Industrial School, one of two proclaimed UNIA colleges in South Africa;[2] he also protested state taxation and dipping regulations.[3] His kraal became a meeting place for UNIA concerts, church programs, and Wellington-led UNIA meetings that drew followers from Basutoland and the surrounding districts of Matatiele, Herschel, Mount Frere, Tsolo, and Qumbu.[4] Defying the magistrate's order to arrest Wellington, Zibi hosted the "American" at his homestead, collected funds for the UNIA, went with Wellington to ANC political meetings, and provided him with horses and money for travel.[5] Regarding Wellington, Zibi vowed, "I will not part with him, wherever he dies, I will die . . . the only thing parting [me] from Wellington will be a bullet."[6]

Edward's UNIA activity deeply disturbed his uncle, the progovernment Hlubi chief Johannes Zibi.[7] Also a government headman, the Lovedale-educated chief had recruited Africans for the South African Native Labour Contingent during World War I. As a former police constable, Zibi had also sided with the government during the protracted antidipping campaigns that had raged in the district's Hlubi locations between 1908 and 1916.[8] In May 1926, Chief Zibi refused Wellington's request to "tell the good news from America" and to establish a UNIA chapter in Mount Fletcher, declaring, "I am a government man."[9] With greater powers granted to chiefs, the 1927 Native Administration Act bolstered Chief Zibi's authority to administer and enforce government directives, which overshadowed the chieftainship's traditional role of reflecting the will of the Hlubi people. With Chief Zibi as a faithful state employee, Edward Zibi retorted that he had "sold us to the Government" and that the Americans did not "recognize the authority of any European and Native Chief." Johannes complained to the magistrate that Edward "has been shunning me . . . he treats me with contempt."[10]

Edward Zibi and other UNIA personnel, including African mission school-teachers who had left to teach at UNIA schools, taught children "on American lines."[11] They referred to themselves as "Negroes" linked to "American Negro" liberators who possessed the "American white man's wisdom, skill and education," to "raise the standard of . . . African people."[12] Zibi's UNIA African Christian Church would guide his people "from the dry grass to the green pasture."[13] He proclaimed loudly, "As long as I am a Headman these people [his opponents] will suffer." He reportedly threatened to kill government spies, and UNIA members threatened physical harm to non-UNIA members who paid taxes, enrolled their children in mission schools, and refused to join their organization.[14] Reverend Frederick Keinemann, the Moravian school's principal, lamented: "The power of my church discipline is broken. If I have to act according to my official duty, it begins now to be a custom that people tell me . . . well, I go now to the Americans . . . the old order is destroyed and nobody finds it necessary to obey. It is the fact that this American movement will ruin all existing laws."[15]

Robert Welsh, the Mount Fletcher magistrate, suspended Zibi from his headmanship and revoked his homestead and land allotments.[16] He convicted teachers *and* children from Tsolo for unlawfully entering Mount Fletcher, thereby decreasing the number of St. Welford attendees.[17] He denied UNIA members traveling passes to work in or travel to other districts, as well as firewood-collecting permits to cut thatch grass for their huts or plow their fallow lands. He also prosecuted UNIA members who refused to pay their taxes.[18] But he could not close UNIA schools because they were on the homesteads of UNIA members and thus private institutions exempt from legal measures.[19]

Ferment over the headmanship issue culminated in December 1928 when Edward and other UNIA members plotted an armed revolt. Awaiting the Americans and leading Wellingtonites from Edendale, UNIA members were to cut telephone lines, block incoming traffic, and then attack Mount Fletcher and Tsolo whites and Africans on their "death list." Loyalists were terrified; they refused to venture out at night, and missionaries made preparations to vacate the district. Finally, the Umtata-based Mobile Squadron Police went to the district to enforce government control of the area.[20] The Mobile Squadron, combined with the continued failure of Wellington and the Americans to appear at the designated time, may have muted the apocalyptic fervor, but the district remained hotly contested. Edward Zibi continued to operate UNIA institutions. His supporters, including "American" women wearing black dresses and white aprons adorned with badges and ribbons, agitated for either a separate Zibi-led location or Zibi's reinstatement as Tinana headman. They told Welsh that they did not "want anybody else but Chief E. Zibi."[21] The Americans continued to hold concerts monthly, and the Moravians staged a play in an attempt to win back former congregants. This latest round of millennialism prompted Welsh to remove Edward from the district.[22]

The African newspaper *Izwi lama Afrika* noted in 1931 that Wellingtonism remained strong in Mount Fletcher.[23] Anne Zibi, also known as Ma Wellington, continued to operate a UNIA school as late as 1936. UNIA members referred to themselves as Americans and Amafelandawonye. They held frequent meetings and maintained close contact with Wellington, who was banned from the district but met his followers on the border.[24] By April 1936, the exasperated Mount Fletcher magistrate D. F. Hartmann warned UNIA members "that the law, and not the instructions of Wellington, must be obeyed." But predominately female UNIA members resisted arrest by pelting an African constable and Headman Msi with sticks and stones. The subsequent jailing of twenty-two women and five men did not prevent Ma Wellington from operating the UNIA school as late as 1940, continued testament to the enduring legacy of the UNIA in Mount Fletcher. Local authorities called upon their superiors in Pretoria to prohibit UNIA meetings "by a section of the Native people who call themselves Americans."[25] Even though Edward was ejected from Mount Fletcher, his Garveyism also persisted; in 1938, the Tsolo UNIA chapter listed him as an officer, and he contributed financially to Garvey's Five-Year Plan.[26]

In 1927 in the Transkeian district of Tsolo, Headman Lutshoto Mditshwa heard the gospel of Garveyism from the "wandering American," Wellington. He journeyed to Mount Fletcher, Qumbu, and Basutoland to link with other UNIA divisions; he led UNIA churches and schools; and he held UNIA meetings in his kraal to protest high taxes, stock dipping, and high commodity prices. The government's refusal to recognize his legitimate claim to the Mpondomise chieftainship in Tsolo particularly motivated his UNIA participation.[27] Chief Magistrate W. T. Welsh claimed that the Mpondomise had "killed their own chieftainship" in 1880. That year, the Mpondomise paramount chief Mhlontlo, along with Lutshoto's grandfather Mditshwa, led an Mpondomise uprising against the British that included the murder of Qumbu magistrate Hamilton Hope. British military forces soon conquered the Mpondomise, seized their land, and refused to recognize as chiefs Mhlontlo, Mditshwa, and their descendants in Qumbu and Tsolo districts.[28] Lutshoto and the Mpondomise complained, "The government still holds Hope against us."[29]

With the UNIA, Lutshoto and his followers threatened Tsolo magistrate Edgar Lonsdale that he would meet a fate similar to Hope's as part of a plan to finish Lutshoto's grandfather's mission to expel whites.[30] Lutshoto reportedly was to lead the attack on Tsolo's white community during Wellington's prophesied American Negro invasion in March 1927.[31] He also oversaw the two UNIA schools, held in the kraals of local Africans. These schools had as many as sixty-three students, causing low enrollments at the local government-sanctioned mission school.[32] Philip Payn, a local white trader, complained:

"In the evenings concerts are held and the proceeds go to Dr. Wellington and the people have to pay for the Teachers at these schools and on Sundays the children do a route march carrying Banners with the Stars and Stripes of America on the Banners and they now call themselves Americans."[33] UNIA members called non-UNIA Africans Englishmen and beat them with sticks and burned their huts.[34] Observers reported numerous female followers who were "singing and drilling children" as well as confrontations with police that left an African constable and a female Wellingtonite dead. UNIA members nearly killed a commanding police officer with a bullet that fatally wounded his horse.[35]

The UNIA blurred the lines between the African police, headmen, and government-supported mission teachers, on one side, and those Africans who opposed colonial rule on the other. Lutshoto was one of several headmen who were UNIA leaders, and many mission schoolteachers left to teach at UNIA schools; others were sympathizers who refused to cooperate with investigating state officials.[36] Puzzled by the lack of more detailed information about UNIA activity, magistrates suspected that some African police officers were UNIA members.[37] Exasperated white missionaries declared: "It is impossible to tell who is in it and who is not. Some are said to have joined who have not, and others, who appear not to have joined, have done so secretly, from fear lest anything should happen, so as to be found wearing the badge, when (or if) this great army from America should appear."[38]

As Lutshoto's UNIA involvement continued in 1929, Rev. F. J. Rumsey, who baptized Lutshoto's child, remarked that "the one thing that seems still to block the way in his mind is the Government's refusal to recognize the Chieftainship . . . I can't help feeling that if only the Government would recognize Lutshoto's Chieftainship there would be a great recovery on his part in the ways we so desire."[39] (Lutshoto had already declared "that he was tired of being not recognized by Government and he would like to leave the country.")[40] In 1930, the chief magistrate installed Sigidi, Mhlontlo's grandson, as paramount chief in Qumbu and promised Lutshoto a similar installation in Tsolo if he used his considerable authority to crush the UNIA.[41] Lutshoto complied initially, telling followers that in three years Wellington had not produced the promised teachers and schoolbooks for UNIA schools, American Negro liberators, or African independence. He claimed that he had abandoned Wellington, pressed charges and evicted his former UNIA colleagues from Tsolo, and informed against UNIA members to the Tsolo magistrate.[42]

The chief magistrate equivocated, however, and Lutshoto remained a UNIA vice president. With Wellington, he retained a law firm to advocate for the legality of his chieftainship bid. In 1931, citing Lutshoto's resumed ties with Wellington, the chief magistrate denied him the Mpondomise chieftainship in Tsolo,[43] and he named Lutshoto's son as paramount chief, appointing a regent until the boy reached majority age.[44] Lutshoto's post-1931 UNIA activities seem to have been minimal, which might explain why the state recognized his chieftaincy, effective 1 January 1936. But Paul Gulwa helped keep Garveyism alive in Tsolo.[45]

Gulwa was an educated landowner whose exempted status allowed him free movement around the country. He was one of the Garveyites who kept the faith despite Wellington's failed prophecies and Garvey's political decline and death.[46] Gulwa first met Wellington—and was introduced to Garveyism—in 1926 in Qumbu, during one of Wellington's many trials. He accompanied Wellington to Natal, Bloemfontein, and Pretoria, where they visited the prophetess Nontetha.[47] Gulwa secured a car and driver for Wellington and continued to support him for several years after his failed prophecies.[48] Gulwa wrote to Garvey, addressing him as The Right Honorable President General. He also maintained a UNIA charter for the Tsolo division, which included Edward and Anne Zibi, by regularly sending monthly dues and fees to the parent body.[49] He informed Garvey and American-based UNIA officials that there were UNIA chapters in "Mount Fletcher, Matatiele, Mount Frere and Qumbu, Libode."[50] This UNIA activity concerned authorities. The Bunga issued resolutions in 1936 and 1937 to ban unauthorized UNIA meetings, churches, and schools in Tsolo. The chief magistrate authorized all Transkeian magistrates to enforce wartime emergency regulations against UNIA members and sympathizers.[51]

SEPARATE DEVELOPMENT:
THE 1929 BLACK PERIL ELECTION AND THE
PERSISTENCE OF GARVEYISM IN A WHITE SOUTH AFRICA

The intensification of segregationist policies and ideology in South Africa encouraged some Africans to continue to view American Negroes and Garveyism as the means to establish a separatist African republic. During the South African election in 1929, incumbent prime minister James Hertzog was reelected with the promise of establishing a "white South Africa" if Parliament passed his Native Bills. These bills called for complete African disenfranchisement, continued territorial racial separation, and restrictive laws on African political activity that would make impossible the black peril of African rule. Building upon earlier segregationist legislation and foreshadowing later apartheid-era policies, Hertzog's dream of a white South Africa classified Africans as disenfranchised temporary migrant workers coming from their supposed homes in the reserves, where they could develop "along their own lines." He painted his opponent, Jan Smuts, as an "apostle of a black Kaffir state" that would lead to the extinction of whites in South Africa.[52]

Yet in postelection lectures at Oxford, Smuts also stressed the necessity of separate development both for the survival of whites, who would not be swamped by numerically superior Africans, and for the benefit of Africans, who would not be overwhelmed by white "civilization." He blamed missionary schools for producing "detribalized" and "spoilt" Africans who demanded full citizenship, and he proposed segregation as the means for Africans to preserve their ethnic-based institutions, languages, and culture. In a subsequent trip to the United States, Smuts enraged Du Bois, Robert Moton, and other African Americans when he evoked American Negroes as models for Africans because he believed they exhibited "the patience of an ass" in advancing gradually in America under white trusteeship.[53] Representative of the white electorate, the affirmation of a white South Africa by South Africa's two leading statesmen confirmed for many Africans the futility of interracial cooperation and encouraged continued linkages with American Negroes in the quest for an Africa for the Africans. Smuts admitted that blacks no longer "looked to whites as gods," as blacks in South Africa yearned for the "12 million teachers in America who will come and teach us the true gospel."[54]

Garvey, too, advocated racial nationalism to secure an African republic and avoid racial extermination. In his petition to the League of Nations for African territory, he argued, "Blacks in the Americas, the West Indies and West Africa are far more cultured and advanced, educationally, than the white South Africans." He pointed to Hertzog's Native Bills and other discriminatory laws as evidence of the whites' unfitness to govern Africans.[55] In his newspaper editorials and in his correspondence to South Africans, he said South Africa was "high in racial prejudice against the Negro. In fact, it occupies the higher place for treating the Negro with contempt," adding that "our people are suffering much in South Africa."[56] He wrote several South Africans asking that they send delegates to the 1929 UNIA convention lest the continent become "another United States of America for the white man, and the natives and the black race [be] completely exterminated."[57]

Though the South African government refused to issue passports to allow Africans to attend the conference, Garvey's invitation sparked a lengthy debate among Africans about the liberationist potential of Garveyism and American Negroes. Some Africans like Xhosa cultural historian and poet Samuel Krune Mqhayi felt that American Negroes were useful role models but not liberators. He reminded Africans of Dr. Wellington's failed American Negro liberationist prophecies, dismissed "this ugly Gavi [Garvey]" as a jailbird, and advised Africans to "not rely on gentlemen overseas" for deliverance. Mqhayi suggested instead that Africans liberate themselves: "Our nation is alive, and on top of that, perfectly healthy; we must work amongst our own people in our own nation. That's where our salvation and that of our nation lies."[58]

But other Africans protested "the draconian laws of Hertzog" and "the many abominations and brutal legislation under which the South African black man is suffering."[59] Africans hailed the UNIA conference, the petition to convert former German colonies to African republics, and the UNIA's Africa for Africans mantra as key components of their goal to regain their independence. The Pretoria UNIA elected conference delegates because they wanted to be "free from the shackles of slavery . . . we want a black Africa, a black Republic. Africa is our land."[60] Other Africans felt the conference would facilitate the return of diasporic blacks to their "Homeland, Africa," to create "one of the biggest republics of the world."[61]

Theodore Kakaza was a South African who had graduated from the AME's Wilberforce University in 1901 and become a medical doctor and leader in the Buffalo, New York, UNIA. Writing to *Imvo*, he urged Africans to attend the UNIA conference because Garvey was an apostle of unified racial nationalism and the UNIA was the "new religion" for all blacks.[62] Alexander Njaba saw Garvey as "uniting his African people as an African himself" who was "flesh of our flesh and bone of our bones." Njaba viewed Garvey as a persecuted Jesus-type figure whose fellow blacks had betrayed him and had him sent to prison "just for speaking the truth."[63] J. J. Mole cast Garvey as a modern-day Joseph, calling his long-separated relatives together to create the envisioned African republic. Mole prophesied that God would curse Africans like Mqhayi who relied on whites like Hertzog, nicknamed "Tsalitoro" (the dreamer in Xhosa), who dreamed of a white South Africa.[64] Other Africans agreed that their people "must give up on unity with whites, which they will never get, and hold on to Christianity and turn to God."[65]

In December 1929, while white South Africa celebrated Dingaan's Day to commemorate the Afrikaner defeat of the Zulu in the battle of Blood River in 1838, the ANC and the Communist Party of South Africa held a protest demonstration with a reported fifteen thousand people. Against a backdrop featuring effigies of Smuts and Hertzog, ANC member Daniel P. Adams praised Garvey, to thunderous applause, as "the greatest African living or dead."[66] The ANC newspaper *Abantu-Batho* supported Garvey's advocacy to the League of Nations for African statehood, concluding, "Garvey is indeed a dangerous man for all the great powers that are exploiting Africa. In him, they see a power that is going to shorten the time of their exploits of this fair country of ours."[67]

THE POLITICAL MARGINALIZATION OF MARCUS GARVEY

As Garveyism continued to pervade South Africa, Garvey himself was at a low point. At the time of his release from prison in Manhattan and his deportation to Jamaica in December 1927, his Black Star Line and Black Cross Navigation Company had failed. So, too, had his much heralded attempts to establish colonies in Liberia and in Germany's former African colonies. Britain and France, after the tragic losses of World War I, once again had firm control of their African possessions. Africa seemed no closer to independence than it had a decade earlier when Garvey prophesied African salvation. For the first time in its decade-long existence, the *Negro World*, the newspaper of the UNIA, had no program to promote; it had become a more conventional paper encompassing news of interest to black readers. By 1933, it was defunct.

In Jamaica in December 1927, Garvey struggled to rebuild the UNIA, and the following year, he sailed to England, France, Germany, and Belgium to rally support for new plans to establish a UNIA settlement in Africa. In Geneva, Garvey delivered an updated version of his earlier petition to the League of Nations demanding black control of former German colonies, German East Africa and Southwest Africa, "for the purpose of racial development." He continued, "We feel that if the League will pass over to our control as a race the development of these two German colonies we shall be able within twenty years to prove to the world and to the League our ability to govern ourselves."[68] He was monitored closely by officials of the U.S. Department of State and by British colonial authorities, and his plans for a 1929 UNIA convention in Toronto were dashed when the Canadian government deported him while he was on a visit there.

Relocated to Jamaica instead, the UNIA convention resolved to establish black universities and black businesses, including another steamship line and daily newspapers, as well as embassies in certain countries. It authorized another petition to the League for independent black territories in Africa. In an effort to regain control of the UNIA's American wing, Garvey fired its American-based officials, citing the organization's decline while he was in prison. He reorganized it under a new name, as the UNIA and ACL (August 1929) of the World, with a new Jamaican base to shield him from legal judgments enacted by former officials to recover unpaid salaries. He no longer controlled the editorship of the *Negro World*, and several American leaders refused to acknowledge his authority. William Ware, former head of the Cincinnati UNIA, declared that Garvey had no rights to the UNIA name in America. He arranged for a U.S. Post Office ban on moneys mailed to Garvey and the censorship of all correspondence to or from Garvey.[69] And in Jamaica itself, Garvey's hold slipped as well. He failed to be elected to political office and in his plans to run a daily newspaper, the *Blackman*, or sponsor extravagant fund-raising events at his palatial residence, Edelweiss Park. Nor could he persuade the League of Nations to consider yet another petition in 1934 for a black-led state in Africa.

That same year, Garvey moved to London with his second wife, Amy Jacques Garvey, and two sons (Marcus Jr., then four, and Julius, one). In London, he grew increasingly conservative. He advised blacks to be loyal to European and

American governments. He backed legislation to repatriate blacks to Africa, introduced in the U.S. Senate by the racist Mississippian Theodore Bilbo. He even expressed admiration (if grudging) for the abilities of Adolph Hitler and Benito Mussolini to lead an aggressive racial nationalism that he claimed belonged initially to the UNIA, "the first fascists."[70]

In 1935, Mussolini invaded Ethiopia to establish an Italian colonial presence in Africa in order to civilize supposedly barbaric and uncivilized Africans and avenge Ethiopia's defeat of Italy forty years earlier. Garvey initially expressed confidence that Ethiopia would defeat Italy again with "the unconquerable character of the Negro when put to fight." The League of Nations and "broadminded and liberal Englishmen" would also protect Ethiopian sovereignty, he predicted, but he warned that European acquiescence to fascist aggression could unleash another world war.[71]

But in 1936, when the Italians conquered Ethiopia, Garvey cast that nation no longer as a symbol of black sovereignty and courage but as representative of racial hatred and disunity among blacks and their political, economic, and technological weakness worldwide. When Haile Selassie had pressed the League of Nations and England to intervene, Garvey remarked, "The Emperor of Abyssinia allowed himself to be conquered, by playing white, by trusting to white advisors and by relying on white Governments, including the white League of Nations."[72] Selassie refused to meet Garvey and a black delegation in London, whereupon Garvey dismissed him as "a great coward who ran away from his country to save his skin and left the millions of his countrymen to struggle through a terrible war that he brought upon them because of his political ignorance and his racial disloyalty."[73]

Garvey's criticism marginalized him among black activists globally who saw Selassie and Ethiopia as besieged symbols of black nationality and as part of the general protest against the rise of fascism in Spain, Italy, and Nazi Germany. London-based anticolonial activists C. L. R. James and George Padmore heckled Garvey relentlessly when he made his anti-Selassie remarks during public speeches at London's Hyde Park.[74] Future U.S. congressman Adam Clayton Powell Jr., who organized Americans to protest Italy's invasion, expressed admiration for Garvey's past achievements. Yet he declared that Garvey had "signed his death warrant" when he criticized Selassie, an international statesman who represented the larger fight against fascism, colonialism, and racism.[75] London-based West African anticolonial activist I. T. A. Wallace-Johnson noted that the UNIA was a key stepping stone in the advancement of blacks worldwide. But, he lamented, Garvey "is to be pitied" because he "has fallen a thousand degrees below what he was at the period of the inception of the UNIA" and "obviously outlived his usefulness in so far as leading the African peoples may be concerned."[76]

In May 1939, the state charged James Ghazu and Lutoli Semekazi, head of the Qumbu district UNIA, with sedition and inciting public violence for their prophecies that American Negroes would overthrow the South African state. The forty-year-old Semekazi saw the UNIA as the means to replicate the independent black nationality of the African republic of Liberia. He referred to the Qumbu UNIA as the Liberian Division and named his kraal Liberia and adorned it with a UNIA flag. His kraal had a prominent warning to unauthorized visitors: "Nobody is allowed near this gate—he will be in danger—by order of U.N.I.A. and A.C.L." Excluded from formal district politics, the illiterate Semekazi (his wife, Elizabeth, the UNIA secretary and a UNIA schoolteacher, handled correspondence) represented the "people of another nation, here it is Liberia." He asserted that the laws of "the king" Marcus Garvey and the UNIA superseded colonial laws.[77]

In the late 1920s, Wellington had appointed Semekazi as president of the Qumbu UNIA. However, Wellington's ban from the Transkei, the unraveling of his supposed American identity, the unfulfilled American Negro liberationist prophecies, and his failure to provide UNIA schools with needed books and supplies gave Semekazi greater autonomy over local affairs—and the search for new apocalyptic signs of liberation.[78] The approximately seventy-five UNIA members usually held nightly meetings twice monthly to voice enduring complaints about high taxes and cattle dipping.[79] Qumbu members instituted UNIA churches (the Umanyano/Church of Christ) and schools, and they traveled to Tsolo, Mount Frere, and other districts to attend UNIA meetings. They hosted other Transkeian Garveyites like Paul Gulwa, who read letters from Garvey and American UNIA members and distributed UNIA literature.[80]

James Ghazu was a South African who became the primary UNIA organizer in South Africa by 1938.[81] A frequent sailor, he claimed to have read nearly thirty American papers and declared to the Negro World that blacks were under the "gloomy shadow of extermination and perhaps [would be] brutally murdered by the various white governments." He praised Garvey as a great African leader whose UNIA was the only hope for blacks, and he express his dislike of W. E. B. Du Bois and other American Negroes who opposed Garvey, saying West Indians like Garvey were "tough, hard back-boned Negroes, brave and clever."[82]

In addition to the chartered UNIA divisions in Cape Town and Pretoria, Ghazu wanted unofficial UNIA chapters in Vrede, OFS, and the Transkeian districts of Ramlani, Mount Frere, Matatiele, Qumbu, Tsolo, Mount Fletcher, Jokie, Kowe, Ngqamakwe, and Engcobo to have formal links with Garvey's UNIA.[83] He corresponded with Semekazi to charter the Qumbu UNIA, which would give it the official support of Garvey, the chartered UNIA divisions, and

American Negroes. Ghazu could then intervene with the Qumbu magistrate on behalf of official UNIA members, and he could have Semekazi's grievances heard at the 1938 UNIA conference in Toronto; most important, he could initiate a UNIA-led apocalyptic liberation that would restore African rule. Ghazu told Semekazi, "The world is dead, surely it is dead. Warn the people of the Association and inform them that their prayers have been heard by God, the armies of the Association are ready they should be plucky. When the King of the English thinks of us of the Association he trembles." Ghazu predicted "the coming of the black general of Africa . . . the King of the Association says now is the time for the purpose of liberating the blind of Africa, so says the overseas Hon. Marcus Garvey . . . let it come back to its owners."[84] "So help my God they shall pay; they shall not pass. We must take our pen of iron, dip it in the ink of blood, write on the blue sky; peace be on earth Africans, and Africa is free for ever. . . . We must kill from Cape to Cairo to free the land of our forefathers."[85]

The Qumbu UNIA recruited new members with claims that "we have educated men in American Negroes" who would assist Africans in reclaiming their independence. Fascist aggression by the Germans, Italians, Japanese, and rebels in Spain gave legitimacy to Ghazu's prophecy of an impending Armageddon in South Africa. Ghazu told Semekazi, "Overseas the war is raging in Spain; China vs. Japan; people are getting finished, towns being burnt by means of bombs from the aeroplanes—war planes, guns and machine-guns, bombs and tanks. So it is the war of tomorrow among all races and nations of the world. Pray the day of God is near."[86] Ghazu also planned to "settle the dispute between UNIA and ACL divisions and Mr. Wellington's groups once and for all the time."[87]

Semekazi responded eagerly: "Come ye Africans to liberate us . . . under Marcus Garvey's flag," "come at once so that God's work may be done and finished. . . . It should be clear that Yehova has sent his Angels . . . liberating Africa and . . . proclaiming the new Kingdom."[88] "What you said, General Secretary of the UNIA and ACL has been fulfilled in the whole world that you are a messenger of the Heaven. They tremble when they hear of the coming of the King the Hon. General President Marcus Garvey."[89] According to Semekazi, there would be a new Africa "when the Americans come."[90] "My friend, the world is dead here . . . all the servants of the white man want to fight against Liberia [the Qumbu UNIA] alleging that it is fighting."[91] Semekazi spoke of police raids that removed "assegais, guns, sickles, axes, medicines and mufflers" from the huts of UNIA members, fines for possession of weapons, and the burning of a UNIA school. He remained convinced that the Qumbu magistrate had armed "all the Chiefs including the Basuto [who] were coming to attack me."[92] When Ghazu did not immediately go to Qumbu, Semekazi reported anxiety among local UNIA members: "They wonder when you will come, you people who persuaded them to join Wellington's movement."[93]

In late July 1938, Ghazu went to Qumbu to organize that chapter according to official UNIA guidelines. He was to issue membership cards, institute bookkeeping standards, and distribute organizational literature, particularly the two-volume *Philosophy and Opinions of Marcus Garvey*. He was also to record personally the reported two hundred to four hundred letters of complaint from Qumbu members regarding cattle dipping, high taxation, police raids, and the destruction of UNIA property.[94] Loaded down with UNIA paraphernalia, Ghazu arrived in Qumbu to find Semekazi in jail after he had exchanged gunfire with police officers attempting to search his kraal for a fellow UNIA member.[95] Ghazu soon joined his friend; police charged him with failing to pay taxes, and he served a month of hard labor. The police also seized Ghazu's UNIA materials and his correspondence with Semekazi—the basis of their sedition charge. Ghazu immediately wrote to Arthur McKinley, asking him to inform Garvey of his detention and to secure legal funds from the UNIA. But Garvey had already denied that he was an instrument of liberation, saying, "I have no wonders to perform." He urged the black man to "cut loose from the fantasy of exterior help and fall back on his own initiative."[96] Garvey told Ghazu that he would do nothing for Semekazi because the Qumbu UNIA was not a chartered branch, and then he chided Ghazu for running afoul of the law: "When we issue a Charter to a Branch it is taken for granted that the members of that particular Branch are sufficiently intelligent to operate the Association without any offense to the law or without any cause to invite their interference. . . . Whatsoever is done by the Capetown Branch, to which we issued a Charter, must be done intelligently, properly and without offense."[97]

Ghazu and Semekazi were charged with the crimes of conspiring to wage war against "His Majesty, the King," and alternatively with sedition, public violence, and promoting hostility between Europeans and Africans. They remained jailed for several months as state prosecutors established that both men were UNIA members, arguing that the anticolonial sentiment in their letters and in Garvey's *Philosophy and Opinions* proved seditious intent.[98] In May 1939, the circuit court found Ghazu and Semekazi guilty of treason, sedition, and conspiring to public violence, with intent to "take advantage of the unsettled state of world affairs and launch a sudden attack on Europeans with assistance from Negroes in America."[99]

Judge P. C. Gane noted that Garvey's *Philosophy and Opinions* asserted blacks could use military means to claim their inherent right to Africa. Gane denied this, arguing that "Negroes" did not found ancient African civilizations like Egypt and that "the Dutch and the English were both in South Africa long before the negroes ever arrived there." He then dismissed American Negroes as potential liberators, stating that they "were many thousands of miles away from South Africa. They have no merchant vessels, and no ships of war. As far as we know they own no munitions, nor do they own a single trained soldier." He concluded that "the scheme of Marcus Garvey is one of the most preposterous and visionary that has ever been propounded, and it is as well that the natives in South Africa should understand that." Gane sentenced Ghazu and Semekazi to four months of imprisonment at hard labor, to be suspended for three years on condition of good behavior.[100] Semekazi's ultimate fate is unknown; Ghazu died at sea in January 1945.[101]

TRANSCENDING TUSKEGEE:
EDUCATIONAL LIBERATION IN AMERICA

Despite the unfulfilled dream of seeing American Negro liberators arrive to end the oppression of South African blacks, the United States remained for Africans a key venue for acquiring an advanced education. U.S. educational outlets allowed Africans to regain autonomy and control over their lives and become leaders in the fight against segregation and apartheid. The "leading Zulu woman" of her generation, Sibusisiwe Makhanya, was a 1930 graduate of Columbia University who symbolized the growing capacity of Africans to control their own destinies. Makhanya's family members were early converts of the American Board. Her father was a successful commercial farmer, and both her parents, though proud of their traditional Zulu customs, were devout Christians. At school in Inanda and Amanzimtoti, Makhanya was not "quiet and well-behaved like the other girls"; indeed, she was almost expelled from Inanda. Still, her powerful intellect and forceful personality won her a teaching post there. Her parents and kin, now concerned that her fierce independence was unwomanly, urged her to marry, but Makhanya refused. She planned instead to pursue freely her interest in community affairs, and she founded the Bantu Purity League to help restrict the growing number of premarital pregnancies. In 1923, she left her teaching post at Inanda to establish a night school of her own and to continue as traveling secretary of the Bantu Purity League. Her cousin John Dube soothed her parents' anxiety about her living as a single woman in America. Seeking the most advanced social work training, Makhanya accepted a Phelps-Stokes scholarship for study in the United States.[102]

After Washington's death, the white Hampton sociologist Thomas Jesse Jones became the world's leading champion of industrial education in Africa. Jones was also director of the Phelps-Stokes Fund, founded in 1911 to support black education in America and in Africa. He had led a two-year study of African Americans and education, which concluded with an influential report that recommended "simple manual training" for blacks whose supposedly erratic and emotional temperament, suspect intelligence, and poor work ethic made them virtually uneducable in the liberal arts. Jones and Phelps-Stokes convinced most northern philanthropists to fund exclusively schools on the Hampton/Tuskegee model. Much to the dismay of blacks like Du Bois, Jones continued the Washingtonian practice of controlling the direction of black education by directing northern philanthropic dollars to industrial schools. These educational ideas emerged within a growing international sociology of race that emphasized not the biological but the cultural inferiority of blacks and thus provided intellectual justification for white-over-black regimes in colonial Africa and the United States.

Makhanya's activities also attracted the attention of Charles T. Loram, a Columbia PhD and the most influential educator in South Africa. Loram was one of more than seventy white South Africans with degrees from Columbia's Teachers College. In the early years of the century, these educators returned to South Africa to staff universities, run secondary schools, or take government appointments in education. Based on his research on Hampton and Tuskegee, Loram's 1917 PhD dissertation, "The Education of the South African Native," was regarded as the leading study on African education for decades. Back in South Africa, he became the inspector of schools for Natal and a key adviser to the Phelps-Stokes Fund and the Carnegie Foundation, sponsors of South African students in American universities.[103] But Loram, who also edited an abbreviated version of Booker T. Washington's *Up from Slavery* that circulated widely in South Africa, understood African education through the prism of the Hampton/Tuskegee industrial education model. Having visited both schools, he concluded that similar methods should be used in South Africa to educate Africans, and he applied successfully for philanthropic dollars from Phelps-Stokes and other American sources, thereby facilitating a model of colonial education that buttressed colonial rule.[104]

Like other white "race experts" and "friends of the native" such as Jones, YMCA official Oswin Bull, and South African author Maurice Evans, who had traveled throughout the American South and wrote comparative works on race relations in the U.S. South and South Africa, Loram exerted tremendous influence over black education on both sides of the Atlantic. These individuals globalized the Jim Crow American South, viewing it as a laboratory in which to study race relations and apply those lessons to colonial regimes in Africa.

Loram and his colleagues believed that Hampton, Tuskegee, and South Carolina's Penn School offered a Christian-based training in industrial and agricultural skills that prepared blacks to be productive workers who would not challenge the racial status quo. Africans like Makhanya, Loram was convinced, should train at such schools for leadership roles within the rural tribal reserves he regarded as the natural home of Africans in segregated South

Africa. These reserves, Loram felt, were appropriate spheres for Africans' 'separate development" at their own pace without threatening white minority rule. As he put it, "If possible, let the teachers be of the same tribe and language as the children they teach. Require them to live in the villages where their schools are located . . . let not European tradition dominate too much. Which is really more important in the African villages today—practical hygiene or the ability to read? Elementary agriculture or geography? Wise recreation or arithmetic?"[105] Loram believed his critics attacked him much as American foes had attacked Booker T. Washington, whom he noted had been "accused by some of his own people of trying to keep his people down, of not approving of higher education."[106]

Tuskegee president Robert Moton had recommended that Makhanya enroll at a black liberal arts university, Atlanta University's School of Social Work. However, Loram and the Phelps-Stokes director, Thomas Jesse Jones, decided that Makhanya and a colleague, Amelia Njongwana, would instead attend the Penn School, an industrial education center on South Carolina's St. Helena Island. There, they were to learn how to establish rural-based community training centers in South Africa.[107] Both women had intended to use their training to develop new courses in white mission centers—Makhanya at Inanda, Njongwana at the Lovedale Institute in the Cape Colony.[108] But no one had consulted them, despite their maturity and extensive social work experience. The Penn School's rudimentary curriculum and rural environment were not what they wanted. They hoped to address the needs of Africans who had migrated to cities because of the increasing landlessness, heavy taxation, and the general unsustainability of an agriculturally based rural society. Phelps-Stokes, in response to their complaints, enrolled the women at Tuskegee for a ten-week summer session, but they knew more than their teachers and considered their training inferior to that of leading white universities. Tuskegee's president, Moton, agreed with their wishes to leave his school and praised their intellect, maturity, and clarity of purpose, explaining to Jones that Makhanya "has her own ideas." Njongwana accepted Jones's offer to enroll her in the Atlanta School of Social Work, which Moton had recommended earlier. However, Makhanya was infuriated that she was given limited choices, and she severed her ties to Phelps-Stokes, though she had no funds for another school or for return passage.[109] Jones and American Board officials promptly cut off her access to funds, protesting that she had broken her contract and "gone about the country telling half-truths."[110]

Makhanya, in no way ashamed of her behavior, said loftily to Loram, "In as much as you and the Phelps-Stokes foundation do not entertain the idea of giving me a hearing too, in a matter that I claim concerns me, I have deemed it fit that I take such a step as I have taken." She and Loram were both fellow travelers on the road of racial uplift, "pushing up the wagon of progress and light among my people." Yet Makhanya appropriated Loram's claim of native expertise, saying, "My life is to be spent in this field so hinder me not as I pick up what will make me serve efficiently." With great satisfaction, she informed him that she was now attending the Congregational-affiliated Schauffler Missionary School in Cleveland, which "gives a very fine course in Social Service Work covering many phases of it.": "I am enjoying my course every day."[111]

When she arrived in America, Makhanya had told African Americans that black South Africans "are always interested in, and so eager to read about, anything you American Negroes are doing. Don't forget us—come over and help us. I think that perhaps your being brought here to America, even as you were, was a part of God's plan."[112] African Americans, among them the *Chicago Defender's* publisher Claude Barnett—a Tuskegee graduate—and the *Boston Chronicle's* editor, Alfred Houghton, helped her immensely after she left Phelps-Stokes. They publicized her public lectures on Zulu life and customs that, along with wages she earned from cleaning bathrooms, covered her tuition at Schauffler. There, she studied youth community service, work that led to the founding of the Bantu Youth League on her return to South Africa. But she did not go home immediately. After Schauffler, friends arranged a national speaking tour for her that garnered enough funds to continue her studies at Columbia University, ironically and fittingly the alma mater of both Charles Loram and Thomas Jesse Jones.[113]

At Columbia, Makhanya studied with Mabel Carney, who became one of several American donors who helped finance her 1930 return to South Africa.[114] Makhanya would open a pipeline of African students to Columbia for graduate-level courses on black education, where they met black leaders like Du Bois, E. Franklin Frazier, and Mary McLeod Bethune. Among the African students who moved through that pipeline were former Ohlange pupils Reuben Caluza, who became South Africa's most popular composer, and Don M'timkulu. M'timkulu earned an MA in English from Fort Hare/Rhodes University and taught at the American Board's Adams College before a Carnegie fellowship helped him earn an MA in social anthropology from Yale. Caluza joined Ohlange's faculty and composed hundreds of pieces of American jazz and ragtime, including "Silusapho Lwase Afrika" (We Are the Children of Africa), the first official anthem of the African National Congress. He led the Ohlange choir on yearly fund-raising tours throughout South Africa to keep the school afloat. Caluza's 1930 London recording of 150 songs, including 44 of his own compositions, brought him international renown. Also in 1930, the Phelps-Stokes Fund provided a Hampton Institute scholarship for Caluza to study with Nathaniel Dett, perhaps the world's leading authority on African American spirituals, to compare Zulu folk music with African American sacred music. Caluza toured New England with his African Quartet and performed for President Franklin Roosevelt. After getting his BS from Hampton in 1934, he enrolled at Columbia, where he advised the noted anthropologist Franz Boas on African music and culture, earning an MA in 1935.

After no doubt receiving positive reports from Makhanya about Columbia, John Dube arranged for his nephew, Frederick Dube, to attend the black liberal arts school Morehouse College, to be followed by an MA from Columbia. Frederick returned to South Africa with an African American wife who taught music at Adams College. Eva Mahuma Morake earned a BA from Wilberforce University and an MA in rural education from Columbia University and became the first principal of Wilberforce Institute in South Africa. Under Francis Gow, Wilberforce was a Tuskegee-like industrial school, with government subsidies and white liberal support. White liberals went to the school on Sundays to hear the Wilberforce Singers perform African American spirituals.

Makhanya became a leading figure in Natal. She established, with Dube as chair, the Bantu Youth League to preserve Zulu cultural traditions and to champion the Christian wholesomeness of Zulu youth in twenty-five branches in Natal. She also set up several secondary and night schools and a popular community center in Umbumbulu. The Phelps-Stokes Fund had spurned her in the United States, but its patron, Anson Phelps Stokes, did not. When he visited her in Natal in 1932, he recommended to his fund that it support her work with a modest grant of up to $100. Makhanya's initiation of the Columbia educational pipeline allowed Africans to bypass permanently the Hampton/ Tuskegee Jim Crow–colonial network. She personified the growing desire of Africans to define their own interests and to use American education and the support of American Negroes for their personal and collective advancement.

JOE LOUIS, "UP FROM SLAVERY," AND THE BEGINNINGS OF THE GLOBAL ANTIAPARTHEID ALLIANCE

For the majority of blacks in South Africa, American Negroes remained significant models of racial advancement, even if few any longer expected them to arrive as liberators. But as happened with Jack Johnson a generation earlier, South African blacks pointed to the triumphs of an African American boxer over whites as proof of their inherent racial equality. Africans celebrated Joe Louis's boxing victories and long reign as heavyweight champion (1937–1949) as further evidence of African American progress from slavery, and saw it as a reason to champion the United States, at least in comparison to South Africa, as a country more willing to allow equal competition between blacks and whites. In 1938, when Joe Louis avenged his earlier defeat against German Max Schmeling, South African blacks claimed his victory as their own. Louis was further proof that blacks could be the equal and sometimes the superior of whites if given equal opportunity. Many blacks saw segregation as protecting whites from true and fair competition and thus exposing the lie of white supremacist claims of racial superiority. The African newspaper *Umteteli wa Bantu* exemplified this feeling when Louis won a close decision against the British champion Tommy Farr, writing: "There had been a persistent rumor that a man of Louis's race when once beaten is cowed, couldn't come back and lacked an essential Anglo-Saxon quality—that of never knowing when you are beaten." "Out of this second Negro heavyweight champion of the world, [the first was Jack Johnson] along with the astonishing Olympic records of Negro athletes [Jesse Owens et al. in 1936], there should develop an increased mutual respect between the two races that fate has joined together in the making of an America with justice for all."[115]

Louis, widely acknowledged by boxing historians as the greatest heavyweight of all time, became a folk hero for blacks. "When Joe Louis was going to fight, Africans would get up early in the morning so that they could hear it over the short wave radio."[116] After future ANC president James Moroka made airplane reservations to see Louis box, the government blocked his trip. Traveling through South Africa for three months beginning in September 1937, noted Howard University political scientist Ralph Bunche also met two "colored bedding boys on our train" who were "all very proud of American Negro fighters like Armstrong and the Louises" (a reference to the first black light heavyweight champion, John Henry Lewis). "It would pep these people up if they could develop, say, even one or two outstanding native athletes. They take such pride in the American Negro athletes—especially Jesse Owens and Joe Louis."[117]

An ANC speaker, likely Garveyite Arthur McKinley, praised Joe Louis as a "great man—a black man and world champion: No white man in all of Africa can challenge him."[118] "We were intensely interested in a young man in America who was making a name for himself as a prizefighter," said black South African writer Peter Abrahams. Blacks "stuck photographs of this young man on the walls near their beds. They never tired of talking about him. They knew the details of every fight he had been in, the time in which he had beaten an opponent. To them, he was the most important man in the world, the greatest hero of our time." Louis and other boxers could legally do what Africans could not: beat a white man to a pulp with impunity.[119]

In 1927, after fourteen years in the United States and England, Alfred B. Xuma had returned to South Africa to set up his medical practice. Arriving at Tuskegee as a young man from rural South Africa, Xuma had earned degrees from Tuskegee, Minnesota, and Northwestern universities and completed additional medical training at the University of Edinburgh in Scotland. Like John Nembula decades earlier, Xuma, as one of few African medical doctors, was also prepared for racial leadership. After initial attempts at interracial cooperation, he broke from Charles Loram and other white liberals because they did not adequately protest government segregation and because they championed programs of two-tiered education, designed to train Africans as "medical aides," not as fully credentialed medical doctors.

Xuma concluded that American Negroes would be more faithful partners in his goal of achieving full citizenship and equal rights for all Africans. Though Xuma was intimately aware of the subordinate position of blacks in America, he had deep respect for their progress and considered them models of success and potential partners in African strategies to "unloosen the shackles that bind us . . . [in] jail.[120] Xuma felt Africans should model the ideals of racial self-reliance and solidarity that he saw in Booker T. Washington and at Tuskegee. He maintained close friendships with prominent African Americans, among them the future NAACP executive director Roy Wilkins, the YMCA missionary Max Yergan, Ralph Bunche, and Paul and Eslanda Robeson. He hosted Eslanda and her son, Paul Jr., during the Johannesburg leg of their 1936 trip to Africa. He was a trustee and treasurer of Wilberforce Institute, a secondary school in South Africa run by the African Methodist Episcopal Church that was an important model for Africans "because it is an institution that is run by non-whites."[121]

Xuma's second wife, Madie Hall-Xuma, a black North Carolinian schoolteacher and graduate of Columbia University, became the first president of the ANC Women's League (the ANC opened membership to women in 1942). She had met Xuma at Columbia in 1937 after a speech he had given, and she arrived in South Africa not only to marry but also because she felt divinely ordained to go to there and propagate the providential design narrative of African American history, likening African Americans to the biblical Israelites. Even though Hall-Xuma was from the Jim Crow American South, she was still shocked by the extent of racial segregation in South Africa. In her opinion, the way out, at least partially, was to emulate the American Negro story of progress from slavery to freedom. Both Madie and Alfred used their ANC leadership posts to speak throughout South Africa about the trials and lessons of American slavery, giving due credit to whites like Abraham Lincoln but also asserting that "the Negroes themselves had taken an active part in making emancipation possible."[122]

In 1890, the Virginia Jubilee Singers had introduced to South Africans the American Negro up from slavery historical narrative. More than fifty years later, in 1943, Madie Hall-Xuma produced *The American Negro Revue: The Progress of a People*, a play in the tradition of the same up from slavery narrative of African American history. The revue, performed in Johannesburg and Bloemfontein over six months, began with enslaved American Negroes picking cotton and singing Negro spirituals. It demonstrated American Negro progress through the lives of, among others, Paul Robeson, Joe Louis, George

Washington Carver, and Marian Anderson. And it ended with depictions of modern, entrepreneurial, cosmopolitan American Negro families, black celebrities, and political leaders.[123]

The revue raised over £200 for the ANC, a crucial contribution to its financial sustainability, and it continued African traditions of portraying the up from slavery narrative. The Bantu Men's Social Center featured groups that performed scenes of slavery and of Harlem's Cotton Club, including several acts that imitated American stars such as Fats Waller and the Mills Brothers.[124] In 1934, the writer and Ohlange graduate R. R. R. Dhlomo wrote a play not on the end of South African slavery but on *African American* emancipation. "Native children and adults . . . made the past live by their realistic performance of the suffering of the American Negroes on the slave market, in the cotton fields, and at home until the joyful news of liberation."[125]

When Xuma became ANC president in December 1940, it was a dying, bankrupt organization comprising a few hundred Western-educated, urban-based African elites with little control over its provincial branches. After paying the organization's outstanding debts with personal funds, Xuma developed the ANC infrastructure, opened the first national ANC office, established equal membership rights for women, traveled widely to set up new branches, increased membership and revenues, created an internal committee to handle daily affairs, appointed official ANC organizers, and coordinated the ANC's agenda of fighting against segregation by exerting more control over wayward provincial branches. Xuma also placed the ANC on sound financial footing with fund-raising efforts like the *American Negro Revue* and by soliciting grants from white liberals. By 1943, the ANC had over £700 in the bank. In his efforts to broaden the membership base, Xuma also presided over the formation of the ANC Youth League, which included future antiapartheid leaders Nelson Mandela, Walter Sisulu, and Oliver Tambo. For these efforts, one African praised Xuma as the "new Moses."[126]

Under Xuma, the ANC engaged in the burgeoning anticolonial movements that demanded racial equality in the post–World War II world. In August 1941, British prime minister Winston Churchill and American president Franklin Roosevelt issued the Atlantic Charter, which, in establishing a blueprint for a postwar world order, asserted the right of self-determination for all peoples. The charter planted the seeds of decolonization and the end of apartheid, as people of color seized upon this language to press for racial equality. Under Xuma's leadership, the revived ANC published *African Claims*, which adopted the democratic, self-determinist language of the Atlantic Charter to demand the repeal of all segregationist laws and full citizenship rights for black South Africans.

Prime Minister Jan Smuts dismissed *African Claims* as radical propaganda and refused to meet with Xuma, but the doctor found an ally in the Council on African Affairs (CAA), an African American anticolonial, anti-imperialist organization that, like Garvey decades earlier, targeted South Africa's system as a particularly noxious form of white supremacy. Prominent leaders of the CAA included Max Yergan, Paul Robeson, and W. E. B. Du Bois. The Xumas were close friends with Yergan, an African American YMCA missionary in South Africa from 1921 to 1936. In October 1926, Charles Loram told his Tuskegee audience that Yergan was "one of God's good men. Yergan has done it, by common sense, real goodness and by his wisdom. He is doing in our country what Booker T. Washington and Dr. Moton have done for you."[127] But like Makhanya, Yergan moved beyond the Tuskegee model. South Africa's Black Peril election in 1929 disillusioned him: "As a result of the elections Africans are more discouraged than I have observed them to be in a long time. . . . How can one lay a foundation when one is by law prevented from buying land or selling one's labour wherever one desires, or when one is denied facilities for advanced education, or even good elementary education as is the case here with few exceptions?"[128]

By 1932, Yergan was leading a double life as YMCA missionary by day and communist mentor to Fort Hare students by night. Future ANC stalwart Govan Mbeki credited Yergan with his radicalization, achieved via "utterly convincing" procommunist arguments, particularly on the long road trips they took together.[129] The passage of Hertzog's Native Bills was the immediate impetus for Yergan's departure from South Africa and his resignation from the YMCA in 1936. Stopping in England en route to the United States, he met with Paul Robeson, and the two soon cofounded what became the CAA, the first antiapartheid organization in the United States. Xuma would meet Robeson in London in 1938 while protesting successfully against South Africa's bid to incorporate British protectorates Bechuanaland (present-day Botswana), Basutoland (present-day Lesotho), and Swaziland.

The noted actor, singer, lawyer, and all-American football player Paul Robeson was another long-admired African American in the up from slavery tradition who partnered with the ANC. In 1935, the editors of *Bantu World* explained that they admired African Americans like Robeson "not because they expect American Negroes to deliver them from the thralldom of European oligarchy, but because their achievement has exploded the story that the black man is mentally not the equal of the white man." For the *Bantu World*, Robeson "brought a message of hope from men and women who have emerged from the crucible of slavery to a position of importance in American [society]."[130]

Robeson expressed a strong affinity for Africa: "Where I live is not important. I am going back to my people in the sense that for the rest of my life I am going to think and feel as an African—not as a white man. . . . Frankly years ago I would not have said—as I do now—that I am proud to be Negro.

I did not know that there was anything to be proud about. Since then I have made many discoveries."[131] Robeson's reediting and rewriting of the narration of the film *My Song Goes Forth* transformed it from its original intent of glorifying white rule in South Africa to documenting South African racism.[132] The film, which included Robeson singing and speaking on behalf of Africans, anticipated his later antiapartheid work.[133] At his request, Xuma sent a telegram detailing South African abuses to a CAA conference to support African decolonization. In 1943, the CAA had raised over $5,000 and sent over twenty-two thousand cans of food to the ANC in support of its drought-relief campaign for Africans suffering in the Eastern Cape, and in 1946, the organization gave wide publicity and support to the ANC-led mineworkers' strike that the government brutally crushed. The two organizations also partnered to block South Africa's attempts to incorporate its southern African neighbors and in the campaigns to apply the Atlantic Charter to African countries and to free Ethiopia from Italian occupation.[134]

In 1945, Jan Smuts emphasized the importance of human rights while drafting the preamble to the charter of the new United Nations. Smuts exemplified the contradiction between, on the one hand, offering rhetorical support for democracy, equality, and human rights, particularly to justify war efforts, and, on the other hand, dismissing black demands for racial equality. For African Americans, he had exacted a "Nazi-like domination" over South African blacks, and Du Bois pointed to the irony of "the foremost exponent of the suppression of the Negro calling for a preamble to the UN Charter, which recognized human rights."[135] Xuma went to America to join with the CAA to protest South Africa's proposal to incorporate Southwest Africa. He wrote and circulated a detailed memorandum entitled "South West Africa: Annexation of United Nations Trusteeship?" a searing attack on South African segregation. At a reception in New York when a surprised Smuts asked Xuma why he was in the United States, Xuma retorted, "I have come to be near my Prime Minister. I have had to fly 10,000 miles to meet my Prime Minister. He talks about us but he won't talk to us."[136]

The UN General Assembly voted 37 to 0 (with 9 abstentions) to reject South Africa's incorporation plan, stating that South African racial policies violated the terms of UN trusteeship. Finally, these policies were under international scrutiny. Defeated, an embarrassed Smuts wailed, "Color queers my poor pitch everywhere." He was wrong again; he and others like him had queered the South African pitch by drawing the color line. But he did offer some final prophetic words: "South Africans cannot understand. Color bars are to them part of the divine order of things. But I sometimes wonder what our position in years to come will be when the whole world will be against us."[137] In 1948, the UN General Assembly did enshrine his human rights rhetoric into the Universal Declaration of Human Rights. Though no state could claim to have met its standard at that moment, the declaration set a common standard of human rights that antiapartheid activities would appeal to in the coming years.

Xuma had linked the ANC and the rejuvenated African freedom struggle in South Africa to larger international freedom struggles, helping lay the groundwork of the global antiapartheid struggle. Though American blacks remained important models for Africans after World War II, this transnational relationship became one between equals, with no more apocalyptic prophecies of liberation. After 1945, Africans led the Pan-African movement, and they spurred the wave of African decolonization that served as a model to American Negroes fighting American Jim Crowism, who said "proudly we can be Africans."[138]

In 1949, former Fort Hare students Nelson Mandela, Oliver Tambo, and Govan Mbeki, along with the new ANC secretary-general, Walter Sisulu, were the driving forces behind the ouster of Xuma, who was unwilling to engage in the programs of civil disobedience and, eventually, armed struggle that proved necessary to combat apartheid. In 1953, Fort Hare professor Z. K. Matthews, after a year in the States, returned to South Africa with the idea of drafting a freedom charter, an update of Xuma's *African Claims*, that would serve as the guiding policy for the antiapartheid struggle; it became the basis for the present constitution in the newly democratic South Africa. When South African government officials established Fort Hare partially to stem radicalizing influences from the United States, they did not imagine that students there would transcend the initial Hampton/Tuskegee model and that the institution would become a training ground for Africans dedicated to ending apartheid. The dream of American Negro liberation remained fantasy and did not halt segregation, but the sustained and multifaceted links between Africans and diasporic blacks did plant the seeds of liberation by attacking the global color line, thereby propelling forward the struggle against forms of white supremacy in America and in South Africa.

Tragically, white supremacy continued apace in South Africa even as the counternarrative of transnational black liberation strengthened. Nazi Germany was a tragic consequence of the white supremacist racial theories that Du Bois had lamented in his 1910 "Souls of White Folk" essay. As the dream of American Negro liberation faded at the outset of World War II, some desperate Africans looked to Nazi Germany, an enemy of Britain, as a potential liberator. New prophecies claimed, "Hitler and the Germans are coming here. . . . Hitler will rule this country [and] . . . will open schools for children. . . . Hitler is going to overcome the English people in this war and . . . the people must not obey this Government as there is a new Government coming, and . . . that government will be a very good one and Hitler will not ill treat the people."[139]

During the war, many Afrikaners used Hitler as a model to construct an anti-British, anti-African Afrikaner nationalism that extolled apartheid, a more comprehensive form of racial segregation. After his 1948 defeat of the aged Smuts, National Party leader D. F. Malan had claimed that only apartheid could save the white race from being overwhelmed by people of color. For Malan, the central question was whether white society could "maintain its rule, its purity, and its civilization, or will it float along until it vanishes without honor in the black sea of South Africa's non-European population?"[140] The Nationalists were completing the work of Smuts and Hertzog and Louis Botha, the three Afrikaner generals who were defeated in the South African War but had ruled South Africa since 1910, instituting a segregationist program that was the necessary foundation to apartheid. Western powers like the United States, for economic and Cold War geopolitical reasons, supported South Africa's claim of state sovereignty on its racial matters and, more important, implicitly sanctioned the right of whites to rule.

But what of Garvey and the legacies of Garveyism? While Garvey was in Canada in 1938 on UNIA business, Amy Jacques Garvey—weary of his imperious and demanding manner, tired of the constant financial instability, and concerned that the damp London climate worsened son Julius's asthma—returned to Jamaica with the children. An enraged Garvey never spoke to his wife again; he sent letters, money, and sweets to his children but never saw them again either. On the eve of World War II, Amy Ashwood Garvey, his first wife, who also lived in London, remembered that Garvey was a diminished figure unable to rouse Hyde Park audiences with either his message or his oratory. This image was in stark contrast to the charismatic figure who, in the aftermath of World War I, put forth "Africa for the Africans" as the electrifying slogan of the black world in response to President Woodrow Wilson's doctrine of self-determination for all peoples. As another great war began, Garvey was silent; he died in London on 11 June 1940 from a massive stroke, reportedly after reading erroneous reports of his death from a smaller stroke he had suffered the previous month.

African newspapers responded to news of Garvey's death with reflective obituaries. The *Bantu World* argued that he, like Hitler and Mussolini, was a product of the last great war, which created conditions for aggressive racial nationalism. More than any other person, Garvey energized and organized blacks dissatisfied that that war's promise to extend so-called civilization and democracy did not extend to blacks, even those who had fought for white nations. The *Bantu World* remembered Garvey as a racial separatist uninterested in equal rights between races in the Western Hemisphere but more concerned with blacks' "equal status in the world." Perhaps aware of continued prophecies of American liberation from South African Garveyites, the paper cast Garvey as a master propagandist who appealed to the raw passions, rather than the intelligence, of his followers. Like Judge Gane and other opponents of Garvey, the *Bantu World* ridiculed his promises of African liberation and the prophecies of his followers who believed in liberation from American Negroes "without an army, a navy, and an Air Force." The paper expressed amazement that "thousands of black men in America and Africa believed that this 'miracle' could happen, that Garvey, as the 'Moses' of their race, had the magic rod of the Prophet of Israel."[141] *Imvo Zabantsundu* pointed out Garvey's catastrophic financial failings but praised his "deep inspiration and indomitable courage" in contributing to racial advancement "despite his outstanding faults, which need not be turned to monuments against his service."[142]

Garvey died, but Garveyism survived, as at least two South African Garveyites prophesied "the 'Americans' are coming here."[143] Garvey's death did not discourage Gulwa, who declared, "As black race and members of the UNIA and ACL of South Africa we are sorry but God's work shall never die."[144] Gulwa continued to remit membership dues, fees, and donations to the American-based UNIA, and surviving letters demonstrate his ongoing correspondence with American officials until 1942.[145] The religious character of prophetic Garveyism remained intact. Tsolo UNIA meetings opened with a hymn and prayer; Gulwa founded his Umanyano Church featuring a Garveyite red, green, and black flag waved at its services, and he used Romans 8:31 to affirm divine deliverance: "When God is for us, who can be against us?"[146] In Kimberley, Joseph Masogha and his coworkers apparently managed to weather the storm of hostility for many years after Garvey's death: the House of Athlyi, or some remnants thereof, is reported to have been in existence as late as the 1980s.

South African UNIA chapters in Johannesburg and Cape Town were active as late as the early 1950s, and South African Garveyites continued to write to American UNIA officials, to donate to UNIA-related causes, and to graduate from the UNIA's School of African Philosophy, a program to prepare blacks for racial leadership.[147] As happened during Garvey's lifetime, his ideas transcended UNIA chapters. In the 1940s, ANC Youth League president Anton Lembede quoted frequently from *The Philosophy and Opinions of Marcus Garvey* to develop his nationalist Africanism ideas of racial pride and self-reliance. Lembede pointed to Du Bois and Garvey as examples of black men "developing to the same extent of the white man."[148] In 1944, Jordan Ngubane had coauthored with Lembede the Youth League Africanist manifesto that pushed the ANC toward the more aggressive politics of the apartheid period. Ngubane had been a longtime reader of the *Negro World*, proclaiming in one issue that Africans were "patiently waiting with open arms to welcome our brothers and sisters who are sending a message through the UNIA that they are coming back to their fatherland."[149]

In 1959, those in the Africanist wing of the ANC, concerned about what they perceived to be too much white influence in the leadership ranks, broke away and founded the Pan-Africanist Congress. Ngubane joined them, becoming part of a more overtly Africanist grouping that remained attuned to Garveyist ideas of African nationalism. The Black Consciousness Movement of the 1970s also articulated ideals associated with Garveyism—ideals that circulate today in fledgling UNIA chapters, popular music, art, and an informal settlement outside Cape Town named Marcus Garvey. The settlement is appropriately named, not just because of the revered status of Garvey among its residents but also because it is a community founded by Rastafarians, a religious group with origins in Garvey's native Jamaica. In Rastafarianism, Garvey remains a prophetic figure and the *Holy Piby*, the black man's Bible that circulated in South Africa during Garvey's 1920s heyday, remains a foundational text read today among South African Garveyites.

Apartheid South Africa was arguably the most vicious regime on earth since Nazi Germany, and the study of this system, along with the antiapartheid movement, has attracted considerable attention. Yet chroniclers of this period invariably begin their story with the onset of apartheid in 1948 even though, as this book demonstrates, apartheid was actually the logical conclusion of the longstanding problem caused by the global color line. But just as apartheid did not emerge from a vacuum, neither did the global antiapartheid movement. The genie of transnational liberationist thought and action had been out of the bottle since 1890, when the Virginia Jubilee Singers traveled to South Africa to sing their jubilant spirituals of liberation. Marcus Garvey and the many Africans who took up the Garveyist banner added depth and dimension to the counternarrative of transnational black liberation. Garveyism animated African anticolonial politics, moving it away from the dead-end politics of deputations and petitions. Though the dream of American Negro liberation died with Marcus Garvey, the deep local reverberations of Garveyism in South Africa helped sustain the transatlantic links between Africans and American Negroes, the foundation for the ultimately successful global antiapartheid movement. As Garveyism declined in the Americas, Africans revitalized it in South Africa, joining Garvey-influenced anticolonial leaders Kwame Nkrumah, Nnamdi Azikiwe, and Jomo Kenyatta in a long but ultimately successful freedom struggle against white colonialism. In South Africa in 1994, at long last, Africa would be for the Africans but without the color line, as the early ANC vision of full citizenship rights for all, regardless of color, in a unitary South Africa finally came to pass.

Essay on Sources and Methodology

The Americans Are Coming! has benefited from a range of archival sources, manuscript collections, and newspapers in southern Africa, the United States, and England. Of great help, too, was the research I conducted for the book in government archives in Pretoria, Cape Town, and Pietermaritzburg, South Africa, in 1998, 2000, and 2003.

The records of the Department of Native Affairs and the Department of Justice were particularly helpful in reconstructing the story of Wellington Butelezi, as well as in substantiating the government's general awareness of and response to the Garvey movement during the interwar years. These sources revealed that Garveyism was an active political force not only in large cities like Johannesburg, Cape Town, and Durban but also in rural environs like the former Transkei region. In government archives in Cape Town, I reviewed methodically colonial records that document political activity in each of the twenty-nine Transkeian districts. These archives yielded a tremendously rich vein of evidence. In the Public Records Office in London, I found documents originating with the British Colonial Office that revealed marked concern about Garveyism in the British Commonwealth, including in South Africa.

In the South African Library in Cape Town, I scoured newspapers, among them the weeklies of the Coloured community, the *APO*, the *Cape Standard*, and the *Sun*; white dailies, the *Cape Times* and *Cape Argus*; leftist publications, the *Guardian*, *Liberator*, and *Inkululeko*; and available copies of African newspapers, such as the Garveyist-oriented *Black Man*, *Abantu Batho*, *Umteteli wa Bantu*, and the *Workers Herald*. For the *Black Man*, there are extant copies only from July to December 1920, but they chronicle the formation of the first UNIA branch in the Cape Town area, the heavily Garveyist presence in virtually unprecedented trade union activity, the extraordinary influence of Caribbean immigrants on these activities, and South African Garveyites' awareness of events in the United States.

The *APO*, in its cautious and then hostile critiques of Garveyism, allowed me to build on information gleaned from letters in the *Negro World*, which slowed considerably after 1925. The *Cape Standard*, the *Sun*, the *Guardian*, and the

Liberator were important sources on continuing and former Garveyites and on organizing in trade unions and in Communist and Socialist groups during the 1930s. The *Cape Standard* and the *Sun*, particularly, provided accounts of the educational and political endeavors of the Caribbean community, with obituaries and profiles that proved especially useful.

Interviews with descendants of the West Indian sailing community who were at the forefront of Garveyism offered additional context on interwar black life in South Africa. These individuals shared with me UNIA, ICU, and ANC documents of their fathers and grandfathers. Armed with a list of names for approximately twenty-five Cape Town Garveyites unearthed in archival and newspaper sources, I had conferred with local historians in hopes of finding surviving members or, more likely, their descendants. Vincent Kolbe, a curator at a local museum, was particularly helpful. Kolbe had written a newspaper article about American Negroes that he remembered from his childhood in the early 1940s, and he was able to provide phone numbers for two children of UNIA members. I supplemented his leads by searching the Cape Town phone book for names that matched my list, a search that yielded a self-proclaimed Garveyite and two children of members, one of whom pointed me to two other Garveyite children. Of these seven persons, six, including the surviving Garveyite, agreed to taped interviews.

I prepared for the interviews with ice-breaking phone conversations and then followed up with home visits. All the interviewees insisted that I come to their homes for weekend lunches. Relatives would appear mysteriously to witness the exotic "American who has come all this way to find out about Daddy." As lunch extended into dinner, I learned that the children, most born during the 1920s, had common memories of their fathers. Too young to recall specific UNIA meetings or activities, they talked of the close-knit West Indian community and shared vivid accounts of Sunday gatherings that mixed Caribbean-style food and drink with boisterous talk of politics, sport, and the "old country." They recalled their fathers' admiration for American Negroes such as Garvey, George Washington Carver, Joe Louis, and Paul Robeson. They spoke of fundraising drives for educational scholarships, of the adoption of children left by deceased friends, and of membership in the local AME church.

My interview questions centered on these issues and on biographical details related to their fathers, including their home islands, stories of their sailing careers, and the factors that motivated them to settle in Cape Town — all valuable context for the UNIA activities of these Caribbean immigrants. The children shared with me photographs of their fathers and surviving documents, including in several instances UNIA membership cards, Black Star Line stock certificates, and other papers attesting to their fathers' political, fraternal, economic, and educational activities. An interview with former ANC secretary-general Walter

Sisulu yielded valuable insights about Wellington Butelezi's "American" schools, at which his own mother taught and which he attended briefly. An interview with trade union luminary Ray Alexander confirmed the continuance of Garveyism in South Africa in the 1930s.

In the United States, I conducted research in archives and research repositories, including the Schomburg Center for Research in Black Culture in Harlem and the Moorland-Spingarn Research Center in Washington, D.C. In research trips to the Schomburg Center for Research in Black Culture beginning in 1998, I examined the UNIA Central Division Records and a nearly complete run of the primary UNIA paper, *Negro World*, which was essential to this book. South Africans sent more letters to the *Negro World* than did readers from any other African country. Many were accounts of UNIA meetings; others were from passionate pro-Garvey sympathizers. These letters were an invaluable source of information about the founding of the UNIA, as well as the strong religious character and the activities of individual Garveyites and their UNIA chapters. They reflected the pervasive views among blacks in Africa that American Negroes were a chosen people, destined to rise from the horrors of slavery to be exemplars of black progress and potential liberators of Africa. The *Negro World* captured the centrality of southern Africa to the UNIA's anticolonial agenda, as well as various perspectives about Africa prevalent in the diaspora.

Another collection of primary documents I searched included the massive *Marcus Garvey and UNIA Papers* at the University of California—Los Angeles (UCLA). The directing editor, Robert A. Hill, provided relevant documents, offered cogent advice on field research, and in several discussions deepened my understanding of South African Garveyism. I also reviewed several newspaper archives housed at UCLA, among them the *Negro World* and *Imvo Zabantsundu*. In the African American Collections in the Manuscript, Archives, and Rare Book Library at Emory University in Atlanta, I searched the papers of longtime UNIA president Thomas Harvey, which provided insight into the continuance of international Garveyism into the 1970s.

Notes

INTRODUCTION

1. "Some American Bishops in Africa and Natives," *Negro World*, 22 November 1924; "Mr. Marcus Garvey in South Africa," *Negro World*, 7 February 1925.

2. Daniel W. Alexander, "Poem Dedicated to Marcus Garvey," *Negro World*, 7 February 1925.

3. *Negro Churchman*, March 1923, in folder 204, box 17, Alexander/AOC Papers, African Orthodox Church Records (AOC), RG 005, Archives and Manuscripts Department, Pitts Theology Library, Emory University; "What Is That in Thy Hand?," *Negro World*, 9 August 1924.

4. African diasporic studies remain overwhelmingly oriented toward the North Atlantic triangle of North America, the Caribbean, and Europe. For the focus on key North Atlantic sites of transnational black organizing like London, Paris, and Harlem, see Brent Edwards, *The Practice of Diaspora: Literature, Translation, and the Rise of Black Internationalism* (Cambridge, MA: Harvard University Press, 2003); Hakim Adi, *West African Students in Britain* (London: Lawrence and Wishart Press, 1998); and Winston James, *Holding Aloft the Banner of Ethiopia: Caribbean Radicalism in Early Twentieth-Century America* (New York: Verso Press, 1998). The lack of serious engagement of Africa within African diasporic studies is noted in the "African diaspora" special issue of *African Studies Review* 43, no. 1 (April 2000), and the recent "transnational black studies" issue of *Radical History Review* 87, no. 3 (Fall 2003), as well as in Patrick Manning, "Africa and the African Diaspora: New Directions of Study," *Journal of African History* 44, no. 3 (November 2003): 487–506. See also the special issue on the African diaspora in *Radical History Review* 103, no. 4 (Winter 2009). However, while there are few monographs that center Africa and Africans in African diaspora studies, there are some recent edited collections by Africanists that have this focus. See, for example, Livio Sansone, Elisee Soumonni, and Boubacar Barry, *Africa, Brazil and the Construction of Trans Atlantic Black Identities* (Trenton, NJ: Africa World Press, 2008); Toyin Falola, Niyi Afolabi, and Aderonke Adesola Adesanuya, eds., *Migrations and Creative Expressions in Africa and the African Diaspora* (Durham, NC: Carolina Academic Press, 2008); Paul Tiyembe Zeleza, *Barack Obama and African Diasporas: Dialogues and Dissensions* (Athens: Ohio University Press, 2009); and Tejumola Olaniyan and James H. Sweet, eds., *The African Diaspora and the Disciplines* (Bloomington: Indiana University Press, 2010).

5. I use the term *black* to describe both Africans and the mixed-race people known in South Africa as Coloureds in situations where members of both groups were participants in the events described. Of course, there were significant differences between the two groups; I specify African or Coloured when greater specificity is necessary and more accurate.

6. Edwards, *Practice of Diaspora*.

7. A recent monograph on Garveyism in Africa is Ibrahim Sundiata, *Brothers and Strangers: Black Zion, Black Slavery, 1914–1940* (Durham, NC: Duke University Press, 2003), which focuses on Liberia. For recent books on Garveyism in the American South, see Mary Rolinson, *Grassroots Garveyism: The Universal Negro Improvement Association in the Rural South, 1920–1927* (Chapel Hill: University of North Carolina Press, 2007); Claudrena Harold, *The Rise and Fall of Garveyism in the Urban South* (New York: Routledge, 2007); Jarod Roll, *Spirit of Rebellion: Labor and Religion in the New Cotton South* (Champaign: University of Illinois Press, 2010); and Steven Hahn, *A Nation under Our Feet: Black Political Struggles in the Rural South from Slavery to the Great Migration* (Boston: Belknap Press, 2005). For a new study on the economic aspects of Garveyism, see Ramla Bandele, *Black Star: African American Activism in the International Political Economy* (Champaign: University of Illinois Press, 2008). See also a recent biography of Garvey by Colin Grant, *Negro with a Hat: The Rise and Fall of Marcus Garvey* (New York: Oxford University Press, 2008).

8. See, for instance, George Fredrickson, *Black Liberation: A Comparative History of Black Ideologies in the United States and South Africa* (New York: Oxford University Press, 1995).

9. W. Keith Hancock, *Smuts*, vol. 1, *The Sanguine Years, 1870–1919* (Cambridge: Cambridge University Press, 1962), 55–56. For a more current reading of Smuts's racial thought, see Shula Marks, "White Masculinity: Jan Smuts, Race and the South African War," *Proceedings of the British Academy* 111 (2001): 199–223.

10. James Stewart, *Dawn in the Dark Continent* (Edinburgh: Oliphant Anderson and Ferrier, 1903), 364.

11. Lothrop Stoddard, *The Rising Tide of Color against White World Supremacy* (New York: Charles Scribner, 1920).

12. Clifton Crais, *The Politics of Evil: Magic, State Power, and the Political Imagination in South Africa* (Cambridge: Cambridge University Press, 2002), 8.

13. Exceptions include James Campbell, *Songs of Zion: The African Methodist Episcopal Church in the United States and South Africa* (New York: Oxford University Press, 1995); Robert R. Edgar and Hilary Sapire, *African Apocalypse: The Story of Nontetha Nkwenkwe, a Twentieth-Century South African Prophet* (Athens: Ohio University Press, 2000); Robin D. G. Kelley, "The Religious Odyssey of African Radicals," *Radical History Review* 51, no. 3 (Fall 1991): 5–26; and Wallace G. Mills, "Millennial Christianity, British Imperialism, and African Nationalism," in *Christianity in South Africa: A Political, Social, and Cultural History*, ed. Richard Elphick and T. R. Davenport, 337–47 (Berkeley: University of California Press, 1997).

1. There was, of course, no state named South Africa before the Union of South Africa was established in 1910; I use the term in accounts of pre-1910 events to place them within the geographical space that became the Union of South Africa. Before the South African War of 1899 to 1902, there were two Afrikaner-dominated republics, the Orange Free State and the Transvaal, and two English colonies, Natal and Cape Colony. With the British victory, the two Afrikaner republics were incorporated into the Union of South Africa until 1960, when the Republic of South Africa declared independence from the British Commonwealth.

2. For the development of minstrelsy in the United States, see Eric Lott, *Love and Theft: Blackface Minstrelsy and the American Working Class* (Oxford: Oxford University Press, 1993).

3. Zine Magubane, *Bringing the Empire Home: Race, Class and Gender in Britain and Colonial South Africa* (Chicago: University of Chicago Press, 2004), 154.

4. Veit Erlmann, *African Stars: Studies in Black South African Performance* (New York: Oxford University Press, 1991), 21–53; Erlmann, *Music, Modernity and the Global Imagination* (Chicago: University of Chicago Press, 1999), 144–66.

5. Eddie S. Glaude Jr., *Exodus! Religion, Race, and Nation in Early Nineteenth-Century Black America* (Chicago: University of Chicago Press, 2000); Allen Dwight Callahan, *The Talking Book: African Americans and the Bible* (New Haven, CT: Yale University Press, 2008); W. E. B. Du Bois, "Of the Sorrow Songs," quoted in Du Bois, *Souls of Black Folk*, 143–67 (1903; repr., New York: Vintage, New American Library, 1990); James W. Johnson and J. Rosamond Johnson, *The Books of American Negro Spirituals* (1925; repr., New York: Da Capo, 2002); and Eileen Southern, *The Music of Black Americans*, 3rd ed. (New York: Norton Press, 1997).

6. For the Fisk Jubilee Singers generally, see J. B. T. Marsh, *The Story of the Fisk Jubilee Singers, with Their Songs* (1881; repr., New York: Negro Universities Press, 1969). For Orpheus McAdoo's accounts of his travels with the troupe, see his "From a Hampton Graduate in Australia," *Southern Workman* 15 (November 1886): 118, and "Letters from Hampton Graduates," *Southern Workman* 16 (April 1887): 41. In 1883, the U.S. Supreme Court declared the 1875 Civil Rights Act unconstitutional on the grounds that Congress had no power to regulate individual conduct.

7. McAdoo, "Letters from Hampton Graduates," 41.

8. The group included sopranos J. S. Ball, Belle Gibbons, and Josie M. Jackson; tenor Richard Collins; Moses Hodges, a baritone; Mamie Harris, the group's contralto; accompanist Lucy Moten; and a female tenor named Mattie Allan, McAdoo's future wife.

9. See Bruno Chenu, *The Trouble I've Seen: The Big Book of Negro Spirituals* (Valley Forge, PA: Judson Press, 2003).

10. "The Jubilee Singers," *Transvaal Advertiser*, 9 February 1891.

11. "The McAdoo Singers," *Southern Workman* 19 (October 1890): 104.

12. Editorial, *Imvo Zabantsundu*, 16 October 1890; "Mr. McAdoo's Jubilee Singers," *Imvo Zabantsundu*, 19 December 1895.

13. Editorial, *Imvo Zabantsundu*, 16 October 1890.

14. *Kaffrarian Watchman* (KingWilliamsTown, n.d.), quoted in *Southern Workman* 18, no. 20 (January 1891): 12.

15. *Leselinyana*, 1 October 1890, quoted in Erlmann, *African Stars*, 44. The McAdoo troupe inspired Semouse to join the African choir that toured in England.

16. Erlmann, *African Stars*, 45; "The Jubilee Singers," *Imvo Zabantsundu*, 21 August 1890.

17. "The Jubilee Singers," *Natal Advertiser*, 17 November 1890.

18. For an example of how eager Africans were to attend Hampton, see "Charles Kumkani and Samuel Cakata to Samuel C. Armstrong," *Southern Workman* 18 (February 1891): 146.

19. The Natives Land Act rendered millions of Africans landless, forcing them to sell their labor cheaply to white-owned mines, farms, and industries. The Natives (Urban Areas) Act undergirded a policy that sharply controlled and restricted Africans' movement from country to town, allowing entry into urban centers only insofar as their labor was necessary to "minister to the white man's needs."

20. "The Jubilee Singers," *Southern Workman* 17 (February 1891): 146.

21. McAdoo to Samuel Armstrong, in "A Letter from South Africa: Black Laws in the OFS in Africa," *Southern Workman* 17 (November 1890): 120.

22. Veit Erlmann, "'A Feeling of Prejudice': Orpheus McAdoo and the Virginia Jubilee Singers in South Africa, 1890–1898," *Journal of Southern African Studies* 14, no. 3 (Fall 1988): 331–50; *Times of Natal*, 30 March 1898.

23. J. D. Huyser, "Die Naturelle-Politiek van die Suid-Afrikaanse Republiek" (PhD diss., University of Pretoria, 1936), 167.

24. *Natal Witness*, 28 September 1875; *Standard and Mail*, 12 October 1875.

25. William Van Ness to Dr. Leyds, Transvaal Secretary of State, 15 January 1893, Consular Dispatches, Johannesburg, South Africa, Record Group (RG) 59 microfilm publications, T 191, roll 15, Cape Town General Records of Department of State, NARA. George Hollis to Josiah Quincy, May 9 1893; Van Ness to Leyds, 18 September 1893; and John Ross to Leyds, 16 September 1893, all in Consular Dispatches, Johannesburg, South Africa, RG 59 microfilm publications, T 191, roll 15, NARA; Clement Keto, "Black Americans and South Africa, 1890–1910," *Current Bibliography of African Affairs* 5 (1972): 387–88.

26. 3 July 1896 and 23 July 1896, Consular Dispatches, Cape Town, A 668, National Archives and Records Administration, College Park, Maryland (hereafter cited as NARA).

27. Henry M. Turner, "My Trip to South Africa," in *Respect Black: The Writings and Speeches of Henry McNeal Turner*, ed. Edwin Redkey, 178–81 (New York: Arno Press, 1971); Willard B. Gatewood Jr., "Black Americans and the Boer War, 1899–1902," *South Atlantic Quarterly* 75 (1976): 231. See also the AME's foreign mission newspaper, *Voice of Missions*, 1 June 1898.

28. Harry Dean, *The Pedro Gorino* (New York: Houghton Mifflin, 1929), 213.

29. E. De Waal, "American Black Residents and Visitors in the South African Republic before 1899," *South African Historical Journal* 6 (1974): 52–55.

30. "A Letter from South Africa: Black Laws in the Orange Free State in Africa," *Southern Workman* 19 (November 1890): 120.

31. Erlmann, *African Stars*, 42.

32. Erlmann, *Music*, 152.

33. The first independent African churches were Nehemiah Tile's Thembu Church (1883); a Lutheran Bapedi church (1889); Joseph Kanyane Napo's African Church (1890); Mbiyana Ngidi's Zulu Mbiyana Congregational Church (1891); Jonas Goduka's African Native Church (1892); and Mokone's Ethiopian Church (1893).

34. J. Mutero Chirenje, *Ethiopianism and Afro-Americans in Southern Africa, 1883–1916* (Baton Rouge: Louisiana State University Press, 1987); George Shepperson, "Ethiopianism: Past and Present," in *Christianity in Tropical Africa*, ed. C. G. Baeta, 249–68 (London: Oxford University Press, 1968). See also Bengt Sundkler, *Bantu Prophets in South Africa* (London: Oxford University Press, 1961); and editorial, *Cape Times*, 31 July 1893, quoted in Chirenje, *Ethiopianism and Afro-Americans*, 24. The Afrikaner Bond was a culturally oriented political movement of Afrikaners, who were descendants of seventeenth-century Huguenot settlers.

35. Absalom Jones, "A Thanksgiving Sermon, Preached January 1, 1808, In St. Thomas's, or the African Episcopal Church, Philadelphia: On Account of The Abolition of the African Slave Trade, on That Day, By The Congress of the United States (Philadelphia 1808)," in *Early Negro Writing, 1760–1837*, ed. Dorothy Porter, 335–42 (Boston: Beacon Press, 1971).

36. Editorial, *Richmond Planet*, 2 December 1899; Charles S. Morris, "A Work for American Negroes," in *Ecumenical Missionary Conference, New York, 1900: Report of the Ecumenical Conference on Foreign Missions*, 1:469–71 (New York: American Tract Society, 1900).

37. James Campbell, *Songs of Zion: The African Methodist Episcopal Church in the United States and South Africa* (New York: Oxford University Press, 1995), 135.

38. "Enough Negroes There!," *Indianapolis Freeman*, 26 October 1895.

39. "Chalk-Marked His Back: How the Boers Treated Colored People in the Transvaal," *Cleveland Gazette*, 20 September 1902.

40. "Foreign Shores," *Cleveland Gazette*, 1 December 1900.

41. For black American disapproval, see "American Negroes Making Mischief in South Africa," *Missionary Review of the World* 16 (May 1903): 396–97.

42. "The Ethiopian Movement," *Lagos Weekly Record*, 1 July 1905.

43. South African Native Affairs Commission (hereafter cited as SANAC), *Minutes of Evidence and Reports*, 5 vols. (Cape Town: Cape Times, 1905), 2:969–70.

44. For the Black Peril as a supposed sexual threat that black men posed to white women, see Timothy Keegan, "Gender, Degeneration and Sexual Danger: Imagining Race and Class in South Africa ca. 1912," *Journal of Southern African Studies* 27, no. 3 (September 2001): 455–77.

45. SANAC, *Minutes of Evidence and Reports*, 2:973.

46. Roderick Jones, "The Black Peril in South Africa," *Nineteenth Century and After* 55 (May 1904): 712–23; Jones, "The Black Problem in South Africa," *Nineteenth Century and After* 56 (May 1905): 770–76.

47. For the Bambatha rebellion, see Benedict Carton, *Blood from Your Children: The Colonial Origins of Generational Conflict in South Africa* (Pietermaritzburg: University of Natal Press, 2000), and Shula Marks, *Reluctant Rebellion: The 1906–08 Disturbances in Natal* (New York: Oxford University Press, 1970).

48. Neville Chamberlain, "Speech at Wanders' Hall, Johannesburg, South Africa, 17 January 1903," in *Mr. Chamberlain's Speeches*, ed. Charles Boyd, 2:112 (London: Constable, 1914).

49. Harry Dean and James Brown to Secretary of State, 22 September 1903, Consular Dispatches, Cape Town, RG 59, M 179, 1182, NARA.

50. Proffit to Loomis, 8 August 1904, Consular Dispatches, Pretoria, RG 59, T 660, roll 3, NARA.

51. Thomas J. Noer, *Briton, Boer, and Yankee: The United States and South Africa, 1870–1914* (Kent, Ohio: Kent State University, 1978), 115–18. The judge suspended Brown's sentence.

52. Secretary of Native Affairs, Transvaal Colony, 1906, box 310, files 101, 106, 108, 109, National Archives of South Africa (hereafter cited as NASA), Pretoria. I am grateful to Amanda Kemp for sharing the NASA reference with me. For a similar case, see also J. De Roos to American Consul Johannesburg, 3 October 1910, Justice Dept. box 30, file 3/33/10, NASA, Pretoria.

53. Department of Justice, February 1913, box1, file 136, NASA, Pretoria. Phthisis, also known as silicosis, causes a hardening of the lungs through excessive exposure to dust. In 1907, rock-drilling miners had an expected annual mortality rate of 100 deaths per 1,000. See Elaine Katz, *The White Death: Silicosis on the Witwatersrand Gold Mines, 1886–1910* (Johannesburg: Witwatersrand University Press, 1994).

54. Proffit to Loomis, 28 December 1903, Consular Dispatches, Pretoria, RG 59, T 660, roll 2, NARA.

55. Proffit to Loomis, 8 August 1904, Consular Dispatches, Pretoria, RG 59, T 660, roll 2, NARA.

56. Geoffrey C. Ward, *Unforgivable Blackness: The Rise and Fall of Jack Johnson* (New York: Alfred A. Knopf, 2004), 122–28.

57. *Richmond (Va.) Planet*, 9 January 1909. The *Detroit Free Press* advised, "Draw the color line in everything if we are to avoid being whipped individually and collectively." "The Caucasian's Plight," *Detroit Free Press*, reprinted in "Afro-American Journal," *New York Age*, 14 January 1909.

58. Donald Denoon, *A Grand Illusion: The Failure of Imperial Policy in the Transvaal Colony during the Period of Reconstruction, 1900–1905* (London: Longmans, 1973), 107.

59. Governor-General to Secretary of State, 2 February 1908, Colonial Office 886/1/85, National Archives of the United Kingdom, London, England.

60. Ward, *Unforgivable Blackness*, 112–15.

61. "Black v. White Prize-Fighters," *Bloemfontein Friend*, 29 December 1908.

62. Dan Streible, "Jack Johnson Fight Films," in *The Birth of Whiteness: Race and the Emergence of U.S. Cinema*, ed. Daniel Bernardi, 173 (New Brunswick, NJ: Rutgers University Press, 1996). Johnson earned a percentage of the film's general distribution fees and personal prints; he distributed the film to several outlets, including black-owned theaters like Chicago's famed Pekin. When he traveled, he carried film clips to illustrate his live narrations in vaudeville style. His merging of sport and entertainment and his example of what blacks could achieve if given equal opportunity created a potent "New Negro" depiction of black power and black masculinity. Between 1903 and 1915, more than 95 percent of "black" male representations in film were actually white men in blackface.

63. "'Black Coolie' to Editor," *Times of Natal*, 5 July 1910.

64. "A Review of the World," *Current Literature* 48 (June 1910): 606.

65. Editorial, *Literary Digest* 41, no. 3 (16 July 1909): 85.

66. Robert H. de Coy, *Jack Johnson: The Big Black Fire* (Los Angeles: Holloway House, 1991), 114.

67. *Afro-American Ledger*, 30 April 1910.

68. *Chicago Tribune*, 5 July 1910.

69. David Krasner, *A Beautiful Pageant: African American Theatre, Drama, and Performance in the Harlem Renaissance, 1910–1927* (New York: Palgrave Macmillan, 2002), 23.

70. Gail Bederman, *Manliness and Civilization: A Cultural History of Gender and Race in the United States, 1880–1917* (Chicago: University of Chicago Press, 1995), 3.

71. "'Black Coolie' to Editor," *Times of Natal*, 8 July 1910.

72. "'Fair Play' to Editor," *Bloemfontein Post*, 7 July 1910.

73. "What Is Civilization?," *Ilanga lase Natal*, 15 July 1910; "Prize-Fighting," *Ilanga lase Natal*, 22 July 1910.

74. "Far-Reaching Effects," *Times of Natal*, 6 July 1910.

75. "Black vs. White," *Bloemfontein Friend*, 6 July 1910; "The Inevitable Sequel," *Bloemfontein Post*, 7 July 1910.

76. "Inevitable Sequel."

77. Ibid.

78. For the ban in southern theaters, see Robert J. Norrell, *Up from History: The Life of Booker T. Washington* (Cambridge, MA: Harvard University Press, 2009): 413.

79. Jordan to Lansing, 15 June 1917, and Jordan to Hughes, 13 April 1921, RG 59, T 583, roll 14, Department of State Records of British Africa, NARA.

80. James East, *Outline for Mission Study Classes, 1876–1932* (Nashville, TN: National Baptist Convention, 1920), 83; Gladys East, interview by author, 26 December 1995, Philadelphia.

81. The deposit required of the Paynes was to guarantee to the South African government that they would leave the country; it was to be refunded upon the missionaries' departure.

82. Brian Willan, *Sol Plaatje: South African Nationalist, 1876–1932* (Berkeley: University of California Press, 1984), 205. Plaatje had some political capital from his recruitment of African troops for the South African military contingent that fought for Britain in World War I, but this was a relatively small victory. Plaatje remained in Cape Town for two weeks to rally (unsuccessfully) support for efforts to derail legislation that eventually became the Native Administration Bill.

83. Payne to George Murphy, 22 February 1917; Murphy to South African Department of Interior, 23 February 1917; and Department of the Interior to Murphy, 26 February 1917, all in RG 59, T 583, roll 14, Department of State Records of British Africa, NARA.

84. Murphy to Department of the Interior, 1 March 1917, RG 59, T 583, roll 14, Department of State Records of British Africa, NARA.

85. Murphy to State, 12 March 1917; Pisar to State, 27 November 1922; both in RG 59, T 583, roll 14, Department of State Records of British Africa, NARA.

86. L. G. Jordan, "Rev. and Mrs. H. A. Payne to be banished from So. Africa," June 1917, RG 59, T 583, roll 14, Department of State Records of British Africa, NARA.

87. Jordan to Polk, 26 July 1917; Carr to Jordan, 2 August 1917; Department of Interior to Murphy, February 1917; and Murphy to American Department of State, 7 July 1917, all in RG 59, T 583, roll 14, Department of State Records of British Africa, NARA.

88. Murphy to the South African Governor-General, 15 January 1918; Governor-General Department, file 3/2542/36, vol. 124, NASA, Pretoria; Murphy to State, 26 September 1917, RG 59, T 583, roll 14, Department of State Records of British Africa, NARA.

89. Virginia Theological Seminary graduates included the Paynes' classmate Vernon Johns, a tireless civil rights activist and Martin Luther King Jr.'s predecessor at Dexter Avenue Baptist Church in Montgomery, Alabama. Patrick L. Cooney and Henry W. Powell, *The Life and Times of the Prophet Vernon Johns* (Vernon Johns Society, 1998), http://www.vernonjohns.org (accessed May 28, 2011).

90. James East, "Excerpts from Brief Report on the Middledrift Mission," *Mission Herald*, February 1923, 25.

91. Ibid., 22–23.

92. Gladys East interview.

93. "Rev. J. East Appointed," *Imvo Zabantsundu*, 12 November 1918.

94. James East, "Our Twenty-First Anniversary," *Mission Herald*, September 1919 (reprinted in the October 1919 edition); Alexander Kerr, *Fort Hare, 1915–48: The Evolution of an African College* (New York: Humanities Press, 1968), 23, 69.

95. R. Hunt Davis Jr., "John L. Dube: A South African Exponent of Booker T. Washington," *Journal of African Studies* 1, no. 2 (1975): 497–528; Willan, *Sol Plaatje*, 278–79. Plaatje proudly displayed pictures of his friend Robert Moton, Washington's successor as Tuskegee president.

96. D. D. T. Jabavu, *The Black Problem: Papers and Addresses on Various Native Problems* (1920; repr., New York: Negro Universities Press, 1969), 97; Booker T.

Washington to Reverend John Harris, 9 September 1913, reel 353, Booker T. Washington Papers, Library of Congress, Washington, D.C. See also D. D. T. Jabavu, "A Report on the Tuskegee Institute, Alabama, U.S.A., for the Minister of Native Affairs, South African Union Government," typescript, app. 1, pp. 36–37, Helen Nontando Jabavu Crosfield Collection, London. A condensed version of the report is found in Jabavu, *Black Problem*, 27–70.

97. For NFA activities, see Catherine Higgs, *Ghost of Equality: The Lives of D. D. T. Jabavu* (Athens: Ohio University Press, 1997); Farieda Khan, "Rewriting South Africa's Conservation History: The Role of the Native Farmers Association," *Journal of Southern African Studies* 20, no. 4 (December 1994): 499–515; and Jabavu, *Black Problem*, 112–21, 127, 134–36.

98. Gladys East interview.

99. East to Jordan, *Mission Herald*, August 1920; East, "Excerpts from Brief Report"; Gladys East interview.

100. Editorial, *Mission Herald*, April 1921.

101. East, "Excerpts from Brief Report," 46.

102. Ibid., 15, 74.

103. See Leon Litwack, *Trouble in Mind: Black Southerners in the Age of Jim Crow* (New York: Vintage Press, 1999).

CHAPTER 2: THE FAILED DREAM OF BRITISH LIBERATION AND CHRISTIAN REGENERATION

1. Sheila Meintjes, "Family and Gender in the Christian Community at Edendale, Natal, in Colonial Times," in *Women and Gender in Southern Africa to 1945*, ed. Cherryl Walker, 129, 132 (Cape Town: David Philip, 1990).

2. Norman Etherington, *Preachers, Peasants and Politics in Southeast Africa, 1835–1880* (London: Royal Historical Society, 1978), 133–34.

3. Ross Shiels, "John Mavuma Nembula, 1860–1897: First Black Physician in Southern Africa," *Journal of the National Medical Association* 80, no. 11 (1988): 1255–58; and Anne Digby, "Early Black Doctors in South Africa," *Journal of African History* 46 (2005): 448.

4. On African praise for Nembula's accomplishments, see, for example, *Imvo Zabantsundu*, 7 May 1889 and 9 February 1888. The medical missionary was Burt Bridgman. Nembula caught the fancy of a racehorse owner, who, in the late 1890s, ran a horse named Dr. Nembula. Other horses with South African–derived names, such as Kaffir Prince, Prince Zulu, and Pondoland, competed in races during that era.

5. Heather Hughes, "Doubly Elite: Exploring the Life of John Langalibalele Dube," *Journal of Southern African Studies* 27, no. 3 (September 2001): 445–58.

6. Plans to establish a liberal arts college to train African male pastors and a women's college modeled after Mount Holyoke were unfulfilled, as both institutions became only middle schools. R. Hunt Davis Jr., "John L. Dube: A South African Exponent of Booker T. Washington," *Journal of African Studies* 1, no. 2 (1975): 504.

7. Etherington states that Amanzimtoti taught "advanced arithmetic, biblical and secular history, geography, zoology, English grammar and reading in English and Zulu." Cape Colony governor George Grey imported the industrial education model, which had spread throughout the British Empire, to South Africa in 1855, after having done similar work among New Zealand's Maori peoples. Etherington, *Preachers, Peasants and Politics*, 28–29, 130; Myra Dinnerstein, "The American Board Mission to the Zulu, 1835–1910" (PhD diss., Columbia University, 1971), 8; Etherington, "Mission Station Melting Pots as a Factor in the Rise of South African Black Nationalism," *International Journal of African Historical Studies* 9, no. 4 (1976): 594.

8. John Dube, *The Zulu's Appeal for Light and England's Duty* (London: Evans Bros., 1910), 27–28.

9. William Wilcox, "The Booker Washington of South Africa," *Oberlin Alumni Magazine*, March 1927, in Wilcox Papers, Oberlin College Archives, Oberlin, OH; John Dube, *A Familiar Talk upon My Native Land and Some Things Found There* (Rochester, NY: R. M. Swinburne and Co., 1892), in Oberlin College Library Special Collections, Oberlin, OH. The Chautauqua circuit was designed to expose rural Americans to the important political and socioeconomic questions of the day in the form of multiday lectures, debates, community discussions, and forms of entertainment. Begun in rural New York in the late nineteenth century, the Chautauqua circuits spread throughout the United States, reaching their peak of popularity in the 1920s.

10. In 1892, the Cape Colony used the Mississippi legislation to disenfranchise virtually all Africans. In Natal by 1900, there were only 280 enfranchised Africans and Indians in a total electorate of 9,300. President Cleveland vetoed the U.S. Immigration Restriction Act.

11. The American Board's control mirrored colonial policies that segregated Africans, restricted their movements and landownership opportunities, denied them the franchise (except in the British Cape Colony), and ruled them as lesser "tribes." Lindley was to supervise the Inanda mission and the surrounding land reserves, which the Natal government had earlier reserved as part of mission land for the Qadi peoples, Dube's relatives. Because Lindley and the non-Christian Qadi chief Mqhawe had an amicable relationship, the question of control of the land had not become an issue. Pixley, however, employed the Native Administration Act of 1875 to extend American Board authority over Mqhawe and the Qadi. The Natal secretary for native affairs at the time, Theopolis Shepstone, enacted the segregationist policies; the act had made easier the indirect rule of Africans by white magistrates appointed to oversee African chiefs and headmen who had, in turn, been appointed by the government to administer and enforce colonial law. Amakholwa, who were classified as tribes in the act, became subject to a separate and subordinate governing structure, and Pixley acted as the magistrate of the Inanda mission station.

12. W. Manning Marable, "African Nationalist: The Life of John Langalibalele Dube" (PhD diss., University of Michigan, 1976), 82–83. After James Dube's death in 1878, Pixley appointed a headman, Klaas Goba, not an ordained clergyman, to

lead the amakholwa at Inanda. With Goba's own assertion about being "chief" bolstered by the Natal Code of 1891, he claimed authority over the entire mission reserve, including the lands controlled by Mqhawe and the Qadi since 1856. From the 1890s, colonial laws banned chiefs from distributing land without the permission of magistrates, and Pixley undermined Mqhawe's authority by offering his lands to new American Board converts who acknowledged Goba as their chief. See Hughes, "Doubly Elite," 457.

13. Hughes, "Doubly Elite," 457. In this regard, they were like other Africans establishing their own "Ethiopian" churches and schools, for example, Samungu Shibe and his Zulu Congregational Church in 1896.

14. Marable, "African Nationalist," 33.

15. *Montgomery Advertiser*, 28 May 1897; *Birmingham News*, 28 May 1897, cited in W. Manning Marable, "Booker T. Washington and African Nationalism," *Phylon* 35, no. 4 (1974): 401.

16. John Dube, "Need of Industrial Education in Africa," *Southern Workman* 27 (July 1897): 141–42, in Hampton University Archives, Hampton, VA.

17. Robert Norrell, *Up from History: The Life of Booker T. Washington* (Cambridge, MA: Harvard University Press, 2009), 30.

18. James Campbell, "Models and Metaphors: Industrial Education in the United States and South Africa," in *Comparative Perspectives on South Africa*, ed. Ran Greenstein, 96–97 (New York: St. Martin's Press, 1998); Armstrong attended Williams College, whose earlier graduates had founded the American Board, which Williams continued to maintain.

19. Booker T. Washington, *Up from Slavery* (Garden City, NY: Doubleday, 1963); Louis Harlan, *Booker T. Washington: The Making of a Black Leader, 1856–1901* (New York: Oxford University Press, 1975); Harlan, *The Wizard of Tuskegee, 1901–1915* (New York: Oxford University Press, 1983); and Norrell, *Up from History*. Members of the African American community in Franklin County had organized their own schools. After graduation, Washington had returned to Hampton to train Native Americans captured in Indian wars in the West. He was selected based on the assumption that black Americans, schooled in the civilizing mechanisms of slavery and Hampton industrial education, were well positioned to transmit civilization to persons supposedly more backward than themselves. African Americans could not be a vanguard for the uplift of other "backward peoples." Thus, Washington's tutelage of Native Americans was a precursor to his later interest in extending the Hampton-Tuskegee educational model to Africa.

20. Norrell, *Up from History*, 8, 154, 167.

21. For increasing literacy rates for blacks in the South, see James Anderson, *The Education of Blacks in the South, 1865–1900* (Champaign: University of Illinois Press, 1988); for increased landownership among black farmers, see Edward Ayers, *The Promise of the New South: Life after Reconstruction* (New York: Oxford University Press, 1992).

22. Norrell, *Up from History*, 3, 132, 275.

23. Ibid., 210–37. For a comprehensive account of the horrors of Jim Crow for African Americans, see Leon Litwack, *Trouble in Mind: Black Southerners in the Age of Jim Crow* (New York: Vintage Press, 1999).

24. *Imvo Zabantsundu*, 8 July 1903; Soga to Washington, 9 December 1903, container 235, Booker T. Washington Papers, Library of Congress, Washington, D.C.

25. Marable, "Booker T. Washington," 400; Davis, "John L. Dube," 501.

26. Booker T. Washington, *The Story of the Negro: The Rise of the Race from Slavery* (1909; repr., New York: Negro Universities Press, 1969).

27. John Dube, "A Zulu's Message to Afro-Americans," typescript, John Bruce Papers, Schomburg Center for Research in Black Culture, New York Public Library, New York.

28. John Dube, "Are Negroes Better Off in Africa? Conditions and Opportunities of Negroes in America and Africa Compared," *Missionary Review of the World* 27 (August 1904): 583–86; Report re "John Dube" of Inanda Mission Station, Chief Commissioner of Police, 13 December 1902, file 1/4/12, C6/1903, South African Government Archives, Pietermaritzburg, South Africa; Hughes, "Doubly Elite," 457. In 1897, during his second American sojourn, he placed Charles at Wilberforce College, affiliated with the African Methodist Episcopal Church, newly engaged in South African mission work. Other students placed in American colleges and universities by Dube included John Mdima, his brother-in-law, Mqhawe's son and heir Mandlakayise, Mabhelubhelu, and Qandyana, and Pixley and Lindley Seme.

29. Joseph Booth, *Africa for the African* (1897; repr., Lilongwe, Malawi: Kachere Press, 1996), 14.

30. For Booth's remarkable life, see the scholarly biography by his grandson Harry Langworthy, *Africa for the African: The Life of Joseph Booth* (Blantyre: Christian Literature Association in Malawi, 1996).

31. Though the careful and discreet Washington rarely attached his name publicly to such anticolonial projects, he expressed cautious support for Booth's plans over several years of friendly correspondence.

32. Booth, *Africa for the African*; *Imvo Neliso Lomzi*, 1 October 1896.

33. Dube, *Zulu's Appeal*, 20.

34. Richard Elphick, "Evangelical Missions and Racial Equalization in South Africa, 1890–1914," in *Converting Colonialism: Visions and Realities in Mission History, 1706–1914*, ed. Dana L. Robert (Cambridge, UK: William Eermans, 2008), 112–33. In a 1904 poll, 38 of 45 white men who expressed an opinion on the subject of African education expressed open hostility to the idea. During SANAC hearings that same year, only 37.7 percent of white officials of the African administration and 13.3 percent of white farmers expressed the opinion that education benefited Africans; Davis, "John L. Dube," 517. The American Board was part of an evangelizing process that produced an estimated 322,763 black Protestants, educating 175,747 black children in Protestant schools and 14,206 in Catholic schools in 1911.

35. Davis, "John L. Dube," 76.

36. Marable, "African Nationalist," 136. When Dube established Ohlange, there were "182 state-aided African schools that had an enrollment of 10,725 students and received government grants totaling 5,659 pounds."

37. Ibid., 108.

38. Editorial, 25 December 1903, and editorial, 20 May 1904, *Ilanga lase Natal*. See also editorial, *New York Age*, 1 February 1912. Dube worked closely with black American missionary Simon Crutcher, of the Gospel Workers of the World, which was known as the "Black Moody" after Dwight Moody, a popular white American evangelist. Blackburn was at Ohlange from 1912 to 1915.

39. Editorial, *Ilanga lase Natal*, 25 December 1903.

40. Andre Odendaal, *Vukani Bantu! The Beginnings of Black Protest Politics in South Africa to 1912* (Cape Town: David Philip, 1984), 30.

41. G. B. Pyrah, *Imperial Policy and South Africa, 1902–1910* (Oxford: Clarendon Press, 1955), 91.

42. In 1868, the British annexed Basutoland. Ten years later, after nine wars, the British subdued the Xhosa. By 1894, they had annexed all of the Transkeian territories. In 1879, the British defeated the Pedi and the Zulu, and in 1885, they claimed Bechuanaland as a protectorate.

43. W. Keith Hancock, *Smuts*, vol. 1, *The Sanguine Years, 1870–1919* (Cambridge: Cambridge University Press, 1962), 148–49.

44. Milner to Asquith, 18 November 1897, in Herman Giliomee, *The Afrikaners: Biography of a People* (Charlottesville: University of Virginia Press, 2003), 261; George Fredrickson, *White Supremacy: A Comparative Study in American and South African History* (New York: Oxford University Press, 1981).

45. Saul Dubow, "The Elaboration of Segregation Discourse in the Inter-war Years," in *Segregation and Apartheid in Twentieth-Century South Africa*, ed. William Beinart and Saul Dubow, 148–49 (London: Routledge, 1995).

46. Alfred Milner, *The Nation and the Empire: A Collection of Speeches and Addresses* (London: Constable Press, 1913), 296–97.

47. Ntongela Masilela, *The Cultural Modernity of H. I. E. Dhlomo* (Trenton, NJ: Africa World, 2007), 100.

48. Shula Marks, *Reluctant Rebellion: The 1906–8 Disturbances in Natal* (New York: Oxford University Press, 1970), 75. Dube's exemption from native law was one reason authorities who complained about his Ethiopianism restrained themselves, on advice from the attorney general.

49. Odendaal, *Vukani Bantu!*, 119.

50. Resolutions of the South African Native Congress, 10 April 1906, in the *Aborigines' Friend*, reprinted in *From Protest to Challenge: A Documentary History of African Politics in South Africa*, ed. Thomas Karis and Gwendolen M. Carter, vol. 1: *Protest and Hope* (Stanford, CA: Hoover Institution Press, 1972), 46–48.

51. Resolutions of the South African Native Convention, 24–26 March 1909, in *Izwi Labantu*, reprinted in Karis and Carter, *Protest and Hope*, 53.

52. House of Commons Debates, 5th ser., vol. 9 (1909), colls. 966–67, 1001–2, 1025.

53. The land division for Africans by province was: Transvaal, 3.5 percent; Natal, 29.7 percent; the Orange Free State, 0.5 percent; and the Cape, 7.5 percent. The act was invalidated in the Cape, since land restrictions interfered with property requirements for the franchise for Africans. The 1936 Natives Representation Act disenfranchised Africans in the Cape in exchange for 6 percent more land.

For contemporary views of the devastating effects of the Natives Land Act, see Sol Plaatje, *Native Life in South Africa* (New York: Negro Universities Press, 1969). For historical accounts, see generally Tim Keegan, *Rural Transformations in Industrializing Southern Africa: The Southern Highveld to 1914* (New York: Macmillan, 1987); Keegan, *Facing the Storm: Portraits of Black Lives in Rural South Africa* (Athens: Ohio University Press, 1988); Marian Lacy, *Working for Boroko: The Origins of a Coercive Labor System in South Africa* (Johannesburg: Ravan Press, 1981); and Charles Van Onselen, *The Seed Is Mine: The Life of Kas Maine, a South African Sharecropper, 1894–1985* (New York: Hill and Wang, 1999).

54. Silas Molema, *The Bantu Past and Present: An Ethnographical and Historical Study of the Native Races of South Africa* (Edinburgh: W. Green and Son, 1920), 245, 259.

55. Hughes, "Doubly Elite," 457. Dube placed several Zulu students also, including Isaac (Pixley) Seme, his cousin and future cofounder of the ANC. Dube paid half of Seme's $100 school fees, a considerable sum in 1897; despite his difficulties with Dube, Pixley paid the other half and convinced associates to pay the fees in succeeding years. Seme expressed his gratitude by changing his first name from Isaac to Pixley. Seme graduated from Mount Hermon in 1902, and his brother attended South Carolina's Benedict College.

56. Pixley Seme, "The Regeneration of Africa," in *African Abroad*, 5 April 1906, reprinted in Karis and Carter, *Protest and Hope*, 69–71. Seme's romantic rhetoric contrasted with his observations of African Americans made to James Stuart in 1925: "Negroes of America are like balls blown up, by which he means that they have no definite status of their own, but are content merely aping the white man, dressing and behaving like him. Having lost their own peculiar traditions and customs, they have become like parasites. Natives of South Africa, on the other hand, are respected for what they are, what they retain of the natural mode of life inherited from a far-off past." See Colin de B. Webb and John B. Wright, eds., *The James Stuart Archive*, vol. 5 (Pietermaritzburg: University of Natal Press, 1979), 276.

57. Seme to Washington, 29 January 1907, in *The Booker T. Washington Papers*, ed. Louis Harlan and Raymond Smock, vol. 9 (Champaign: University of Illinois Press, 1980), 204–5; Mary Benson, *The African Patriots: The Story of the African National Congress of South Africa* (London: Faber and Faber, 1963), 33.

58. Pixley Seme, "Native Union," *Imvo Zabantsundu*, 24 October 1911.

59. Peter Walshe, *The Rise of African Nationalism in South Africa: The African National Congress, 1912–1952* (Berkeley: University of California Press, 1971), 34.

60. Odendaal, *Vukani Bantu!*, 273.

61. Dube, *Zulu's Appeal.*

62. Selby Ngcobo, interview by Davis, quoted in Davis, "John L. Dube," 498n2.

63. Dube to "Chiefs and Gentlemen of the South African Native Congress," 2 February 1912, S 18, D 2/3, Anti-Slavery and Aborigines Protection Society (hereafter cited as APS) Papers, Rhodes House, Oxford University, Oxford, UK.

64. Walshe, *Rise of African Nationalism*, 38–39.

65. Ibid., 45; Dube to Buxton 24 October 1913, S 22, G 203, APS Papers.

66. "Petition to King George V, from the South African Native National Congress, July 20, 1914," reprinted in Karis and Carter, *Protest and Hope*, 125–30; "An Appeal to the Members of the Imperial Parliament and Public of Great Britain," in Karis and Carter, *Protest and Hope*, 130–33.

67. Walshe, *Rise of African Nationalism*, 62; Norman Clothier, *Black Valour: The South African Native Labour Contingent, 1916–1918, and the Sinking of the Mendi* (Pietermaritzburg: University of Natal Press, 1987), 865. Africans lost their lives in World War I, including 615 when the troop supply ship *Mendi* sank off the English coast.

68. Brian Willan, *Sol Plaatje: South African Nationalist, 1876–1932* (Berkeley: University of California Press, 1984), 228.

69. Karis and Carter, *Protest and Hope*, 140.

70. Martin Chanock, *Unconsummated Union: Britain, Rhodesia, and South Africa, 1900–1945* (Manchester, UK: Manchester University Press, 1977), 132.

71. Dube also cofounded the Natal Native Congress in 1901, and after his ouster as SANNC president in 1917, he was the guiding force in this provincial organization until his death in 1946.

72. *Natal Witness*, 13 February 1928, quoted in Shula Marks, *The Ambiguities of Dependence: Class, Nationalism, and the State in Twentieth-Century Natal* (Johannesburg: Ravan Press, 1986), 50.

73. "Petition to King George V, from the South African Native National Congress, 16 December 1918," reprinted in Karis and Carter, *Protest and Hope*, 137–42.

CHAPTER 3: THE RISE OF MARCUS GARVEY AND HIS GOSPEL OF
GARVEYISM IN SOUTHERN AFRICA

1. For earlier scholarship on Garveyism in southern Africa, see Robert Trent Vinson, "In the Time of the Americans: Garveyism in Segregationist South Africa, 1920–1940" (PhD diss., Howard University, 2001); Robert R. Edgar, "Garveyism in Africa: Dr. Wellington and the American Movement in the Transkei," *Ufahamu* 6, no. 3 (Spring 1976): 31–57; Robert A. Hill and Gregory A. Pirio, "Africa for the Africans: The Garvey Movement in South Africa, 1920–1940," in *The Politics of Race, Class and Nationalism in Twentieth-Century South Africa*, ed. Shula Marks and Stanley Trapido, 209–53 (New York: Longman, 1987); and Michael O. West, "Seeds Are Sown: The Garvey Movement in Zimbabwe in the Interwar Years," *International Journal of African Historical Studies* 35, nos. 2–3 (2003): 335–62. There were eight UNIA chapters in South Africa, chartered from UNIA headquarters in New York; at least sixteen others were organized under the UNIA banner but had no official affiliation. Chartered UNIA chapters in the Cape Town area included Cape Town, Woodstock, Claremont, West London (present-day Athlone), and Goodwood-Parow. Chartered UNIA chapters in the Pretoria-Johannesburg area included Pretoria and Evaton, Johannesburg, and additional chapters in this area were in Sophiatown and Waterpan. There was one unchartered UNIA chapter in Vrede, Orange Free State. The majority of unchartered UNIA chapters were clustered in the rural former Transkei region of South Africa, including Ramlani, Mount Frere, Matatiele, Qumbu, Tsolo, Mt. Fletcher, Libode, Jokie, Kowe,

Nqamakwe, Engcobo, Maclear, Xalanga. Most of these chapters were organized under the Wellington movement, discussed in chapter 5. In neighboring Southwest Africa (present-day Namibia) there were two chartered chapters in Luderitz and Windhoek and one chartered UNIA chapter in Basutoland (present-day Lesotho).

2. Mary G. Rolinson, *Grassroots Garveyism: The Universal Negro Improvement Association in the Rural South, 1920–1927* (Chapel Hill: University of North Carolina Press, 2007), 3.

3. Lawrence Levine, "Marcus Garvey and the Politics of Revitalization," in *Black Leaders of the Twentieth Century*, ed. John Hope Franklin and August Meier, 106–9 (Champaign: University of Illinois Press, 1982).

4. Garvey's formal education ended at Standard Six.

5. Rupert Lewis, *Marcus Garvey: Anti-colonial Champion* (London: Karia Press, 1987), 21, 23–24.

6. Garvey publicized these conditions in *La Prensa*, another of his newspapers. See also Winston James, *Holding Aloft the Banner of Ethiopia: Caribbean Radicalism in Early Twentieth-Century America* (New York: Verso Press, 1998), 15; Elizabeth Thomas-Hope, *Explanation in Caribbean Migration: Perception and Image—Jamaica, Barbados, St. Vincent* (London: Macmillan, 1992); and Barry B. Levine, ed., *The Caribbean Exodus* (New York: Praeger Books, 1987). Also see Amy Jacques Garvey, *Garvey and Garveyism* (New York: Atheneum, 1969), 7. Some 146,000 black Jamaicans—limited by lack of access to sustainable landownership, rampant unemployment, low wages, and racial discrimination—left the island between 1881 and 1921. They represented more than half of all Caribbean migrants during that period.

7. Marcus Garvey, "The British West Indies in the Mirror of Civilization: History Making by Colonial Negroes," *African Times and Orient Review* 2 (October 1913): 158–60, reprinted in Robert A. Hill, ed., *The Marcus Garvey and Universal Negro Improvement Association Papers* (Berkeley: University of California Press, 1983–), 1:27–33.

8. Marcus Garvey, "The Negro's Greatest Enemy," *Current History Magazine* (September 1923), reprinted in Amy Jacques Garvey, ed., *Philosophy and Opinions of Marcus Garvey* (New York: Atheneum, 1992), 2:126.

9. "Address by Marcus Garvey," *Daily Chronicle*, 26 August 1915, in Hill, *Garvey Papers*, 1:134.

10. Marcus Garvey, "A Talk with Afro-West Indians: The Negro Race and Its Problems," July–August 1914, in Hill, *Garvey Papers*, 1:55–64. The references to imperialism in the ACL title suggest a desire to replicate the European imperialism criticized by future black rivals like socialists Hubert Harrison and A. Philip Randolph and communists like Cyril Briggs.

11. "UNIA Memorial Meeting for Booker T. Washington," *Daily Chronicle*, 24 November 1915, in Hill, *Garvey Papers*, 1:166.

12. Ibrahim Sundiata, *Brothers and Strangers: Black Zion, Black Slavery, 1914–1940* (Durham, NC: Duke University Press, 2003), 18.

13. Marcus Garvey, "West Indies in the Mirror of Truth," *Century Magazine*, January 1917, reprinted in John H. Clarke, ed., *Marcus Garvey and the Vision of Africa* (New York: Vintage Books, 1974), 89–91.

14. Born in 1883 in St. Croix, Danish West Indies, an orphaned Harrison went to New York in 1900, where he finished at the top of his high school class despite working full-time. He eventually found work as both a postman and a writer for the *New York Times*. In 1910, however, Washington retaliated for articles that were critical of the Wizard by using his considerable connections to engineer Harrison's dismissal. Harrison then became a leading organizer in the Socialist Party, working closely with "Big Bill" Haywood, Elizabeth Gurley Flynn, and others in the International Workers of the World, particularly during the Paterson silk strike of 1913. Harrison initiated the storied Harlem tradition of delivering political speeches from street corner stepladders, a local variant of the People's Parliament in London's Hyde Park. For Harrison's compelling life, see Jeffrey B. Perry, *Hubert Harrison: The Voice of Harlem Radicalism, 1883–1918* (New York: Columbia University Press, 2009).

15. W. A. Domingo, interview by Theodore Draper, 18 January 1958, New York, preliminary listing as box 20, folder 7, "Negro Question for Vol. 1 (cont.)," notes re W. A. Domingo, Theodore Draper Papers, Robert W. Woodruff Library for Advanced Studies, Emory University, Atlanta, GA; Amy Ashwood, "First Amy Tells All, Portrait of a Liberator," manuscript, 3, quoted in Colin Grant, *Negro with a Hat: The Rise and Fall of Marcus Garvey* (New York: Oxford University Press, 2008), 185.

16. Marcus Garvey, "The Conspiracy of the East St. Louis Riots," speech delivered at Lafayette Hall, NY, 8 July 1917, reprinted in Hill, *Garvey Papers*, 1:212–20.

17. W. E. B. Du Bois, "Close Ranks," *Crisis* 16 (July 1918): 111. Despite criticism regarding his position from prominent blacks like A. Phillip Randolph, Chandler Owen, and Cyril Briggs, Du Bois maintained his stance throughout the war. See the *Crisis* articles entitled "A Philosophy in Time of War" and "Our Special Grievances," published in August and September 1917. For racial discrimination overseas, see Bernard Nalty, *Strength for the Fight: A History of Black Americans in the Military* (New York: Free Press, 1986), 101–24.

18. "Marcus Garvey at the Bar of United States Justice," Associated Negro Press (c. early July 1923): 2-4; reprinted in Jeffrey B. Perry, ed., *A Hubert Harrison Reader* (Middletown, CT: Wesleyan Press, 2001), 196–97. See also Perry, *Hubert Harrison: The Voice of Harlem Radicalism*.

19. Garvey, "Conspiracy of the East St. Louis Riots"; James, *Holding Aloft*, 95; Malcolm McLaughlin, "Reconsidering the East St. Louis Race Riot of 1917," *International Review of Social History* 47, no. 2 (August 2002): 187–212.

20. *UNIA Declaration of Rights of the Negro Peoples of the World*, 13 August 1920, reprinted in Hill, *Garvey Papers*, 2:571–80.

21. Interview of Julius Wright by Stanley Nelson, *Look for Me in the Whirlwind*, PBS, 2001, available on DVD.

22. Liberia was one of three independent black states, but Haiti was not in Africa and was effectively occupied by the United States and Ethiopia was a remote, arid, and feudal society located in the Horn of Africa, far from the ancestral home of most diasporic blacks in west and west-central Africa.

23. Hill, *Garvey Papers*, 2:128.

24. Ibid., 4:12.

25. Hubert Harrison, "The Negro and the War," in *When Africa Awakes*, ed. Hubert Harrison, 25–38 (Baltimore, MD: Black Classic Press, 1997); W. E. B. Du Bois, "The African Roots of War," *Atlantic Monthly*, May 1915, 707–14; R. Walter to Viscount Milner, 31 July 1919, Colonial Office, file 123/295, Public Records Office, London (Walter is quoting from the *Negro World*, 26 October 1918).

26. Quoted in Rolinson, *Grassroots Garveyism*, 5; "Bureau of Investigation Reports," 5 December 1918, in Hill, *Garvey Papers*, 1:305; Ida B. Wells, *Crusade for Justice: The Autobiography of Ida B. Wells* (Chicago: University of Chicago Press, 1991), 379.

27. *Negro World*, 5 November 1921.

28. As a young man, Plaatje had seen the Virginia Jubilee Singers, thus beginning a lifelong engagement with American Negroes.

29. See "Negro Martyrs," *Negro World*, 7 January 1922; "South African Natives Alive to Interests," *Negro World*, 2 August 1924; H. D. Tyamzashe, "South Africa's Native Question Discussed by a Man on the Spot," *Negro World*, 12 November 1927; and Edwin Mofutsanyana, "South Africa," *Negro World*, 3 June 1933.

30. Grant, *Negro with a Hat*, 198.

31. *Garvey v. United States*, 8317 (2d Circuit 1925), Government's Exhibit 1, reprinted in Hill, *Garvey Papers*, 441–44; Hill, *Garvey Papers*, 2:xxxi. Between July 1919 and February 1922, the Black Star Line sold nearly 153,026 shares of stock at $5 per share to roughly 35,000 stockholders and raised a total of $756,130. Of course, there were many other attempts to create a black-owned shipping line, dating back to Paul Cuffe and most recently Chief Sam and Prince U. Kaba Rega, but Garvey transcended all because he had a propaganda organ in the *Negro World*, a stock investment option, and his own charisma and magnetism. These moneys allowed the organization to acquire the cargo ship *Yarmouth*, promptly renamed the *Frederick Douglass*; the excursion vessel SS *Shadyside*; and the SS *Kanawha*, renamed the *Antonio Maceo*. The *Frederick Douglass* made two trips to the Caribbean, the *Shadyside* ran excursions around Manhattan Island, and the *Kanawha* was a converted yacht.

32. Grace Jordan McFadden, "Septima P. Clark and the Struggle for Human Rights," in *Women in the Civil Rights Movement: Trailblazers and Torchbearers, 1941–1965*, ed. Vicki L. Crawford and Jacqueline A. Rouse, 87 (Bloomington: Indiana University Press, 1993).

33. Theodore Kornweibel, *"Seeing Red": Federal Campaigns against Black Militancy* (Bloomington: Indiana University Press, 1998), 112.

34. W. E. B. Du Bois, "Marcus Garvey," *Crisis* 21, no. 2 (December 1920): 57–60, and no. 3 (January 1921): 112–15.

35. The *Negro World* was also the most consistent source of revenue for the UNIA.

36. Edmund David Cronon, *Black Moses: The Story of Marcus Garvey and the Universal Negro Improvement Association* (Madison: University of Wisconsin Press, 1955), xvii; C. L. R. James, *The Black Jacobins* (New York: Random House, 1963), 397.

37. Grant, *Negro with a Hat*, 137.

38. *New York Times*, 2 August 1924.

39. Grant, *Negro with a Hat*, 174.

40. In addition to being the sites of most UNIA events, Liberty Halls served as multipurpose community centers that temporarily sheltered the homeless, fed the hungry, helped the unemployed find work, offered educational classes, and hosted dances and concerts.

41. L. Levine, "Marcus Garvey," 131.

42. *New York Times*, 2 August and 4 August 1924; Rolinson, *Grassroots Garveyism*, 156; and "Report of the Convention," in Hill, *Garvey Papers*, 2:644–45. Some Garveyites also saw in Garvey a reincarnation of the Old Testament prophet Ezekiel, the long-suffering messenger of God who told oppressed Israelites in Babylon that their God had allowed their subjugation because of their sins but had not abandoned them and would soon deliver them into their own homeland. UNIA officials took an oath on a Bible to uphold the values and objectives of the UNIA and the Declaration of Rights.

43. "Report of the Convention," 2:614; *Negro World*, 28 August 1920.

44. Hill, *Garvey Papers*, 2:457; *Negro World*, 8 May 1920.

45. William Pickens, *Nation*, 28 December 1921.

46. Rolinson, *Grassroots Garveyism*, 3.

47. See ibid., 95. The UNIA headquarters took advantage of the explosive growth of the UNIA by allowing formation of UNIA divisions that did not meet every official requirement for membership.

48. For Pelem, see Thomas Karis and Gwendolyn M. Carter, eds., *From Protest to Challenge: A Documentary History of African Politics in South Africa*, vol. 2: *Hope and Challenge, 1935–1952* (Stanford, CA: Hoover Institution Press, 1973), 102; see also Silas Molema, *The Bantu Past and Present: An Ethnographical and Historical Study of the Native Races of South Africa* (Edinburgh: W. Green and Son, 1920), 352, and W. E. B. Du Bois, *Darkwater: Voices from within the Veil* (New York: Harcourt, Brace and Howe, 1920), 49–50, 60.

49. Secretary for Justice to Secretary for the Interior, 18 October 1920, Interior Department, Reports on Bolshevism, Department of Native Affairs (NTS) 168/74B, vol. 2, file 7/168/74, NASA.

50. Affidavit of "Golifili" to Kentani Assistant Magistrate, 14 December 1920, 1/KNT, box 40, file N1/9/2, Cape Province Depot (hereafter cited as CA), NASA.

51. Secretary for Justice to Secretary for the Interior, 18 October 1920, Interior Department, Reports on Bolshevism, NTS 168/74B, vol. 2, file 7/168/74, NASA.

52. Hill and Pirio, "Africa for the Africans," 211.

53. Josiel Lefela, article excerpt, *Naledi*, 18 November 1921, found in Colonial Office Records, Public Records Office, London (England), 417/665/02597.

54. Jan Smuts quoted in the *Cape Argus*, reprinted in *Negro World*, 27 December 1924.

55. *Negro World*, December 15, 1922; Hill and Pirio, "Africa for the Africans," 225.

56. *Cape Argus*, 29 January 1923.

57. H. Selby Msimang quoted in *Umteteli wa Bantu*, 13 August 1921.

58. Robert Trent Vinson, "'Sea Kaffirs': American Negroes and the Gospel of Garveyism in Segregationist South Africa," *Journal of African History* 47, no. 2 (July 2006): 281–303.

59. The conference report protested the treatment of disenfranchised African migrant workers exploited in the gold and diamond mines and "sacrificed to the greed of gold, their liberties taken away, their family life debauched." See *Report of the Pan-African Conference, held on the 23rd, 24th, and 25th July, 1900, at Westminster Town Hall*, Westminster S.W. London (London: n.p., 1900), 10–12.

60. *Cape Argus*, 26 August 1904, in National Library of South Africa, Cape Town.

61. *Cape Argus*, 26 August 1904. For more on Williams's South African sojourn, see Christopher Saunders, "Henry Sylvester Williams in South Africa," *Quarterly Bulletin of the National Library of South Africa* 55, no. 4 (2001); James Hooker, *Henry Sylvester Williams, Imperial Pan-Africanist* (London: Collings, 1975); and Owen Mathurin, *Henry Sylvester Williams and the Origins of the Pan-African Movement, 1869–1911* (Westport, CT: Greenwood Press, 1976). Upon his return to London, Williams also represented the Transvaal Native Congress, BaSotho chiefs, and other groups in land disputes; hosted visiting South Africans like Walter Rubusana and Josiah Gumede; and likely mentored Pixley Seme and Alfred Mangena, two African law students who became founding members of the ANC.

62. Mathurin, *Henry Sylvester Williams*, 118.

63. Levi Coppin, *Observations of Persons and Things in South Africa, 1900–1904* (Philadelphia: A.M.E. Book Concern, n.d.); James Campbell, *Songs of Zion: The African Methodist Episcopal Church in the United States and South Africa* (New York: Oxford University Press, 1995), 234–35. Over time, the Woodings clashed with the Cape Education Board that maintained authority over the school; eventually, they moved to Newark, New Jersey. See also Mathurin, *Henry Sylvester Williams*, 113; Mohamed Adhikari, "Voice of the Coloured Elite: APO, 1909–1923," in *South Africa's Alternative Press: Voices of Protest and Resistance, 1880s–1960s*, ed. Les Switzer (New York: Cambridge University Press, 1997), 127–46.

64. After his return to England, Williams unsuccessfully sought election in the British Commons. He had hoped to represent black South African interests within the British Parliament; instead, he became a de facto representative and lobbyist for the Transvaal Native Congress, protesting bans on African landownership and BaSotho chief Lerotholi who wanted lands illegally seized by Afrikaners to be returned to his people. Williams also maintained relationships with Pixley Seme and Alfred Mangena and with Josiah Gumede, founding member of the ANC and its future president-general.

65. Unfortunately, there are few surviving copies of *Abantu-Batho*, the ANC newspaper, and the ICU's *Workers Herald*; consequently, the chronicling of ANC and ICU activities in the *Negro World* becomes even more significant.

66. *African World*, 3 May 1925.

67. *Negro World*, 14 June 1924 and 1 November 1930. Rufus Letsaolo, the West London division president, expresses similar sentiments.

68. *Negro World*, 20 November 1926.

69. *Negro World*, 14 June 1924.

70. D. Lyner, interview by the author, 10 July 1998; *Black Man*, August 1920. It is unclear exactly when the Cape Town UNIA branch began; its members helped organize the Claremont chapter in February 1922. *Negro World*, 18 March 1922. H. L. Davids, who succeeded Robertson as president of the Goodwood division, also helped to establish the Cape Town UNIA and was the first speaker at the UNIA charter unveiling of the West London branch. *Negro World*, 8 November 1924. This chapter's actual location was probably in the now razed District Six section of Cape Town. The western section of Cape Town was razed by the apartheid government during the 1960s and 1970s, but at that time, many West Indians also lived in the polyglot District Six along with Coloureds, Africans, whites, and foreigners.

71. See, for example, *Negro World*, 22 July 1922 and 8 November 1924. It is also possible that William Chaswell, the division's treasurer and musical director, was of Caribbean origin as well. West Indian officers included William Jackson (president), J. Caesar Allen (general secretary), Arthur Emile Wattlington (secretary), and James Gumbs (advisory board).

72. One example is in *Negro World*, 27 January 1923.

73. Monthly Police Report, 11 August 1922, Department of Interior, NTS, file 3/1064/18, NASA.

74. *Guardian*, 25 July 1940. There is scant evidence for the ethnic composition of the membership, although a Colored man named "Brother Jantjes" was a prominent member. *Negro World*, 29 November 1924.

75. J. J. Samuels was president, a Mrs. W. Samuels was treasurer and secretary, and a Rev. Schuman was the division chaplain. *Negro World*, 8 November 1924. Claremont, the founding place of the APO, was predominantly Colored; Woodstock was mostly working-class Colored; West London (present-day Rondebosch) was also primarily Coloured, and suburban Goodwood and Parow became increasingly white by the 1940s. See John Western, *Outcast Cape Town* (Minneapolis: University of Minnesota Press, 1981), 71.

76. *Negro World*, 13 February 1926. Johnson was en route to South America.

77. In addition to the Cape Town UNIA chapters, there were also chapters in Pretoria, Evaton, and New Clare. UNIA membership cards, UNIA Central Division (New York) files, Schomburg Collection, New York Public Library, New York. Though Garvey disavowed any connection to Butelezi, several of these UNIA chapters paid dues to UNIA headquarters, and their officers corresponded directly with Garvey. UNIA chapters were reported in East London and Marabastad in 1921.

78. Hill, *Garvey Papers*, 9:337. George Alexander McGuire, the UNIA's chaplain, compiled *The Universal Negro Ritual, Containing Forms, Prayers, and Offices for Use in the U.N.I.A.* in 1921. This organizational guidebook included the Universal Prayer.

79. For examples, see *Negro World*, 18 March and 4 November 1922.

80. Cape ANC meeting, 1923, NTS, file 3/1064/18, NASA.

81. *Negro World*, 3 June 1923, Governor-General files 1556, NTS no. 50/1058, NASA. The slogan "One God, One Aim, One Destiny," a UNIA invention, was on UNIA-printed material like the *Negro World*.

82. *Negro World*, 25 February 1922, 14 June 1924, and 20 June 1925.

83. *Negro World*, 20 November 1926.

84. The *Universal Negro Catechism* echoed biblical scripture. This was particularly true in the assertions that God, Jesus, and other prominent biblical characters were, at least partially, black and that God's kingdom was multiracial: "There before me was a great multitude that no one could count, from every nation, tribe, people and language, standing before the throne . . . and they cried out in a loud voice: 'salvation belongs to our God, who sits on the throne'"; see Revelation 7:9–10.

85. *Black Man*, August 1920.

86. The reference to a "Siloam Pool" was made by Cape Town UNIA vice president Richard Ndimande in a letter to the *Negro World*, 22 November 1924. The "deaf, dumb and half-dead" reference was from ANC member Nathaniel Ntengo, quoted in the *Negro World*, 23 August 1924.

87. Harry Dugmore, "Becoming a Somebody," *African Studies* 51, no. 1 (1992): 22.

88. *Negro World*, 22 July 1922 and 27 January 1923. There is virtually no extant evidence that describes the occupations of Claremont members. However, the relatively high economic status of Caribbeans, their UNIA fellows, and the purchase of musical instruments and lessons suggest there was some disposable income and/or a collective effort to save moneys for these items.

89. "AME Church and Negro Movement," *Black Man*, October 1920; "Negro Movement in America," *Black Man*, November 1920; "Glorious Africa," *Black Man*, October 1920.

90. C. Kadalie to S. Ncwana, 20 May 1920, J. S. Marwick Papers, Killie Campbell African Library, University of Natal, cited in Hill and Pirio, "Africa for the Africans," 215. Kadalie later claimed that he aggressively opposed West Indian Garveyite attempts to turn the ICU into a "UNIA auxiliary."

91. "Negro Movement in America."

92. Hill and Pirio, "Africa for the Africans," 215.

93. Peter Wickins, *The Industrial and Commercial Workers Union of South Africa* (Cape Town: David Philip, 1978), 205.

94. Alan G. Cobley, "Forgotten Connections, Unconsidered Parallels: A New Agenda for Comparative Research in Southern Africa and the Caribbean," *African Studies* 58, no. 2 (1999): 135; Clements Kadalie, *My Life and the I.C.U.: The Autobiography of a Black Trade Unionist in South Africa* (New York: Humanities Press, 1970), 220.

95. H. D. Tyamzashe, *Summarized History of the ICU*, 48, A1178–79, file B5-1941, A. L. Saffery Papers, University of the Witwatersrand, Johannesburg, South Africa.

96. Ibid., 48–49.

97. Kadalie, *My Life and the I.C.U.*, 45, 99, 220; Wickins, *Industrial and Commercial Workers Union*, 79, 114, 156; Helen Bradford, *A Taste of Freedom: The ICU in Rural South Africa, 1924–1930* (Johannesburg: Ravan Press, 1987), 126.

98. For Gumbs's organizational affiliations, see J. Mancoe, *First Edition of the Bloemfontein Bantu and Coloured People's Directory* (Bloemfontein: A.C. White, 1934), 70. For Lyner, see his membership certificates, now in the author's possession. For King, see *Black Man*, August 1920, and documents in the author's possession. For Wattlington, Jackson, and Allen, see *Negro World* issues from 12 November 1921 to 4 November 1922, as well as documents in the author's possession.

99. *Negro World*, 8 October 1921.

100. *Negro World*, 9 August 1921. Though promising to relieve Africans from harsh German rule, South Africa leaders had imported their own segregationist laws to the territory; they reserved less than 3 percent of the land in central and southern Southwest Africa for blacks, who represented 90 percent of the population. Restrictions on land, stock, and firearms; grazing fees; hefty taxes; and vagrancy laws pushed most Africans into reserves, which became, in effect, reservoirs of forced black labor for the colonial economy, especially for fisheries, meat-processing plants, and diamond mines. Africans who were compelled to live in separate locations were required to carry passes.

101. Fitz Headly to Joseph Hailand, 14 November 1922, in Hill, *Garvey Papers*, 9:684–85.

102. A copy of the UNIA petition to the League of Nations appears in Hill, *Garvey Papers*, 9:532–38.

103. *Missionblat*, February 1922, National Archives of Namibia, Windhoek, Namibia, 1851, box 396, file 13.

104. Jan-Bart Gewald, *Herero Heroes: A Socio-political History of the Herero of Namibia, 1890–1923* (Athens: Ohio University Press, 1999), 230.

105. Hill, *Garvey Papers*, 9:204.

106. Headly to Mr. Barnabas, 25 January 1922, box 50, file 32, National Archives of Namibia, Windhoek, Namibia.

CHAPTER 4: TRANSNATIONAL MARTYRDOM AND THE SPREAD OF GARVEYISM IN SOUTH AFRICA

1. Colin Grant, *Negro with a Hat: The Rise and Fall of Marcus Garvey* (New York: Oxford University Press, 2008), 229.

2. Hugh Mulzac, *A Star to Steer By* (New York: International Publishers, 1972), 79.

3. W. E. B. Du Bois, "The Black Star Line," *Crisis* 24 (September 1922): 210–14; Du Bois, "Back to Africa," *Century Magazine* 105 (February 1923): 539–48. In one particularly unfortunate instance, inexperienced Black Star Line agents accepted $11,000 from a client for a cargo run worth $100,000. Garvey's use of the line for political, instead of economic, capital was, in Mulzac's view, "a helluva way to run a steamship." Mulzac wrote a three-part article detailing the organizational and financial problems of the Black Star Line in the *Cleveland Gazette*, from 6–27 October 1923. See also Mulzac, *A Star to Steer By*, 80.

4. *Negro World*, 10 September 1921.

5. The KKK was founded in 1867 by ex-Confederate general Nathan Bedford Forrest to terrorize and intimidate blacks in order to maintain a white supremacist social order. It had been dormant since the 1880s, resurfacing in 1915 after the film *Birth of a Nation* portrayed Klan members as heroic patriots who had saved the Reconstruction South from corrupt and incompetent black rule. The KKK had killed an estimated three thousand African Americans during its existence, which made it public enemy number one among black people. For examples of southern black men murdering and assaulting white men and black women engaged in interracial sexual encounters, see Mary Rolinson, *Grassroots Garveyism: The Universal Negro Improvement Association in the Rural South, 1920–1927* (Chapel Hill: University of North Carolina Press, 2007), 139–41.

6. "Hon. Marcus Garvey Tells of Interview with Ku Klux Klan," *Negro World*, 15 July 1922.

7. McCallum's bill passed by a 3–1 vote in the state senate, but the house rejected it. See Michael W. Fitzgerald, "'We Have Found a Moses': Theodore Bilbo, Black Nationalism, and the Greater Liberia Bill of 1939," *Journal of Southern History* 63, no. 2 (May 1997): 293–320.

8. Amy J. Garvey, ed., *Philosophy and Opinions of Marcus Garvey* (New York: Atheneum, 1992), 2:339–49. After the Liberian fiasco and Garvey's imprisonment, Virginia UNIA divisions linked with white supremacists Earnest Sevier Cox and John Powell, who shared their vision of black repatriation to Africa. Cox and Powell were not dissimilar to members of the American Colonization Society a century earlier, a group dominated by white slaveholders who wanted to rid the country of free blacks and thus helped to establish Liberia. Both groups found common ground as racial nationalists whose goals included race separation and racial purity, and both also viewed miscegenation as the primary threat to the growth and survival of their respective envisioned racial nations. Garvey opposed the antilynching bill, which, had it passed, would have subjected lynchers to federal prosecution. He argued that southern law enforcement officials would not enforce it.

9. Speech of Marcus Garvey, July 14, 1921, New Orleans, Louisiana, in Robert A. Hill, ed., *The Marcus Garvey and Universal Negro Improvement Association Papers* (Berkeley: University of California Press, 1983–), 3:529–30.

10. *Negro World*, 5 August 1922; *New York Times*, 7 November 1921; *Negro World*, 22 April 1922. Garvey rationalized that any white assistance that helped UNIA members realize their African dream, even if their methods and motivations were decidedly different from those of the UNIA, was appropriate. His reasoning was influenced by nineteenth-century debates between free blacks and the American Colonization Society.

11. *New York Times*, 7 August and 21 August 1922.

12. Jeffrey B. Perry, ed., *A Hubert Harrison Reader* (Middletown, CT: Wesleyan Press, 2001), 188–91, 198.

13. W. E. B. Du Bois, "A Lunatic or a Traitor," *Crisis* 28 (May 1924): 8–9.

14. Robert Bagnall, "The Madness of Marcus Garvey," *Messenger* 5 (March 1923): 638–64.

15. Theodore Kornweibel, *No Crystal Stair: Black Life and the Messenger, 1917–1923* (Westport, CT: Greenwood Press, 1976), 149.

16. Ibrahim Sundiata, *Brothers and Strangers: Black Zion, Black Slavery, 1914–1940* (Durham, NC: Duke University Press, 2003), 248.

17. Hill, *Garvey Papers*, 5:213.

18. Lawrence Levine, "Marcus Garvey and the Politics of Revitalization," in *Black Leaders of the Twentieth Century*, ed. John Hope Franklin and August Meier, 134 (Champaign: University of Illinois Press, 1982).

19. Grant, *Negro with a Hat*, 219–20.

20. *New York Times*, 11 September 1922.

21. *New York Age*, 14 October 1922, in Hill, *Garvey Papers*, 5:48.

22. Hill, *Garvey Papers*, 5:298.

23. Theodore Kornweibel, *"Seeing Red": Federal Campaigns against Black Militancy, 1919–1925* (Bloomington: Indiana University Press, 1998), 129.

24. *New York Times*, 19 May, 22 May, and 30 May 1923.

25. *Los Angeles Times*, 22 June 1923.

26. *New York Times*, 2 July 1923. For the petitions, see *Washington Post*, 7 July 1923, 3, and 27 July 1923, 17.

27. *New York Times*, 14 September 1923.

28. For the Liberian debacle, see Sundiata, *Brothers and Strangers*. For the perjury indictment, see *New York Times*, 5 August 1924.

29. *Washington Post*, 24 March 1925.

30. *Daily Negro Times*, 20 June 1923.

31. Hubert Harrison, "Marcus Garvey at the Bar of United States Justice," *Associated Negro Press* (c. early July 1923), cited in Perry, *Hubert Harrison Reader*, 198.

32. *New York Times*, 3 December 1927.

33. *Negro World*, 30 April 1927.

34. James Weldon Johnson, *Black Manhattan* (1930; New York: Arno Press, 1968).

35. *Negro World*, 30 April 1927.

36. *Cape Argus*, 21 June 1923; *Bloemfontein Friend*, 22 June 1923, in Cape Magistrate files, box 1471, file 42 B, NASA, CT; South African Police (SAP) files, box 41, file 6/967/23, NASA, CT; Deputy Commissioner, CID to Deputy Commissioner, 2 November 1923, SAP, NASA, Pretoria.

37. Inspector, Divisional CID Witwatersrand Division to Deputy Commissioner, 13 June 1923, SAP, box 266, file 20, Witwatersrand Division, NASA, Pretoria.

38. The UNIA officials were William Ferris and Henrietta Vinton Davis.

39. Undersecretary for the Interior to the Commissioner of Police, 13 June 1923, 20/168/74, NASA; Secretary for the Interior to Postmaster General, Pretoria, 24 June 1924, NASA, Pretoria.

40. H. A. Payne to Thomas Watt, 16 November 1920, file 168/74B, vol. 2 7/168/74, Interior Department, NASA. The secretary for the interior assumed that UNIA literature came into the country through the mails and made inquiries with the postmaster general at Pretoria.

41. James Campbell, *Songs of Zion: The African Methodist Episcopal Church in the United States and South Africa* (New York: Oxford University Press, 1995), 315.

42. *Umteteli wa Bantu*, 14 August 1920; *Umteteli* article reprinted in *New York Times*, 2 October 1921; Les Switzer, ed., *South Africa's Alternative Press: Voices of Protest and Resistance, 1880s–1960s* (New York: Cambridge University Press, 1997), 33–34.

43. Nongqawuse was the teenaged Xhosa girl who claimed that ancestral spirits commanded the amaXhosa to destroy all their livestock and stored food to show faith in ancestral abilities to repel the encroaching British and ensure amaXhosa independence. Most of her people followed these instructions, and when the ancestral spirits did not come, the resultant mass starvation and societal disorder was a significant factor in eventual British conquest.

44. *Imvo Zabantsundu*, 19 July 1921 and 20 June 1922.

45. *Imvo Zabantsundu*, 20 December 1921. Aggrey was born in the Gold Coast and emigrated to the United States for education.

46. "Shaking Hands," *APO*, 26 June 1920. The column also mentioned optimistically a company headquartered in Staten Island, owned by an unnamed African prince, that marketed mahogany wood from the Gold Coast to the American market. For general praise of American Negroes, see "Negro Progress," *APO*, 30 October 1920; "A Gigantic Movement," *APO*, 2 October 1920; and "One Big Union Essential: A Lesson from America," *APO*, 30 October 1920.

47. *New York Tribune*, 18 May 1921 and 9 September 1921; *Washington Bee*, 29 October 1921; and *Crusader*, 22 October 1921.

48. *APO*, 11 February 1922.

49. *Black Man*, October 1920.

50. *Umteteli* article reprinted in *New York Times*, 2 October 1921. Garvey responded to these charges shortly thereafter. See *New York Times*, 8 October 1921; "AME Church and Negro Movement," *Black Man*, October 1920.

51. *Negro World*, 17 November 1923.

52. *Negro World*, 18 March 1922, 27 January 1923, and 21 April 1923.

53. *Negro World*, 19 June, 1923, 2 August 1924, and 29 November 1924.

54. For example, the 1 December 1923 edition of the *Negro World* reported that the Cape Town division contributed $18.12 toward Garvey's Defense Fund, and Fitzherbert Headly's $10 pledge was one of several from Namibian UNIA contributors. *Negro World*, 12 September 1925.

55. *Negro World*, 20 June 1925. In quoting Humble, I am paraphrasing Jeremiah 23:1–8.

56. *Negro World*, 2 May 1925. Headly appears to have adapted a poem by Frances Ellen Watkins Harper, "To the Cleveland Union-Savers," published in abolitionist newspapers (including the *Liberator*) in 1861; Harper's poem is reprinted in *Nineteenth-Century American Women Poets: An Anthology*, ed. Paula Bennett (Malden, MA: Blackwell, 1998), 136–37.

57. *Negro World*, 30 April 1927. For the Pretoria branch, see *Negro World*, 26 January 1929; for the Evaton branch, see *Negro World*, 22 August 1925.

58. *Negro World*, 30 May 1925.

59. *Negro World*, 2 August 1924 and 15 September 1928.

60. *Negro World*, 26 January 1929.

61. *Negro World*, 29 November 1925.

62. *Negro World*, 13 February 1926 and 30 April 1927; Commissioner of Police to Secretary of Native Affairs, 4 December 1928, SAP 74/406/28, NASA, Cape Town Archives Repository (hereafter CT), Cape Town, South Africa.

63. Memorandum of A. W. Richards, Divisional Inspector, Eastern Cape Division, to District Commandants, South African Police, Eastern Cape Division, 16 June 1928; Superintendent, Native Locations, to the Chairman and Members, Locations Committee, 3 October 1925; Detective Constable J. D. Justus to Divisional Criminal Investigation Officer, Kimberley, 14 May 1928, all in NTS 1455, file 128/214, NASA, CT.

64. *Negro World*, 18 April 1925.

65. *Negro World*, 13, 27 September 1924, 14 August 1926.

66. *Negro World*, 14 January 1922.

67. *Negro World*, 27 June 1925, 18 October 1924, 17 January 1925.

68. The Afro-Athlican Constructive Gaathly Mamatic Church Hymn Book, published in 1926, listed "the House of Athlyi, World's Headquarters" at 253 Nyembane St., Kimberley, South Africa. See Robert A. Hill, "Dread History: Leonard P. Howell and Millenarian Visions in Early Rastafari Religions in Jamaica," *Epoche: Journal of the History of Religions* 9 (1981): 30–71.

69. Richard A. Rogers, *Holy Piby: The Black Man's Bible* (Kingston: Research Associates School Times Publications, 2000), 10.

70. Ibid., 6.

71. Ibid., 54–55.

72. Ibid., 25 (emphasis added).

73. There is virtually no scholarship on Rogers, an undeservedly neglected figure in pan-Africanist historiography. The notable exception is Hill, "Dread History." The *Holy Piby* was published on 15 January 1924. It and the Reverend Fitz Ballentine Pettersburgh's *Royal Parchment Scroll of Black Supremacy* were the foundational texts of the emergent Rastafarian religion in 1930s Jamaica. According to Hill, Leonard Howell's more famous text, *The Promised Key*, plagiarized heavily from the Pettersburgh book, which was reputedly published in 1926. The text can be found online at http://www.sacred-texts.com/afr/tpk/index.htm (accessed 1 June 2011).

74. Rogers, *Holy Piby*, 9, 26–27, 30–31, 36–39, 42–46.

75. Ibid., 9–10, 14, 22.

76. Ibid., 45.

77. Ibid., 7–10, 19.

78. Ibid., 64.

79. Applications for Church Site, 20 April 1926, NTS 1455, file 128/214, NASA, CT.

80. Masogha to Secretary for Native Affairs, 30 June 1925; undated letter of R.A. Rogers to Secretary for the Interior; Secretary for Native Affairs to Secretary for the Interior, 26 May 1926; Superintendent, Native Locations, to Joseph Masogha, 24

October 1925; Superintendent, Native Locations to Native Locations Department, 20 May 1926, in NTS 1455, file 128/214, NASA, CT.

81. Eddie Khaile, ANC national secretary, to A. W. G. Champion, 20 September 1927, Karis-Carter Collection, Joseph Regenstein Library, University of Chicago, reprinted in Hill, *Garvey Papers*, 10:398.

82. G. Rupert Christian, "Garveyism and What It Teaches," *Abantu-Batho*, 20 July 1922.

83. *Negro World*, 30 April 1927; "Another Victory," *Abantu-Batho*, 1 May 1930.

84. A. Kemp and R. T. Vinson, "Poking Holes in the Sky: Professor James Thaele, American Negroes and Modernity in Segregationist South Africa," *African Studies Review* 43, no. 1 (April 2000): 141–59.

85. Michael Ashley, "Features of Modernity: Missionaries and Education in South Africa, 1850–1900," *Journal of Theology for Southern Africa*, 38 (1982), 49-58.

86. Leonard L. Bethel, "The Role of Lincoln University in the Education of African Leadership: 1854–1970" (PhD diss., Rutgers University, 1975), 4. The emphasis is in the original text. Downington opened in 1905, founded by, among others, African Americans John Trower, a wealthy caterer, and William Creditt, a prominent Baptist minister who was also involved in Joseph Booth's African Christian Union. Creditt, as principal, and Mary Tribitt, as financial agent, were crucial and tireless workers for the school during its early years. See *Philadelphia Tribune*, 25 May 1912.

87. Bethel, 155–57.

88. Hill interview by Leonard Bethel, 16 October 1973, New York, quoted in Bethel, "Role of Lincoln University," 76. Hill notes that Lincoln's location above the Mason-Dixon line may have influenced some Africans to attend that school instead of southern schools such as Hampton and Tuskegee. Bethel, "Role of Lincoln University," 232.

89. Many Lincoln students studied four years of Latin and three years of Greek; Lincoln trained more ministers than any other black college up to 1930. Bethel, "Role of Lincoln University," 327–28.

90. Nnamdi Azikiwe, a student during the 1930s, noted the continuance of "woofing" during bull sessions, a form of verbal bullying. One particularly adept "woofer" was Thurgood Marshall, future U.S. Supreme Court justice. See Azikiwe, *My Odyssey* (London: Hurst, 1970).

91. *Negro World*, 22 August 1925 and 4 November 1922.

92. *Umteteli wa Bantu*, 30 July 1925.

93. *African World*, 3 May 1925, 23 May 1925, and 8 August 1925; *Negro World*, 4 July 1925.

94. Reports on Bolshevism, Department of Interior, NTS, file 3/1064/18, NASA; *Negro World*, 18 July 1925 and 24 October 1925. One example is a Woodstock UNIA meeting on 2 January 1927. See *Negro World*, 5 March 1927. For a few more examples, see *Negro World*, 20 June 1925, 4 July 1925, 22 August 1925, 6 March 1926, 5 March 1927, 18 July 1925, 24 April 1926, and 1 December 1923.

95. *Negro World*, 17 November 1923 and 30 May 1925.

96. *Negro World*, 16 May 1925.

97. *Negro World*, 2 May 1925. Mothiba quote is from *Negro World*, 11 July 1925. "The Gates of Africa" refers to Revelation 21:25, the fulfillment of God's prophecy to Isaiah 60:11.

98. *Negro World*, 15 November 1924.

99. *Negro World*, 12 September 1925, 30 April 1927, 23 August 1924, and 14 February 1925. For McKinley, see Robert R. Edgar, *An African American in South Africa: The Travel Notes of Ralph J. Bunche* (Athens: Ohio University Press, 1992).

100. *Negro World*, 17 May 1924.

101. *Negro World*, 20 June 1925.

102. W. Keith Hancock, *Smuts*, vol. 2, *The Field of Force* (Cambridge: Cambridge University Press, 1968), 146–47.

103. Peter Wickins, *The Industrial and Commercial Workers Union of South Africa* (Cape Town: David Philip, 1978), 77–79. Since there were an estimated 5 million blacks and 1.5 million whites, a 50-50 split still would have been inequitable.

104. Ibid., 77–80; Clements Kadalie, *My Life and the I.C.U.: The Autobiography of a Black Trade Unionist in South Africa* (New York: Humanities Press, 1970), 58–60; *Cape Times*, 30 June 1924.

105. *African World*, 10 October 1925.

106. *African World*, 3 October 1925 and 9 January 1926.

107. *The APO*, 8 April 1922. Thaele was the general secretary of the African Land Settlement Scheme, and Samuel Ncwana was the president. In a January 1922 letter to Cyril Briggs, Ncwana denounced Garvey, but in July 1922, he journeyed to Southwest Africa to collaborate with Garveyites there.

108. *African World*, 20 June 1925. Papu was a longtime Baptist minister, trained by African American missionaries James East and Herbert Payne. See *Mission Herald* 51 (November–December 1949): 17–18. For an overview of East and Payne, see chapter 1.

109. *African World*, 9 January 1926. Thaele also chastised ANC president Z. R. Mahabane for attending this conference. Mahabane attended on his own accord, not as an official ANC representative.

110. For more information on the Hertzog bills and interwar segregation, see generally S. Dubow, *Racial Segregation and the Origins of Apartheid in South Africa, 1919–1936* (New York: Palgrave Macmillan, 1989). See also R. Edgar, *Because They Chose the Plan of God: The Story of the Bulhoek Massacre* (Johannesburg: Ravan Press, 1988); G. Lewis, "The Bondelswaarts Rebellion of 1922" (master's thesis, Rhodes University, 1977); and *Negro World*, 16 August 1924. Ndimande claimed that black support for Hertzog was crucial to his election. For a view at variance with Ndimande's interpretation, see Wickins, *Industrial and Commercial Workers Union*, 79–80.

111. *African World*, 12 September 1925.

112. Oswald Pirow, *James Barry Munnik Hertzog* (Cape Town: Howard Timmons, 1957), 196–97.

113. *African World*, 23 May 1925.

114. Peter Walshe, *The Rise of African Nationalism in South Africa: The African National Congress, 1912–1952* (Berkeley: University of California Press, 1971), 257; Alan Cobley, *Class and Consciousness: The Black Petty Bourgeoisie in South Africa, 1924 to 1950* (Bridgeport, CT: Greenwood Press, 1990), 187.

115. *African World*, 23 May 1925.

116. *African World*, 1 August 1925.

117. *African World*, 4 July 1925, 1 August 1925, and 8 August 1925; Statement by Native Sergeant Halele, 21 February 1926, NTS 7603, file 25/328, NASA, CT. Originally a Muslim term for an unbeliever of Islam, *kaffir* is a derogatory word for blacks, particularly in South Africa.

118. *African World*, 11 July 1925.

119. *African World*, 24 July 1926.

120. *African World*, 4 July 1925.

121. *South African Worker*, 31 June 1929, quoted in Edward Roux, *Time Longer Than Rope: A History of the Black Man's Struggle in South Africa* (Madison: University of Wisconsin Press, 1964), 236–37.

CHAPTER 5: "CHARLATAN OR SAVIOR?"

1. W. D. Cingo, "Native Unrest," *Kokstad Advertiser*, 30 September 1927.

2. *Umteteli wa Bantu*, 15 January 1927, 1/TSO (Tsolo district), box 5/1/19, file 3/16/6, NASA, CT. During the 1920s, the Griqua leader Abraham Le Fleur protested taxation, cattle dipping, and pass laws in the Transkei, but he never identified himself with Garvey and never collaborated with Wellington. See Robert R. Edgar and Christopher Saunders, "A. A. S. Le Fleur and the Griqua Trek of 1917: Segregation, Self-Help, and Ethnic Identity," *International Journal of African Historical Studies* 15 (1982): 201–20.

3. Wellington follower Paul Gulwa purchased this car by putting up his land as security. The car allowed Wellington to move quickly through the region and avoid the costs and conspicuousness of train travel. At other times, Wellington had a fleet of cars and horses, one horse bearing the name Sedition.

4. Another document gives his birthdate as 1 January 1899 and his education as taking place at Ekutuleni-Lovedale College and Swits College in Delagoa Bay, Portuguese East Africa. See R. D. Lyle, Pietermaritzburg Magistrate, to Natal Chief Native Commissioner, 30 January 1928, NTS 7602, file 25/328 pt. 2, NASA, CT. Still another document records his birthplace as near Eshowe, Zululand. Allen Lea, "Bantu Leadership: The Escapade of Wellington," *East London Dispatch*, 29 November 1927.

5. Statement by J. E. Hallendorff, Church of Sweden missionary, Ekuteleni, Zululand, 5 February 1927, NTS 7603, file 25/328, NASA, CT.

6. Letters of Exemption, petition of Wellington Butelezi, NTS 7602, file 26/328 (A) pt. 1 (A), NASA, CT; "Application of Elias Butelezi for Exemption from Native Law," Butelezi to Natal Chief Native Commissioner, 9 August 1920 and 20 September 1920, RG CNC 348, file 271/19, NASA, CT.

7. Additional Magistrate, Umgeni Court, PMB, to Chief Native Commissioner, Natal, 1 February 1921, CNC, file 1/30/28, NASA, CT. Wellington became a minister in the Faith Apostolic Church.

8. Robert R. Edgar, "African Educational Protest in South Africa: The American School Movement in the Transkei in the 1920s," in *Apartheid and Education: The Education of Black South Africans*, ed. Peter Kallaway, 184 (Johannesburg: Ravan Press, 1984); undated article by Rev. Allen Lea, 2/SPT (Sterkspruit) 15, file N1/9/2, NASA, CT.

9. He was convicted for representing himself falsely as a general medical practitioner. He had also identified himself as an assistant in America to a Dr. C. G. Cobb. W. R. Lovett to Divisional CID officer, 10 August 1924; NTS 7602, file 26/328 (A) pt. 1 (A), H. B. Wellington to the Secretary of the Interior, 21 July 1924, NTS 7602, file 26/328 (A) pt. 1 (A), NTS Criminal Investigation Division. In 1928, the government passed the Medical, Dental and Pharmacy Act No. 13, which banned African herbalists from practicing outside Natal.

10. See *Umteteli wa Bantu*, 11 November 1926, Wellington file, 2/SPT 16, NASA, CT.

11. Wellington cited religious reasons for the requested name change and did so during his unsuccessful attempt to study medicine at Oxford. P. Nkala, Secretary to B. H. Wellington, to the Secretary for Native Affairs, 16 July 1926, 2/SPT 16, file N1/9/3, NASA, CT; Philip Nkala for B. H. Wellington to the Natal Commissioner of Native Affairs, CNC 348, file 271/19, NASA, CT. See *Umteteli wa Bantu*, 11 November 1926, Wellington file, 2/SPT 16, NASA, CT. B. H. Wellington to Secretary for Native Affairs, 16 July 1926, NTS 7603, file 25/328, NASA, CT.

12. Sworn Statement of B. H. Wellington, 15 January 1926, NTS 7603, file 25/328, NASA, CT.

13. Robert A. Hill, ed., *The Marcus Garvey and Universal Negro Improvement Association Papers* (Berkeley: University of California Press, 1983–), 10:351. The biblical reference refers to Jesus's promise of a return to earth to inaugurate the Apocalypse and the new Jerusalem and also to 2 Kings 2:11 accounts of Elijah being swept up to heaven in a chariot of fire.

14. Lonsdale to Tsolo Magistrate, 12 March 1927, NTS 7603, file 25/328, NASA, CT, and Helen Bradford, *A Taste of Freedom: The ICU in Rural South Africa, 1924–1930* (Johannesburg: Ravan Press, 1987), 217–18.

15. See Bradford, *Taste of Freedom*, 63–87; Paul la Hausse de Lalouviere, *Restless Identities: Signatures of Nationalism, Zulu Ethnicity and History in the Lives of Petros Lamula and Lymon Maling* (Pietermaritzburg: University of Natal Press, 2000), 259–64; and Phil Bonner, "The Transvaal Native Congress, 1917–1920: The Radicalisation of the Black Petty Bourgeoisie on the Rand," in *Industrialisation and Social Change in South Africa: African Class Formation, Culture, and Consciousness, 1870–1930*, ed. Shula Marks and Richard Rathbone, 270–313 (London: Longman, 1982).

16. Clifton Crais, *The Politics of Evil: Magic, State Power, and the Political Imagination in South Africa* (Cambridge: Cambridge University Press, 2002), 8.

17. Jeff Peires, *The Dead Shall Arise: Nongqawuse and the Great Cattle Killing Movement* (Johannesburg: Ravan Press, 1989).

18. See Terence Ranger, "The Myth of the Afro-American Liberator," seminar paper, University of California, Los Angeles, 1971; John Higginson, "Liberating

the Captives: Independent Watchtower as an Avatar of Colonial Revolt in Southern Africa and Katanga, 1908–1941," *Journal of Social History* 26, no. 1 (Fall 1992): 55–80; and Sean Redding, *Sorcery and Sovereignty: Taxation, Power and Rebellion in South Africa, 1880–1963* (Athens: Ohio University Press, 2006), 136.

19. Gilbert Matshoba to Enoch Mgijima, August 1920, RG Governors General 1728, file 51, 6670, NASA, Pretoria. Matshoba was referring to the 14 August 1920 edition of *Umteteli wa Bantu*, which had reported on the 1920 UNIA convention in New York City that took place that month. Mgijima was a former leader of the South African branch of the African American Church of God and Saints of Christ.

20. Robert R. Edgar, "The Prophet Motive: Enoch Mgijima, the Israelites and the Background to the Bulhoek Massacre," *International Journal of African Historical Studies* 15, no. 3 (1982): 401–22; Edgar, *Because They Chose the Plan of God: The Story of the Bulhoek Massacre* (Johannesburg: Ravan Press, 1988).

21. Statement by Sinono Maneli, Headman Ngcabassa location, KingWilliamsTown, 15 May 1923, SAP, box 41, NASA, CT.

22. Mayford Mambhalu, Principal, Pauleni School, Middledrift, 26 April 1923, SAP box 41, NASA, CT.

23. Robert R. Edgar and Hilary Sapire, *African Apocalypse: The Story of Nontetha Nkwenkwe, a Twentieth-Century South African Prophet* (Athens: Ohio University Press, 2000), 31.

24. W. G. Norman, Sub-inspector, SAP, to District Commandant, SAP, East London, 1 November 1923, SAP, box 41, NASA, CT.

25. Edgar and Sapire, *African Apocalypse*, 117. Locusts are central to the Eighth Plague in the story of the plagues of Egypt (see Proverbs 30:27). In Revelation, locusts with scorpion tails and human faces torment unbelievers for five months when the fifth trumpet sounds. The Book of Joel is written in the context of a recent locust plague. Magistrates wanted locusts cleared because swarms could strip fields and damage crops. Other Africans claimed that the locusts would have iron heads.

26. Affidavit of Samuel Nkwali, 5 January 1927; James Coombs, Qumbu Sergeant, to SAP District Commandant, 18 January 1927; Statement by Milton Majola, Matatiele CID detective, 12 December 1928; and Allen Lea, "Bantu Leadership," all in NTS 7603, file 25/328, NASA, CT.

27. Cingo, "Native Unrest."

28. Unnamed Transkeian mine clerk quoted in Bradford, *Taste of Freedom*, 216.

29. *Kansas City Call*, 8 December 1922. Vernon presided over the AME's South African missions from 1920 to 1924.

30. Matatiele Magistrate to SNA, 14 August 1926, NTS 7602, file 26/328, NASA, CT. Solomon Zulu, his colleague in the Apostolic Faith Mission, became the chaplain of the Basutoland UNIA.

31. Interview by Robert R. Edgar of C. P. Mathebe, 3 July 1974, Aliwal North, South Africa.

32. William Beinart and Colin Bundy, *Hidden Struggles in Rural South Africa: Politics and Popular Movements in the Transkei and Eastern Cape, 1890–1930* (Johannesburg: Ravan Press, 1987), 253

33. Monica Wilson, *Reaction to Conquest: Effects of Contact with Europeans on the Pondo of South Africa* (London: Oxford University Press, 1961), 316–17.

34. James Coombs, Qumbu Sergeant, to District Commandant, 18 January 1927, NTS 7603, file 25/328, NASA, CT; Undated Affidavit of Frank Nolan Doran; Affidavit of Qumbu Constable Robert John Waldeck, 10 March 1927; Undated Affidavit of Umtata CID detective Joseph Mho; Statement by Constable Obed Sigenu, 8 August 1928, NTS 7602, file 26/328 pt. 2, NASA, CT. Wellington later claimed to be "the doctor in Israel that will heal you of your leprosy." Statement by Eliezer Mguni, Umtata, 31 January 1929, NTS 7602, file 26/328 pt. 2, NASA, CT. For the coloration of the *impundulu* bird, see Wilson, *Reaction to Conquest*, 302.

35. Frank Brownlee, Butterworth Magistrate, to Chief Magistrate, 14 October 1927, NTS 7602, file 26/328 pt. 4, NASA, CT; D. W. Semple to Qumbu Magistrate, 26 November 1927; Ngqeleni Sergeant to SAP District Commandant, 10 December 1927; Nqamakwe Magistrate to Chief Magistrate, 29 October 1927, 1/NKE, file N1/9/2, NASA, CT. According to these documents, the actual day of apocalypse shifted in 1927 from several dates in March, April, and May to 7 November, 5 December, and the vague "before Christmas."

36. Affidavit by Ncanywa Giyose, Nqamakwe, 27 May 1927, NTS 7602, file 25/328, NASA, CT.

37. Undated Affidavit of Joseph Mho, Umtatata CID detective, NTS 7602, file 25/328, NASA, CT; F. N. Doran, Qumbu Magistrate, to Deputy Commissioner of Police, 5 July 1927, NTS 7602, file 26/328, NASA, CT. In two Qumbu locations known for their strong Wellington allegiance, only 142 of 1,600 Africans submitted to vaccination.

38. J. M. Young, Umtata Magistrate, to Chief Magistrate, 23 June 1927; F. C. Pinkerton to Chief Magistrate, 27 August 1927; and Freemantle to Chief Magistrate, 19 September 1927; NTS 7602, file 26/328 pt. 4, NASA, CT.

39. Affidavit of Edgar Lonsdale, Tsolo magistrate, 12 March 1927, NTS 7602, file 26/328 pt. 2, NASA, CT.

40. Statement by Edward Chalmers Bam, 12 March 1927, 1/TSO (Tsolo district), box 5/1/19, file 3/16/6, NASA, CT.

41. *Umteteli wa Bantu*, 8 January 1927; undated correspondence from Enoch Mgushulu to one Mr. Nyembezi, 1/NKE, box 58, file N1/9/3, NASA, CT; R. Fyfe King, Tabankulu Magistrate, to Chief Magistrate, 13 September 1927, NTS 7602, file 26/328 pt. 2, NASA, CT. Red, black, and green were the organizational colors of the UNIA. The killing of pigs was a necessary precondition to American liberation. Such killing had occurred in 1906 during Bambatha's rebellion in Greytown and again in 1910 before the appearance of Halley's Comet. For Wellingtonites, pigs symbolized spiritual degradation, decay, and death because they ate and wallowed in bodily waste and attracted tapeworms, hence parasitic diseases. Despised whites had introduced pigs to the region. Wellington predicted that the Americans

would set pigs afire with burning coals. The Qumbu magistrate Frank Doran reported Africans were slaughtering their pigs, white cattle, and fowl in accordance with the Wellington doctrine that "a ball of fire from Heaven" will burn those that do not kill these animals.

42. Jeff Pieres, personal communication with the author, 3 August 2000.

43. Edgar, "African Educational Protest," 187; Nqamakwe Magistrate A. L. Barrett to Chief Magistrate, 6 October 1927, NTS 7603, file 26/328 pt. 4, NASA, CT; undated report of N. A. Mazwai, NTS 7603, file 26/328 pt. 4, NASA, CT.

44. Umtata Police Report, 6 July 1932; Lady Grey constable to Aliwal North Commandant, 29 January 1929, both in NTS 7602, file 26/328 (A), NASA, CT.

45. SAP Sergeant to SAP District Commandant, 19 December 1927, 1/MFE (Mt. Frere district), box 8/1/14, file 2/12/4, NASA, CT. The sergeant concluded that "it is not the uncivilized native who is keen on joining the organization but the half educated dressed native." However, Wellington did attract some non-Christian, illiterate Africans.

46. Edendale 1/21/28, Det. Head Constable to Cape Native Commissioner, file 1/21/28, NASA, Pietermaritzburg.

47. CID Report, 15 August 1928, 2/SPT, file 16, NASA, CT.

48. Walter Sisulu, interview by the author, 26 April 1998, Cape Town; 47th Annual Report of the South African Missionary Society (1928), cited in Edgar, "African Educational Protest," 187.

49. Magisterial Court documents of Albert Rulashe, 11 June 1928, NTS 7602, file 26/328, NASA, CT.

50. Engcobo district was but one example of these multiple difficulties. See C. C. Harris to Engcobo Resident Magistrate, 10 November 1927; Engcobo Magistrate to Chief Magistrate, 27 March 1928; and the affidavit of Chief Alex Mgudlwa, 20 May 1929, all from 1/ECO (Engcobo district), file 6/1/99, NASA, CT.

51. For example, see Nqamakwe Magistrate A. L. Barrett to Chief Magistrate, 22 June 1928, 1/NKE (Nqamakwe district), file N1/9/3, NASA, CT.

52. Statement by Matatiele CID detective Milton Majola, 12 December 1928, NTS 7602, file 26/328 pt. 2, NASA, CT. However, the insights provided by Majola did not greatly improve upon similar reports filed by less well placed detectives. At other times, colonial officials coerced a few UNIA members into providing information on the movement, though most simply denied any detailed knowledge. For one confession, see Statement by Xadi Sikoti, Mount Fletcher, 12 December 1928, NTS 7602, file 26/328 pt. 2, NASA, CT. Sikoti had been a UNIA member for three years.

53. Tsolo Magistrate to Chief Magistrate, 28 January 1929, NTS 7602, file 26/328 pt. 2, NASA, CT.

54. Herschel Magistrate Munscheid to Mount Fletcher Magistrate Welsh, 11 October 1926, 2/SPT, file N1/9/2, NASA, CT. See also Welsh's similar opinion expressed to the Chief Magistrate, 18 February 1927, 1/MTF (Mt. Fletcher district), file 2/9/1, NASA, CT.

55. Herschel Magistrate Munscheid to Norton, 11 December 1926, 2/SPT, file N1/9/2, NASA, CT. There was no recorded response to Munscheid's demand to

know "what attitude my Department [is] going to adopt to protect me if such a matter ever goes to the Supreme Court."

56. Affidavit of Tsolo Court Interpreter Edward Chalmers Bam, 12 March 1927, NTS 7602, file 26/328 pt. 2, NASA, CT.

57. Affidavit of Mount Fletcher Constable Peter Dicks, 16 March 1927, NTS 7602, file 26/328 pt. 2, NASA, CT.

58. Affidavit of Tsolo Trader Lionel Harris, 11 March 1927, NTS 7602, file 25/328, NASA, CT.

59. Ibid.

60. Ernest Woon, SAP Deputy Commissioner, to the SAP Commissioner, 9 March 1927; undated letter from Woon to James Jokazi; telegraph from Tembu to Umtata, 31 March 1927; Affidavit of Lionel Harris, 18 March 1927; Van Aardt and Adolf Harris to Secretary for Native Affairs, 27 April 1927; Affidavit of Woon, 17 March 1927; Affidavit of Qumbu Constable Robert John Waldeck, 10 March 1927; Affidavit of Julius Matsinya, all in NTS 7602, file 25/328 pt. 2, NASA, CT; and Bradford, *Taste of Freedom*, 325n11.

61. Mahmood Mamdani, *Citizen and Subject: Contemporary Africa and the Legacy of Late Colonialism* (Princeton, NJ: Princeton University Press, 1996), 94. Jan Smuts was prime minister of South Africa from 1919 to 1924 and from 1939 to 1948.

62. Robert R. Edgar, "New Religious Movements," in *Missions and Empire*, ed. Norman Etherington, 165 (Oxford: Oxford University Press, 2005).

63. Ibid., 180.

64. Ivan Evans, *Bureaucracy and Race: Native Administration in South Africa* (Berkeley: University of California Press, 1997), 176; W. J. G. Mears, "A Study in Native Administration in the Transkeian Territories, 1894–1943" (PhD diss., UNISA, 1947), 80; Bradford, *Taste of Freedom*, 220; and Sean Redding, "Government Witchcraft: Taxation, the Supernatural, and the Mpondo Revolt in the Transkei, South Africa, 1955–1963," *African Affairs* 95, no. 381 (1996): 560–61. The state later referred to the hut tax as the "local tax."

65. *Government Gazette*, March 1927.

66. Nqamakwe Magistrate to Chief Magistrate, 29 October 1927, 1/NKE, file N1/9/2, NASA, CT; Governor-General Proclamation, 31 March 1927, NTS 7602, file 26/328 pt. 2, NASA, CT; A. L. Barrett, Nqamakwe Magistrate, to Chief Magistrate, 29 October 1927, NTS 7602, file 26/328 pt. 4, NASA, CT. Magistrates, Bunga councilors, and headmen continued to petition the government for permission to use these expanded powers to summarily evict remaining Wellingtonites from their districts, but their superiors deemed these actions unnecessary. See, for example, Chief Magistrate to Nqamakwe Magistrate, 17 July 1928, 1/NKE, file N1/9/3, NASA, CT.

67. For example, the government convicted UNIA commissioner Joel Bulana in Idutywa on this charge. See Ernest Woon, South African Police Deputy Commissioner, to Chief Magistrate, 10 November 1927, NTS 7602, file 26/328 pt. 2. For a similar conviction against Edward Maqolo of Nqamakwe, see "The Wellington

Movement," *East London Daily Dispatch*, 21 November 1927, reprinted in NTS 7602, file 26/328 pt. 2, NASA, CT. For harried government officials, application of the Native Administration Act was "the only way in which the movement can be suppressed." J. F. Herbst, Secretary for Native Affairs, to the Chief Magistrate, 17 October 1927, 1/NKE, box 58, file N1/9/3, NASA, CT.

68. Housed in the Transkeian capital of Umtata, the General Council, known as the Bunga and headed by the chief magistrate, had used African chiefs as councilors to represent the needs of their African commoners. Though this process was touted as a model of African "self-government," the chief magistrate had veto power over any Bunga resolution. The chiefs' bid for more control anticipated the authoritarian rule of chiefs during the later apartheid era.

69. Councilor Mlandu, "Transkeian Territories General Council Proceedings and Reports of Select Committee at the Session of 1927," *Umtata Territorial News*, 20 April 1927.

70. "Transkeian Territories General Council Proceedings and Reports of Select Committees at the Session of Wednesday, 2 May 1928," *Umtata Territorial News*, 28 May 1928.

71. "Report for the Diocese of St. John, Kaffraria (1927) from the Bishop of St. John's, Bishopsmead, Umtata," *Missionary Reports*, S.P.G. (1927), sect. 30, 4–5.

72. J. G. Locke, "'Dr.' Wellington," *Blythswood Review*, February 1928, 1–2.

73. "Report for the Diocese of St. John, Kaffraria (1928) from the Bishop of St. John's, Bishopsmead, Umtata," *Missionary Reports*, S.P.G. (1928), sect. 31, 4.

74. Locke, "'Dr.' Wellington."

75. CM to SNA, 28 March 1929, NTS 7602, file 26/328, NASA, CT. Welsh shared the concerns of African councilors that the Wellington movement continued to operate and collect funds under the strict guise of a religious movement.

76. Ibid.; Statement by Eliezer Mguni, 31 January 1929.

77. *Negro World*, 30 July 1927. The government, after considerable deliberation, decided not to publicize Garvey's denunciation, not wanting him to benefit from the free advertising. See undated correspondence of the Secretary for Native Affairs to the Chief Magistrate, NTS 7602, file 25/328 pt. 4, NASA, CT. However, rival organizations like the Cape African National Congress utilized Garvey's denunciation in their efforts to discredit Wellington. See article by E. Mdolomba in *Imvo Zabantsundu*, 14 February 1928, reprinted in 17 February 1928, NTS 7602, file 25/328 pt. 2, NASA, CT. Yet such opponents admitted that Wellingtonism could not have flourished without the existence of real grievances. See A. L. Barrett, Nqamakwe Magistrate, to Chief Magistrate, 12 November 1927, 1/NKE file N1/9/3, NASA, CT.

78. Statement of Samuel Michael Bennett Ncwana, August 23, 1928, 2/SPT file N1/9/3, NASA, CT. Ncwana lists Tana Makobeni, who had attended Wellington's meetings, and Headman Phoko of Sterkspruit as his informants. *Ilanga lase Natal*, 25 March 1927. Dube chided the government for sending airplanes to stop American Negro planes and for raising a "hubbub . . . over such a frivolity."

79. Frank Doran, Qumbu Resident Magistrate, to Robert Welsh, Mount Fletcher Resident Magistrate, 15 February 1927, 1/QBU, file 2/17, NASA, CT.

80. Native Constable Sigenu to Herschel Magistrate, 15 August 1928, 2/SPT, box 16, file N1/9/2, NASA, CT; South African Police Report, 24 January 1929, 1/ELN (East London), box 86, NASA, CT.

81. Additional Magistrate, Umgeni Court, PMB, to Chief Native Commissioner, Natal, 30 January 1928, CNC, file 2/1/1921, NASA, Pietermaritzburg. Further, they said, he would have been no older than seventeen when he claimed to have earned an MD degree by correspondence from Rush University in Chicago.

82. Lea, "Bantu Leadership"; Police Report, 29 March 1929, 1/ELN, box 86, NASA, CT.

83. Johnson Matshanda to the Chief Magistrate, 29 April 1928, 1/TSO, box 5/1/21, file L11, NASA, CT.

84. See Shula Marks, *The Ambiguities of Dependence: Class, Nationalism, and the State in Twentieth-Century Natal* (Johannesburg: Ravan Press, 1986), 65–66, for the transformation of Edendale into an overcrowded slum due to the 1913 Native Land Act.

85. Statement by CID detective Solana, 7 August 1928, RG NTS 7602, file 26/328 pt. 2, NASA, CT.

86. Native Constable Sigenu to Herschel Magistrate, 15 August 1928, 2/SPT, box 16, file N1/9/2, NASA, CT.

87. Tandinyanso, "Concerning Herschel," *Umteteli wa Bantu*, 21 April 1928, 2/SPT, box 16, file N1/9/2, NASA, CT.

88. L. H. Wood, a UNIA general secretary, affixed his signature to correspondence written in SeSotho by Wellington, and Joel Mnyimba, a prominent UNIA organizer, witnessed Wellington's frank acknowledgment to government officials of his Zulu birth while attempting to secure a passport to attend the proposed UNIA convention in 1928. See Wellington correspondence to untitled, 4 April 1926, NTS 7602, file 25/328, and 30 January 1928, NTS 7602, file 25/328 pt. 2, both in NASA, CT.

89. The IICU was one of several splinter groupings of the ICU. After resigning from the ICU in 1928 due to fractious leadership disputes, financial mismanagement, and general organizational chaos, Kadalie founded the IICU in April 1929. Its message of black self-sufficiency, liberationist Christianity, and ardent trade unionism remained informed by a continued reverence for Garvey. By 1935, it had declined into organizational insignificance due to Kadalie's erratic leadership, further leadership splinters, and government harassment.

90. Police Report, 25 January 1929 and 1 February 1929, 1/ELN, box 86, NASA, CT; Statement by Eliezer Mguni, 31 January 1929. Wellington, far removed from his East Griqualand strongholds, successfully challenged East London–area audiences to contradict his claim of never uttering millenarian prophecies.

91. SAP report, 1 February 1929; undated report by N. A. Mazwai, both in NTS 7602, file 26/328, NASA, CT. This report was probably filed in mid-January, since the events described took place on 13 January 1929. Wellington initially attracted as many as seven hundred people to his East London meetings; by September 1929, general interest had largely faded.

92. J. J. Labuschagne to DC, SAP, 3 April 1934, NTS 7602, file 26/328 (A) pt. 1, NASA, CT.

93. Lobola, sometimes referred to as "bridewealth," is an arrangement among many Africans that involves the exchange of gifts between the families of a bride and groom that serve to bind the families together socioeconomically.

94. SAT Mkwananzi letter to Umteteli, 15 January 1927, NTS 7602, file 26/328, NASA, CT; Edgar and Sapire, *African Apocalypse*, 32.

95. J. J. Labuschagne to DC, SAP, 3 April 1934, NTS 7602, file 26/328 (A) pt. 1, NASA, CT.

96. Wellington's ban also did not stop the UNIA from continuing to forge links with other political, economic, and religious organizations. Wellington and five African chiefs twice journeyed to Lourenço Marques to ally themselves with the liberationist organization Gremio Africano in protests against the Portuguese colonial authorities. J. R. de Oliveira, Consular General of Portugal in S. A., to J. B. M. Hertzog, Minister for External Affairs, 22 September 1927, NTS 7602, file 26/328 pt. 4, NASA, CT.

97. For global black reactions to the Ethiopian crisis, see Brenda Gayle Plummer, *Rising Wind: Black Americans and U.S. Foreign Affairs, 1935–1960* (Chapel Hill: University of North Carolina Press, 1996), and Joseph E. Harris, *African-American Reactions to War in Ethiopia, 1936–1941* (Baton Rouge: Louisiana State University Press, 1994).

98. CID report, 3 January 1936; CID reports of 6 April 1935, 2 September 1935, and 6 December 1935, all in NTS 7603, file 25/328 pt. 4, NASA, CT. Interestingly, Paul Gulwa, a longtime Wellington disciple, criticized Wellington for dwelling on nonreligious matters and for his customary absences during meetings.

99. Magistrate to the Secretary for Native Affairs, 4 December 1939; B. H. Wellington to Minister of Native Affairs, 23 June 1944, both in NTS 7603, file 25/328 pt. 4, NASA, CT.

100. Secretary for Native Affairs to B. H. H. Wellington, 8 December 1947, NTS 7603, file 25/328 pt. 4, NASA, CT. The interviewer was Lwandle Kunene, who visited his sister, a nun, in Swaziland during the 1970s.

101. Statement of Stanley Tyaliti, Xalanga district, 5 April 1928; Affidavits of Momvana Malote, Stanley Tyalite, Mnguwe Tlanzana, and Fengweni Maqunau, Xalanga district, 5 April 1928, all in NTS 7602, file 25/328 pt. 2, NASA, CT.

102. "The Wellington Movement," *Kaffraria News*, 17 May 1928, NTS 7602, file 25/328 pt. 2, NASA, CT; Statement of Philip Nomruca, Umtata, 22 December 1928; Tsolo Magistrate to Chief Magistrate, 28 January 1929; Tsolo Magistrate to Chief Magistrate, 12 January 1928, NTS 7606, file 46/328, NASA, CT. Mackey shared Wellington's chameleon tendencies; his extensive criminal record details five different names, and at one point, he claimed to be from Mozambique (18 December 1928). Despite this, he apparently had considerable sway over his followers; they quickly raised £25 to pay for a car rental and a rail pass from Mount Frere to Durban, ostensibly to deliver teachers and children to Wellington schools in Natal.

103. Beinart and Bundy, *Hidden Struggles in Rural South Africa*, 199; Affidavit of Melvin Hlamvana, 13 June 1940, NTS 1681, file 2/276 pt. 2, NASA, CT. The African American liberation myth extended beyond Garvey. For example, in 1937, the Transkeian Bunga reported that an unnamed ex-Wellingtonite now followed "the Negro Father Divine, an American about whom there was something in the papers yesterday." See Minutes of the 1937 United Transkeian General Council, NTS 7602, file 25/328, NASA, CT.

CHAPTER 6: A DREAM DEFERRED

1. William Beinart, "Chieftaincy and the Concept of Articulation: South Africa ca. 1900–1950," in *Segregation and Apartheid in Twentieth-Century South Africa*, ed. William Beinart and Saul Dubow (New York: Routledge, 1995), 183.

2. Zibi had previously clashed with authorities over land boundary issues and pay raises. For both the boundary dispute, see Edward Zibi to Resident Magistrate, 3 March 1921 and 5 September 1921, and for Zibi's raise, see Resident Magistrate to Chief Magistrate, 10 September 1925, and Secretary for Native Affairs to the Chief Magistrate, 25 September 1925, 1/MTF (Mt. Fletcher), box 7/38, file N1/1/5, NASA, CT.

3. Welsh to Chief Magistrate W. T. Welsh (hereafter cited as CM Welsh), 5 July 1927, 1/MTF, box 7/16, file 2/9/1, NASA, CT. Sidlai had given the benediction at Wellington's first documented UNIA meeting in Mount Fletcher. See Affidavit of Daniel Mbebe, 4 February 1927, and Affidavit of Otto Ndwandwa, 5 February 1927, NTS 1681, file 2/276 pt. 1, NASA, CT. The permanent UNIA school was to hold fifty students. At this point, there were a reported thirty-six students who had formerly been at Tinana mission school. For Johannes Zibi's report that there was a "goodly sprinkling of educated Natives i.e. Teachers and Headmen" within the movement, see Zibi to Welsh, 28 January 1927, NTS 1681, file 2/276 pt. 1, NASA, CT. For instance, John Sidlai, Pieter's nephew, taught at Wellington's Siqunqwni School in Tsolo. See John Sidlai to R. Welsh, 11 August 1927, 1/MTF, box 7/16, file 2/9/1, NASA, CT. He was to work in Siqungwini location under a man named Ben Mabandla. Mina Lobenga, expelled from Tsolo for teaching in a Wellington school, quickly resurfaced at St. Welford. Affidavit of Samuel Nkwali, 17 January 1927, NTS 1681, file 2/276 pt. 1, NASA, CT; Enclosures within a report from SAP Sergeant R. D. Nortje to R. Welsh, 24 February 1927, 1/MTF, box 7/16, file 2/9/1, NASA, CT. Pieter Sidlai was the primary Mount Fletcher teacher at St. Welford, though a critical mass of mostly female teachers arrived from Tsolo. CA, 1/MTF, box 7/16, file 2/9/1, NASA, CT; Nortje to Welsh, 10 March 1927; Nortje to Welsh, 12 March 1927; Nortje to Welsh, 15 March 1927.

4. Circular letter from Butler Wellington, 15 November 1927, 1/TSO, box 5/1/18, file 2/16/4, NASA, CT. The stationery also notes that Wellington was the president of both the association and "St. Wellford Universal Industrial College." Wellington also used the return address of St. Booker Washington Liberty College in Edendale. Pieter Sidlai had been a Moravian evangelist. Affidavit of Daniel Mbebe, 4 February 1927, 1/TSO, box 5/1/18, file 2/16/4, NASA, CT. An earlier UNIA document lists Theo F. Mye as the secretary-general.

See Charter of UNIA division 849 (Tsolo), 13 April 1927, 1/TSO, box 5/1/18, file 2/16/4, NASA, CT.

5. Lionel Harris, Esinxago trader, to Edgar Lonsdale, Tsolo Resident Magistrate (hereafter referred to as Lonsdale), 11 March 1927, 1/TSO, box 5/1/18, file 2/16/4, NASA, CT; Sworn Statement by Johannes Zibi, 9 February 1927, 1/MTF, box 7/16, file 2/9/1, NASA, CT.

6. Affidavit of Samuel Nkwali, 5 January 1927, 1/MTF, box 7/16, file 2/9/1, NASA, CT. Zibi's willingness to die for Wellington was consistent with his representation of the Hlubi people's tradition of dying together with their chief in battle. See Sworn Statement of Johannes Zibi, 9 February 1927, 1/MTF, box 7/16, file 2/9/1, NASA, CT. The Johannesburg-based African newspaper *Umteteli wa Bantu* detected the rumblings emanating from this remote district: "Dr. Wellington is in high favor at Mount Fletcher and is being assisted by locally prominent Natives who should know better . . . there seems to be a clear call for police action. "Dr. Wellington Re-appears," *Umteteli wa Bantu*, 8 January 1927.

7. William Beinart and Colin Bundy, *Hidden Struggles in Rural South Africa: Politics and Popular Movements in the Transkei and Eastern Cape 1890–1930* (Johannesburg: Ravan Press, 1987), 112. The Hlubi were an ethnic group predominant in the district since their migration to East Griqualand from Natal during the Mfecane. The Mfecane refers to the domino-like displacement of peoples initiated primarily by the formation and consolidation of the Zulu state beginning in 1816. These displacements affected peoples as far north as modern-day Tanzania, but within South Africa, Amahlubi, Mfengu, BaSotho, among other groups, migrated into and settled in the Transkei during the nineteenth century. See Carolyn Hamilton and John Wright, eds., *The Mfecane Aftermath: Reconstructive Debates in Southern African History* (Pietermaritzburg: University of Natal Press, 1995). For the movement of Hlubi into the northern Transkei, see John Wright and Andrew Manson, *The Hlubi Chiefdom in Zululand-Natal: A History* (Ladysmith, South Africa: Ladysmith Historical Society, 1983).

8. Statement by Daniel Mbebe, 18 May 1927, 1/MTF, box 7/17, file 2/9/1, NASA, CT. Mbebe states that Zibi's authority over the Hlubi stretched from the Umzimkulu River to Herschel and the Cape Province. Beinart and Bundy, *Hidden Struggles*, 192, 207.

9. Affidavit of Johannes Zibi, 11 March 1927, 1/MTF, box 7/16, file 2/9/1, NASA, CT.

10. Beinart and Bundy, *Hidden Struggles*, 210. Edward was the son of Johannes's eldest brother. Though pertinent details regarding the selection of the Hlubi chief are not now available, it is possible that the enmity between Johannes and Edward stemmed from a succession dispute. For Wellington's attempts to gain Johannes's permission to hold a UNIA meeting, see Affidavit of Johannes Zibi, 11 March 1927, and Sworn Statement by Johannes Zibi, 9 February 1927, 1/MTF, box 7/16, file 2/9/1, NASA, CT.

11. Unknown to Welsh, 9 April 1927, 1/MTF, box 7/16, file 2/9/1, NASA, CT; Tsolo Sergeant F. Malan to Lonsdale, 22 April 1927, and Reverend Keinemann to Welsh, 22 December 1927, NTS 1681, file 2/276 pt. 1, NASA, CT.

12. Affidavit of Philip Payn, 12 March 1927, and circular letter by B. H. Welling-ton, 15 November 1927, both in 1/TSO, box 5/1/18, file 2/16/4, NASA, CT; Affidavit of Daniel Mbebe, 4 February 1927, NTS 1681, file 2/276 pt. 1, NASA, CT.

13. Welsh to the Officer in Charge, South African Police, 3 November 1926; Welsh to CM Welsh, 11 November 1926; Affidavit of Walter Bourquin, 25 Novem-ber 1926; Sworn Statement by Johannes Zibi, 9 February 1927, all in 1/MTF, box 7/16, file 2/9/1, NASA, CT.

14. Affidavit of Samuel Nkwali, 5 January 1927, and letter from S. A. T. Mkwa-nanzi extracted from *Umteteli wa Bantu*, 15 January 1927, 1/MTF, box 7/16, file 2/9/1, NASA, CT, and Affidavit of Mkwanzi, 4 February 1927, NTS 1681, file 276 pt. 1, NASA, CT. For the need of Mbebe for police protection, see Sergeant Richard Nortje to Welsh, 1 February 1927, 1/MTF, box 7/16, file 2/9/1, NASA, CT; for Zibi's threats, see Affidavit of Otto Ndwandwa, 5 February 1927 and Welsh to S. A. P., 10 March 1927, idem. Moravian Rev. Keinemann to Welsh, 22 December 1927, NTS 1681, file 2/276 pt. 1, NASA, CT; Johannes Zibi to Welsh, 28 January 1927, 1/MTF, box 7/16, file 2/9/1, NASA, CT. The term *whitefoot* was a derisive term for Africans loyal to the colonial government, essentially meaning "sell-outs."

15. Rev. Keinemann to Welsh, 22 December 1927, NTS 1681, file 2/276 pt. 1, NASA, CT.

16. Trial transcript of the Edward Zibi trial, 9 February 1927, 1/MTF, box 7/16, file 2/9/1, NASA, CT; CM Welsh to Secretary for Native Affairs, 17 June 1929, NTS 1681, file 2/276 pt. 1, NASA, CT; Welsh to CM Welsh, 10 January 1928, NTS 1681, file 2/276 pt. 1, NASA, CT.

17. Welsh to CM Welsh, 5 July 1927, 1/MTF, box 7/16, file 2/9/1, NASA, CT.

18. Welsh to Johannes Zibi, 19 July 1927, 1/MTF, box 7/16, file 2/9/1, NASA, CT. Sergeant Nortje suspected that these men wanted to obtain traveling passes to link with Wellington followers in other districts, and he suggested that they immediately report to police stations in the districts of their destinations so that authorities there could maintain a close watch on their activities. See Nortje to Welsh, 20 July 1927, and undated statement by Welsh, 1/MTF, box 7/16, file 2/9/1, NASA, CT. The event described occurred on 4 April 1927. It is possible, perhaps probable, that Sidlai actually sought to consult with Wellington in Natal about the Mount Fletcher situation. For prosecution of tax evaders, see Welsh to CM Welsh, 10 March 1927, 1/MTF, box 7/16, file 2/9/1, NASA, CT.

19. Welsh to CM Welsh, 5 July 1927, 1/MTF, box 7/16, file 2/9/1, NASA, CT. See also Nortje to Welsh, 15 July 1927, 1/MTF, box 7/16, file 2/9/1, NASA, CT. The protective legislation was Proclamation 143 of 1919.

20. Affidavit of Richard Nortje, 13 May 1929; Affidavit of Richard Welsh, 13 May 1929; Welsh to CM Welsh, 15 May 1929, all in NTS 1681, file 2/276 pt. 1, NASA, CT.

21. Welsh to CM Welsh, 6 October 1927, 1/MTF, box 7/38, file N1; 5 September 1927; Johannes Zibi to Welsh, 16 July 1927; Affidavit of Johannes Zibi, 5 September 1927; handwritten document dated 5 February 1928; Members of the UNIA and ACL to Welsh, 23 September 1927, 1/MTF, box 7/16, file 2/9/1, NASA, CT.

22. Members of the UNIA and ACL to Welsh, 23 September 1927, 1/MTF, box 7/16, file 2/9/1, NASA, CT.

23. "Impi ka Wellington," *Izwi Lama Afrika*, December 1931.

24. Undated letters from Wellington to Edward and Anne Zibi, NTS 7602, file 26/328 pt. 4, NASA, CT. Anne Zibi's status as Ma Wellington suggests that she was a respected older woman, perhaps the mother of Edward. *Amafelandonwye* is an isiXhosa term meaning "we die together." See chapter 5 for a brief discussion of their activities in Herschel district.

25. For continued UNIA activity in these districts, see Internal correspondence of the South African Police, 4 July 1940, 1/TSO, box 5/1/23, file 2/12/2, NASA, CT; H. W. Warner, Mount Fletcher Resident Magistrate, to the Chief Magistrate, 16 June 1937, NTS 7602, file 26/328 pt. 4, NASA, CT; H. A. McKitterick, Office of the Public Prosecutor, Kentani, to the Solicitor-General, Grahamstown: Rex vs. James Ghazu and Lutoli Semekazi trial transcript, 7 December 1938, NTS 1681, file 2/276 pt. 2, NASA, CT. For the Bunga resolutions, see Minute 114 of the United Transkeian Territories General Council: Session 1936, NTS 7602, file 26/328 pt. 3, NASA, CT, and United Transkeian Territories General Council: Session 1937, NTS 7603, file 25/328 pt. 4, NASA, CT. Affidavit of African Constable E. Ndaba, 17 April 1936, NTS 7602, file 26/328 pt. 4, NASA, CT; Hartmann to Chief Magistrate Fyfe-King, 18 May 1936; H. W. Warner, Mount Fletcher Magistrate, to Chief Magistrate, 16 June 1937, NTS 7602, file 26/328 pt. 4, NASA, CT. The jailing of the twenty-seven Wellingtonites sparked a flurry of telegrams from Wellington and his wife, Esther, questioning the legality of this action. In 1930, Joel Bulana led a deputation of 300 men and 50 women to meet with Chief Magistrate W. T. Welsh. There, they asked for government funding of UNIA schools, relaxed restrictions on cattle grazing, the return of Wellington to the Transkei, and the reinstatement of "Chief" Edward Zibi to his headmanship. Unsurprisingly, CM Welsh refused these requests.

26. Paul Gulwa to Marcus Garvey, 8 March and 25 June 1938, documents in the personal collection of Robert R. Edgar.

27. Qumbu Magistrate Frank Doran to CM Welsh, 15 January 1927, 1/TSO, box 5/1/18, file 2/16/4, NASA, CT. Lutshoto promised his followers that the current price of thirteen shillings six pence would be reduced to five shillings in the postcolonial order. See Casteling to Lonsdale, 7 March 1927, 1/TSO, box 5/1/18, file 2/16/4, NASA, CT; Lonsdale to CM Welsh, 8 March 1927, Affidavit of Edward Chalmers Bam, 12 March 1927, and Affidavit of SAP Constable Thomas Lansdell, 6 August 1927, all in 1/TSO, box 5/1/18, file 2/16/4, NASA, CT. For Lutshoto's Basutoland excursions, see Affidavit of Lonsdale, 24 August 1927, 1/TSO, box 5/1/18, file 2/16/4, NASA, CT.

28. W. T. Welsh, "No Bigger Than a Man's Hand," *East London Daily Dispatch*, 6 April 1927, 1/MTF, box 7/16, file 2/9/1, NASA, CT. An unnamed government official made similar assertions in briefly retracing the history of the Mpondomise chieftaincy; Undated document, 1/TSO, box 108, file N1/1/3/36, NASA, CT. After Hope's murder, Mhlontlo had fled to Basutoland. Colonial

officials unsuccessfully tried him for murder upon his return to Qumbu in 1903; he died in 1912, though he remained a lightning rod of Mpondomise anticolonial fervor. Mditshwa surrendered soon after Hope's murder and served five years' imprisonment.

29. Beinart and Bundy, *Hidden Struggles*, 109–10. This is a grievance that still resonates in postapartheid South Africa. In contemporary times, the Mpondomise have sought recognition as an autonomous kingdom, and they still hold reverential ceremonies for Mhlontlo. See Phakamisa Ngani, "Tribal Forum to Meet King Sigcau Today," *East London Daily Dispatch Online*, 9 April 1999, and Rufus Zingqi, "Last Warrior Chief Gets Recognition," *East London Daily Dispatch Online*, 25 August 2000, http://www.dispatch.co.za (accessed May 30, 2011).

30. Affidavit of E. Browning, 27 June 1927; Lonsdale to the CM Welsh, 19 July 1927, both in 1/TSO, box 5/1/18, file 2/16/4, NASA, CT.

31. Affidavit of Edward Chalmers Bam, 12 March 1927; Lonsdale to CM Welsh, 8 March 1927; Affidavit of Philip Payn, 12 March 1927, all in 1/TSO, box 5/1/18, file 2/16/4, NASA, CT.

32. Wellington to Edward Zibi, 15 February 1927 and 11 June 1927, ibid. Wellingtonites like Josiah Sigenu held these institutions, having as many as sixty-three students in their kraals, and hosted UNIA teachers from Mount Fletcher and Mount Frere. Several Tsolo residents taught at St. Welford in Mount Fletcher, among them Principal Teacher Elias Msuntwani and teachers Gretha Jokazi and Marian and Gertrude Matchanda; Lonsdale to CM Welsh, 30 August 1927. For Sigenu, see Affidavit of Wiliam Vabaza, 22 March 1927, and for Nogemane and James Jokazi, see Undated affidavit of Lionel Harris, all in 1/TSO, box 5/1/18, file 2/16/4, NASA, CT. Other teachers originating from Tinana location included John Sidlai and Mina Labanga. See Welsh to Lonsdale, 16 March 1927, 1/TSO, box 5/1/18, file 2/16/4, NASA, CT. The surname Jokazi is a consistent thread in the Wellingtonite documents. Thomas Jokazi opened a UNIA school in his kraal, and James, Dorothy, and Kiddy acted as traveling interpreters and teachers for Wellington. At Thomas Jokazi's UNIA School, there were six Jokazi children attending. The kraal of Josiah Sigenu was the site of the Esiqungqwini UNIA School, where Sandi Sigenu was the listed teacher. See also V. Gottsch to Lonsdale, 3 March 1927. For Somfaka, see Statement of Petshana Majaugaza, 25 May 1927. Somfaka may be the person referred to in 2 June 1927 who had been living in Johannesburg for the previous eighteen months. Lonsdale described this person as a "poisonous brute [who] is very cheeky and openly wears the (UNIA) badge," Lonsdale to CM Welsh, 2 June 1927, all in 1/TSO, box 5/1/18, file 2/16/4, NASA, CT.

33. Affidavit of Philip Payn, 12 March 1927; Lonsdale to CM Welsh, 15 February 1927, 19 March 1927; Report of South African policeman Killie Tile, 24 February 1927; Affidavit of Lonsdale, 12 March 1927, all in 1/TSO, box 5/1/18, file 2/16/4, NASA, CT.

34. Affidavit of Phillip Payn, 12 March 1927; Affidavit of Nelton Mabandla, 13 June 1927; Affidavit of Sprigg Madikiza, 13 June 1927, all in 1/TSO, box 5/1/18, file 2/16/4, NASA, CT.

35. Acting Tsolo Magistrate to CM Welsh, 14 January 1929 and 28 January 1929, 1/TSO, box 5/1/21, file L11, NASA, CT.

36. Affidavit by Lonsdale, 2 May 1927, 1/TSO, box 5/1/18, file 2/16/4, NASA, CT. Headmen Joseph Jokazi (Lower Sinxago), Joseph Ncelana (Upper Sinxago), and Lutshoto (Ndibanisweni) were all leaders in Wellington's movement. Mission teachers who left to teach at UNIA schools included Elias Msuntwani, Gretha Jokazi, and Marian and Gertrude Matchanda. R. D. Nortje to Welsh, 12 March 1927, 1/TSO, box 5/1/18, file 2/16/4, NASA, CT; and South African Police to Lonsdale, 22 April 1927; Native Corporal Obed Sigenu to Herschel Resident Magistrate, 3 October 1928, 2/SPT, box 16, file N1/9/2, NASA, CT. The Matchandas had learned weaving at a mission school and had taught this skill at another mission institution before becoming Wellingtonites. Similarly, Msuntwani had taught in Tsolo and in Pondoland before being "dismissed on account of bad character." Christopher Matchanda, possibly related to Marian and Gertrude, taught in a UNIA school in Herschel. Lonsdale to Welsh, 26 January 1927, 1/TSO, box 5/1/18, file 2/16/4, NASA, CT.

37. Statement by African policeman Joseph Nho, 9 May 1927, 1/TSO, box 5/1/18, file 2/16/4, NASA, CT. Abraham Lupalule, a prominent Wellingtonite in Mount Fletcher, had formerly been a policeman in Maclear district.

38. Father F. J. Rumsey, letter dated 25 July 1927, in *Cowley Evangelist*, September 1927.

39. F. J. Rumsey, letter dated 22 January 1929, in *Cowley Evangelist*, April 1929.

40. G. K. Hemming, "No Bigger Than a Man's Hand," *East London Daily Dispatch*, 29 March and 13 April 1927.

41. Beinart and Bundy, *Hidden Struggles*, 129; 1/QBU (Qumbu), box 60, file N1/1/2, NASA, CT.

42. Undated Affidavit of Edwin C. Bam, 1/TSO, box 5/1/21, file L11, NASA, CT. The meeting described took place on 5 October 1929. Mditshwa to Tsolo Resident Magistrate E. W. Bowen, 14 January 1929, 1/TSO, box 5/1/18, file 2/16/6; Bowen to CM Welsh, 28 January 1929, E. W. Wilkins, Tsolo Resident Magistrate, to Chief Magistrate, 11 November 1935, and SAP Sergeant to the District Commandant, SAP, 30 January 1934, all in 1/TSO, box 5/1/21, file L11, NASA, CT.

43. Minutes of Meeting between the CM Welsh and Lutshoto Mditshwa, 23 June 1931, 1/TSO, box 5/1/21, file L11, NASA, CT. Lutshoto sent Sodinga and Ndonda Mtyingizane to Cape Town to confer with the same attorneys who had assisted the Qumbu Mpondomise in the matter of gaining recognition of their chief.

44. Minutes of a meeting held at Mdibanisweni location, 7 July 1931, 1/TSO, box 5/1/21, file L11, NASA, CT. Lutshoto reportedly spiraled into a reclusive depression that the district surgeon diagnosed as "mental confusion." The quoted loyalist headman was Harry Makamba of Magutywa location.

45. J. Hen Boisen, Tsolo Magistrate, to V. M. de Villiers, 17 May 1939; Meshack Mgidlana to de Villiers, 21 May 1939 and 3 April 1939, all in NTS 1681, file 2/276 pt. 2, NASA, CT. Lutshoto, though a committed Christian, seems to have been only marginally cooperative with state authorities. In 1949, the Tsolo magistrate de-

scribed Lutshoto's cooperation with state authorities as "somewhat less than average." See Tsolo Magistrate to Chief Magistrate, 23 March 1949, 1/TSO, box 5/1/18, file 2/16/4. There is also little documentation detailing Lutshoto's actions after this date, though he did prevent Nqamakwe resident Meshack Mgidlana from converting a UNIA branch into an ANC chapter. Gulwa was born in approximately 1893, passed Standard Six in 1911, and owned Fair View Farm in Tsolo district.

46. Document about Paul Gulwa, 7 May 1949, 1/TSO, box 5/1/133, file N1/10/3. Affidavit of Edward Bam, 1 September 1927; Lonsdale to Welsh, 26 January 1927, both in 1/TSO, box 5/1/18, file 2/16/4, NASA, CT.

47. Paul Gulwa, interview by Robert Edgar, 1974, in Tsolo, South Africa. For Nontetha, see Robert R. Edgar and Hilary Sapire, *African Apocalypse: The Story of Nontetha Nkwenkwe, a Twentieth-Century South African Prophet* (Athens: Ohio University Press, 2000).

48. Affidavits of African Detectives Ephraim Ndhlovu, 11 December 1928, and Magende Zondi, 10 December 1928, CNC, box 348, file 1/29/7, NASA, CT. Wilkins to Chief Magistrate, 11 November 1935; G. H. Hayes to Tsolo RM, 29 October 1935, both in 1/TSO, box 5/1/21, file L11, NASA, CT.

49. Paul Gulwa to Marcus Garvey, 8 March 1938, among letters in possession of the author. I would like to thank Robert Edgar for sharing these letters, collected from Paul Gulwa in 1974.

50. Gulwa to Garvey, 25 January 1938, letter in possession of the author. The South African Police, concerned about "subversive" groups, confiscated hundreds of Gulwa's letters during World War II, never returning them. However, Gulwa managed to keep several, which offer this glimpse of continued UNIA connections.

51. United Transkeian Territories General Council, 1936, Minute 114: 30 March 1936, NTS 7602, file 26/328 pt. 3, NASA, CT; R. Fyfe King to Transkeian Magistrates, 30 November 1939, 1/NKE, box 58, file N1/9/3, NASA, CT.

52. James Barber, *South Africa in the Twentieth Century: A Political History* (London: Wiley-Blackwell, 1999), 104.

53. David Anthony, *Max Yergan: Race Man, Internationalist, Cold Warrior* (New York: New York University Press, 2006), 97–98.

54. *Negro World*, 24 January 1931.

55. Renewal of Petition of the UNIA and ACL to the League of Nations, September 1928, reprinted in Robert A. Hill, ed., *The Marcus Garvey and Universal Negro Improvement Association Papers* (Berkeley: University of California Press, 1983–), 10:443–44.

56. Marcus Garvey, "The Negro Problem in South Africa," *Black Man* 2, no. 6 (March–April 1937): 8.

57. Marcus Garvey to Mr. Mobraw, Ex-Secretary of African National Congress, 15 October 1928, in Hill, *Garvey Papers*, 10:473. See also Garvey to Chalmers Nyombolo, *Imvo Zabantsundu*, 5 February 1929.

58. S. E. K. Mqhayi, "Rev. Nyombolo and Mr. Gavi," *Imvo Zabantsundu*, 25 February 1929.

59. Enock Mazilenko, "Africans Must Unite to Form a Nation," *Negro World*, 9 February 1929.

60. "Pretoria Division of UNIA Elects Delegates to Convention," *Johannesburg Star*, 23 November 1928, reprinted in *Negro World*, 26 January 1929.

61. Mazilenko, "Africans Must Unite."

62. See the serialized letters by Theodore Kakaza, "A Cry to the Native South African Tribes," published weekly in *Imvo Zabantsundu*, 11 June–16 July 1929.

63. Alexander Njaba, "Rev. Nyombolo and Garvey," *Imvo Zabantsundu*, 2 April 1929.

64. J. J. Mole, "Garveyism," *Imvo Zabantsundu*, 5 March 1929.

65. "Kad'enta," "Rough Shaking," *Imvo Zabantsundu*, 10 September 1929. *Kad'enta* is Xhosa for "one who has seen a lot and thus knows a lot."

66. "Effigies of Smuts and Hertzog Condemned as Exploiting Parasites," *Negro World*, 25 January 1930.

67. "Another Victory," *Abantu Batho*, 1 May 1930. The *South African Worker*, a communist paper, sympathized with Garvey's conviction, saying that his "schemes may be impracticable and impossible, but no one doubts his honesty of purpose to realize his aims." "Marcus Garvey Convicted," *South African Worker*, 30 September 1929.

68. Renewal of Petition of the UNIA and ACL.

69. Hill, *Garvey Papers*, 7:296–300.

70. Robert A. Hill and Barbara Bair, eds., *Marcus Garvey: Life and Lessons* (Berkeley: University of California Press, 1987), lv, lvii, lviii.

71. "Mussolini and Ras Tafari," *Black Man* 1, no. 7 (June 1935): 16; "Italy and Abyssinia," *Black Man* 1, no. 8 (July 1935): 17.

72. "Italy's Conquest?," *Black Man* 2, no. 2 (July–August 1936): 4.

73. "The Negro Problem in South Africa," *Black Man* 2, no. 6 (March–April 1937): 8.

74. Hill, *Garvey Papers*, 10:647.

75. "Decline of a Great Leader," *Amsterdam News*, 30 January 1937.

76. West Indian Crusader, "Marcus Garvey and the International African Service Bureau," 27 November 1937, in Hill, *Garvey Papers*, 10:647. For international black antifascist activity, see "This Ain't Ethiopia, but It'll Do," in Robin D. G. Kelley, *Race Rebels: Culture, Politics and the Black Working Class* (New York: Free Press, 1994), 123–58.

77. Trial Transcript of Lutoli Semekazi and James Ghazu; Semekazi to Ghazu, 4 January 1938, 6 January 1938, 11 February 1938, and 1 March 1938, all in NTS 1681, file 2/276 pt. 2, NASA, CT. The uneducated character of the Qumbu UNIA leadership differed from virtually all documented UNIA chapters. Nkwekwe Mehlomakulu was a particularly central UNIA figure in Qumbu during the late 1920s, hosting a UNIA school, holding meetings that drew Wellingtonites from all over the Transkei, and consorting with other leading Wellingtonites like Edward Zibi. However, he does not appear in Qumbu documents during the late 1930s. He may have been related to the Mehlomakulu family in Herschel, descended from

the AmaHlubi chief who led that group into Hershel during the Mfecane. In Herschel, Wellington had already injected himself into the roiling disputes between two branches of the Mehlomakulu family over the legitimate claimant to a headmanship. For Nkwekwe's Qumbu activities, see generally D. W. Semple to Frank Doran, Qumbu Magistrate, 28 March 1927, and Doran to Deputy Commissioner of Police, 30 December 1927, NTS 1681, file 1/18/26, NASA, CT. Within Qumbu, UNIA members clustered in Lower Culunca, Upper Culunca, Caba, and Nqayi locations. Semekazi resided in the remote Nqayi location, forty miles from the district's administrative center. Twenty miles from the nearest police post, Nqayi could only be accessed by car from neighboring Maclear district. This remoteness undoubtedly allowed Semekazi to organize more freely, though his consistent refusal to pay taxes attracted the attention of colonial authorities.

78. Qumbu Magistrate to Chief Magistrate, 6 June 1939; and Criminal Record of Lutoli Semekazi, Preparatory Examination by J. Schoeman, 25 April 1939, both in NTS 1681, file 2/276, NASA, CT.

79. Trial Transcript of Lutoli Semekazi and James Ghazu—Affidavit of Drosilah Mgobozi, 14 August 1938; Qumbu UNIA meeting minutes, 31 July 1938, all in NTS 1681, file 2/276 pt. 1, NASA, CT. Gulwa occasionally presided over Qumbu meetings and sent moneys collected from Qumbu overseas, and Tsolo's James Jokazi regularly preached to Qumbu members before his death in 1938. The Qumbu UNIA also attracted non-Mpondomise, as Basotho women, from the primarily Basotho Nqayi location, attended meetings.

80. Semekazi was also in contact with UNIA branches in Ramlani, Maclear, Matatiele, Jokie, Kowe, Xalanga, Nqamakwe, and Mpondoland. The Qumbu UNIA also attracted non-Mpondomise, as Basotho women, from the primarily Basotho Nqayi location attended meetings.

81. An American or Liberian Negro named Mathews had been in Angola and northern Namibia preaching Garveyism. He was writing a letter to "David Mc" in New York. He told a colonial official that he was one of six men chosen to preach to Africans. The others were in Bechuanaland, Natal, Tanganyika, Rhodesia, and the Transvaal. He said his South African headquarters were in Cape Town.

82. James Ghazu, "An African Letter," Negro World, 16 July 1932. It was at McKinley's address, 15 DeKorte Street, that Semekazi wrote to Ghazu. Ghazu corresponded with Garvey, the Jamaican-born St. William Grant, head of the Tiger Division (so named after prosecutors referred to Garvey as "the Tiger"), and the Garvey club in America. Ghazu also worked closely with the Jamaican-born ANC and UNIA officer Arthur McKinley, the "receiver of all people who join the Association."

83. Only the Pretoria and Cape Town divisions appeared to have official charters from the American-based UNIA.

84. Ghazu to Semekazi, undated letter, NTS 1681, file 2/276 pt. 1, NASA, CT.

85. Decision of Judge Gane, Supreme Court of South Africa, Mount Frere Circuit Court, 27 May 1939, Government Supreme Court (GSC), box 245/39, file 1/21/1349, NASA, CT. Jeremiah 17:1: "The sin of Judah is written with a pen of

iron." Jeremiah is warning Judah for breaking God's covenant; the punishment is to be conquered and ruled by another people in a land not their own. Jeremiah was beaten and ostracized for his prophecies.

86. Ghazu to Semekazi, 22 March 1938, NTS 1681, file 2/276 pt. 1, NASA, CT.

87. Ghazu to Semekazi, undated letter, NTS 1681, file 2/276 pt. 1, NASA, CT.

88. Semekazi to Ghazu, 4 January 1938 and 11 February 1938, NTS 1681, file 2/276 pt. 1, NASA, CT.

89. Semekazi to Ghazu, 4 May 1938, NTS 1681, file 2/276 pt. 1, NASA, CT.

90. Transcript of Preparatory Examination, 25 April 1939, NTS 1681, file 2/276 pt. 1, NASA, CT.

91. Semekazi to Ghazu, 6 January 1938 and Semekazi to Ghazu, 11 February 1938, NTS 1681, file 2/276 pt. 1, NASA, CT.

92. Semekazi to Ghazu, 4 January 1938 and 4 March 1938, NTS 1681, file 2/276 pt. 1, NASA, CT.

93. Semekazi to Ghazu, 7 April 1938, NTS 1681, file 2/276 pt. 1, NASA, CT.

94. Trial Transcript of Lutoli Semekazi and James Ghazu, 4 October 1938, and Ghazu to McKinley, 31 August 1938, in NTS 1681, file 2/276 pt. 1, NASA, CT.

95. Affidavits of South African Police Personnel Hans Visser, Samuel Van Niekerk, and Francis William Lamb, 16 February 1939, NTS 1681, file 2/276 pt. 1, NASA, CT. There is little extant evidence on Meya. In another court document, prosecutors claim that he hailed from Cape Town and was the chief organizer, though there is no corroborating evidence for this charge. See Trial Transcript of James Ghazu and Lutoli Semekazi, 1 September 1938, NTS 1681, file 2/276 pt. 1, NASA, CT. As of early June 1939, Semekazi still had seven and a half months remaining on a sentence deriving from his conviction on several charges: resisting the police, pointing a firearm at a person, possession of an unlicensed rifle, failing to report an undomiciled African in his homestead, and failing to pay taxes. See J. O. Cornell, Qumbu Magistrate, to Chief Magistrate, 6 June 1939.

96. "Unpreparedness a Crime," *Black Man* 2, no. 1 (March 1936).

97. Trial Transcript of Lutoli Semekazi and James Ghazu, NTS 1681, file 2/276 pt. 1, NASA, CT; Marcus Garvey to Arthur McKinley, 8 September 1938, letter in the author's position. He also noted that the Cape Town chapter was "only one of the Charters in that great country."

98. They also questioned UNIA members, most notably Arthur McKinley. The Jamaican-born McKinley had arrived in East London in 1900 after concluding his work as a greaser aboard a steamship. He eventually settled in Cape Town, where he joined the Cape Town UNIA in the 1920s. Many Capetonians knew him for his eloquent and humorous pro-Garvey speeches, though detractors claimed that he was an "anti-white agitator of the worst kind . . . a soap box orator who preaches anti-white doctrines." McKinley was also a businessman, acting as agent for the *Bantu World* and Garveyist literature and newspapers while also renting out rooms (including one to Ghazu). Preparatory Examination Transcript of Public Prosecutor McKittrick, NTS 1681, file 2/276 pt. 1, NASA, CT; Robert R. Edgar, ed., *An African American in South Africa: The Travel Notes of Ralph J. Bunche* (Athens:

Ohio University Press, 1992), 113–14, 321.

99. "Two Natives Sentenced for Sedition" in Hill, *Garvey Papers*, vol. 10 (Berkeley: University of California Press, 2006), 672–79.

100. Decision of Judge Gane, 27 May 1939; "Garveyism Much Alive in Transkei," *Imvo Zabantsundu*, 3 June 1939.

101. Death Notice of James Ghazu, 25 April 1945, 2/OBS (obituaries), file 3/1/13, NASA, CT.

102. Shula Marks, *Not Either an Experimental Doll: The Separate Worlds of Three South African Women* (Bloomington: Indiana University Press, 2001), 31.

103. The Cape provincial commission endorsed Loram's ideas by instituting a Hampton/Tuskegee–style curriculum in the Cape Province by 1923. James Campbell, *Songs of Zion: The African Methodist Episcopal Church in the United States and South Africa* (New York: Oxford University Press, 1995), 309.

104. This experience was very familiar to German colonial officials, who saw enough similarities between the Jim Crow South and colonial Africa to translate *Up from Slavery* and other Washington books into German for the benefit of colonial officials and missionaries in Africa. See Andrew Zimmerman, *Alabama in Africa: Booker T. Washington, the German Empire, and the Globalization of the New South* (Princeton, NJ: Princeton University Press, 2009), 187–88.

105. C. T. Loram, *South African Outlook*, 1 October 1927.

106. C. T. Loram, "Education" *Christian Express*, 1 June 1921.

107. Mtombikani Munduna to Robert Moton, 10 April 1921; Malcolm to Moton, 23 August 1926; Moton to Malcolm, 6 October 1926, Phelps-Stokes Fund Records, file B-4, folder Misc. M's, Schomburg Center for Research in Black Culture, New York Public Library, New York.

108. Margaret Walbridge to Thomas Jesse Jones, 6 July 1928; Loram to Jones, 1 June 1932, Anson Phelps-Stokes Papers, box 27, folder 445, Manuscripts and Archives, Sterling Library, Yale University, New Haven, Connecticut.

109. Moton to Jones, 24 September 1928, Anson Phelps-Stokes Papers, box 32, folder 519, Manuscripts and Archives, Sterling Library, Yale University, New Haven, Connecticut.

110. Jones to Moton, 26 September 1928, ibid.

111. Makhanya to Loram, 30 September 1928, ibid.

112. Dorothy P. Cushing, "Miss Makanya in Boston," *Missionary Herald* 123 (1927), in box 39, folder 33, American Board of Commissioners for Foreign Missions, Houghton Library, Harvard University, Cambridge, Massachusetts.

113. Houghton to Barnett, 12 April 1929, and Barnett to Houghton, 14 May 1929, box 176, Education folder, Claude Barnett papers, Chicago Historical Society, Chicago, Illinois; Richard Glotzer, "The Career of Mabel Carney: The Study of Race and Rural Development in the United States and South Africa," *International Journal of African Historical Studies* 29, no. 2 (1996): 309–36.

114. Marks, *Not Either*, 33.

115. *Umteteli wa Bantu*, 11 September 1937.

116. Edgar, *African American in South Africa*, 322.

117. Ibid., 48, 98, 136.

118. Ibid.

119. Peter Abrahams, *Tell Freedom: Memories of Africa* (New York: Alfred A. Knopf, 1954), 225–26. See also Nat Nakasa, "Mr Nakasa Goes to Harlem," in *To Kill a Man's Pride and Other Short Stories from South Africa*, ed. Marcus Ramogale, 85–98 (Johannesburg: Ravan Press, 1996).

120. Amanda Kemp, *"Up from Slavery (1920–1943)* and Other Narratives: Black South African Performances of the American Negro" (PhD diss., Northwestern University, 1997), 212–13. For Xuma generally, see Steven D. Gish, *Alfred B. Xuma: African, American, South African* (New York: New York University Press, 2000).

121. Alfred Xuma to Bishop Richard R. Wright, 30 December 1936, box B, Alfred B. Xuma Papers, University of the Witwatersrand, Johannesburg, South Africa.

122. Iris Berger, "An African American 'Mother of the Nation': Madie Hall Xuma in South Africa, 1940–1963," *Journal of Southern African Studies* 27, no. 3 (September 2001): 555–57.

123. Kemp, *"Up from Slavery,"* 115, 205; *Umteteli wa Bantu*, 19 June 1943.

124. Kemp, *"Up from Slavery,"* 111–13; Edgar, *African American in South Africa*, 187.

125. *Bantu World*, 17 August 1934.

126. Gish, *Alfred B. Xuma*, 126.

127. Anthony, *Max Yergan*, 67–68.

128. Ibid., 93.

129. Ibid., 132.

130. *Bantu World*, 2 February 1935.

131. *Bantu World*, 16 February 1935.

132. Peter Davis, *In Darkest Hollywood: Exploring the Jungles of South African Cinema* (Athens: Ohio University Press, 1996), 142–44; Martin Duberman, *Paul Robeson: A Biography* (New York: New Press, 1995), 202–3.

133. Black South Africa's admiration of Robeson was part of a larger fascination with American Negro music from the years of the Jubilee Singers through their embrace of spirituals and jazz. Urban black South Africans were proudly and self-consciously identifying themselves as actors on the stage of world history. Jazz was a discourse with explicit historical roots in the continent of Africa, and it had been cultivated by people of color — by former Africans — in the United States. Jazz was truly African American music. African vaudeville and minstrel acts incorporated jazz into performances modeled on American acts, and African stage performers impersonated American stars like the musician Fats Waller and the Mills brothers dancers; others claimed to be "the colored Paul Robeson," the "Copper-colored Shirley Temple," and "the black Charlie Chaplin." These acts included the African Darkies, De Pitch Black Follies, Darktown Strutters, African Sonny Boys, Ravan Girls, Revellers, and Merry Makers, as well as the Yankee Lads, the Movie-Tone Cabaret Girls, the Monte Carlo Girls, and the Harlem Babies. The vocalist James Phillips was the "colored Paul Robeson"; child star Doris Shuping was the

"Copper-colored Shirley Temple"; Lucy Phooko, "our Ginger Rogers"; Sullivan Mphahlele was Fats Waller; and Manyaro was the "black Charlie Chaplin." For the tremendous influence of American, particularly African American, cultural production on South Africa, see David B. Coplan, *In Township Tonight! South Africa's Black City Music and Theatre*, 2nd ed. (Chicago: University of Chicago Press, 2008).

134. For a more detailed treatment of CAA activities with African organizations, see Penny Von Eschen, *Race against Empire: African Americans and Anti-colonialism, 1937–57* (New York: Oxford University Press, 1998), and Gish, *Alfred B. Xuma,* 146–49.

135. W. E. B. Du Bois, *The World and Africa* (1946; repr., New York: International Publishers, 1975), 43.

136. Gish, *Alfred B. Xuma,* 148.

137. W. Keith Hancock, *Smuts,* vol. 2, *The Field of Force* (Cambridge: Cambridge University Press, 1968), 473.

138. James H. Meriwether, *Proudly We Can Be Africans: Black Americans and Africa, 1935–1961* (Chapel Hill: University of North Carolina Press, 2002).

139. The two Garveyites prophesying German liberation were Mndindwa Marwanqana and Sandy Sigenu. Hill, *Garvey Papers,* 10:688. Marwanqana was hustled off to jail, where he sent Hertzog his UNIA card and his badge of racial membership and lamented that though God had made him black, South African laws treated his blackness as a virtual crime (690). Other Africans viewed Nazi Germany, with its seeming power to destroy the British Empire, as a new liberator.

140. Hancock, *Smuts,* 2:500.

141. "The Passing of Garvey," *Bantu World,* 3 August 1940.

142. "The Passing of Marcus Garvey," *Imvo Zabantsundu,* 10 August 1940.

143. J. Grobbelaar to District Commandant, South African Police, 4 July 1940, 1/TSO, box 5/1/23, file 2/12/2, NASA, CT.

144. Gulwa to UNIA, 5 August 1940, letter in author's possession.

145. Stewart to Gulwa, 7 January 1942, letter in author's possession, and Gulwa to UNIA Parent Body, 3 July 1942, in Hill, *Garvey Papers,* 10:694. In a 1974 interview with historian Robert Edgar, Gulwa noted that during World War II, South African police, fearful of anti-British seditious sentiment, confiscated virtually all of his correspondence with Garvey and American UNIA officials. They did not return these letters.

146. "Minutes of the UNIA Fairview Farm Division, 30 June 1942," in Hill, *Garvey Papers,* 10:695, 696. Desmond Tutu used this same quote predicting imminent African deliverance from apartheid when he accepted his Nobel Peace Prize in 1984.

147. Meanwhile, James Hannibal in Southwest Africa donated £2 to help fund the *Black Man;* Hill, *Garvey Papers,* 10:653. Mr. H. Illitintro, Entweni College, Port St. Johns, graduated from the School of African Philosophy; Hill, *Garvey Papers,* 10:685. J. N. Mohapi was president of a Cape Town UNIA chapter; 5 July 1943, in Hill, *Garvey Papers,* 10:696–97. The Cape Town UNIA, together with the

ANC, hosted a reception for natives' representatives. James Thaele presided over the meeting and praised those representatives for their recent parliamentary work. One of the representatives was Hyman Basner, who with Alfred Xuma lobbied the UN on behalf of Africans. Francis Lekuakue pledged to spread UNIA ideals and asked about the School of African Philosophy.

148. Nelson Mandela, *Long Walk to Freedom: The Autobiography of Nelson Mandela* (Boston: Little, Brown, 1995), 45.

149. "A South African Sends a Cheerful Greeting," *Negro World*, 2 August 1924.

Bibliography

BOOKS

Abrahams, Peter. *Tell Freedom: Memories of Africa*. New York: Alfred A. Knopf, 1954.

Adas, Michael. *Machines as the Measure of Men: Science, Technology and Ideologies of Western Dominance*. Ithaca, NY: Cornell University Press, 1989.

Adi, Hakim. *West African Students in Britain*. London: Lawrence and Wishart Press, 1998.

Anderson, James. *The Education of Blacks in the South, 1865–1900*. Champaign: University of Illinois Press, 1988.

Anthony, David. *Max Yergan: Race Man, Internationalist, Cold Warrior*. New York: New York University Press, 2006.

Appiah, Kwame Anthony. *In My Father's House: Africa in the Philosophy of Culture*. New York: Oxford University Press, 1992.

Ayers, Edward. *The Promise of the New South: Life after Reconstruction*. New York: Oxford University Press, 1993.

Azikiwe, Nnamdi. *My Odyssey*. London: Hurst, 1970.

Baeta, C. G. *Christianity in Tropical Africa*. Uppsala, Sweden: Uppsala Press, 1968.

Bandele, Ramla. *Black Star: African American Activism in the International Political Economy*. Champaign: University of Illinois Press, 2008.

Bannister, Robert C. *Social Darwinism: Science and Myth in Anglo-American Social Thought*. Philadelphia: Temple University Press, 1979.

Barber, James. *South Africa in the Twentieth Century: A Political History*. London: Wiley-Blackwell, 1999.

Barrett, David, ed. *Kenya Churches Handbook*. Kisumu, Kenya: Evangel Publishing House, 1973.

Bederman, Gail. *Manliness and Civilization: A Cultural History of Gender and Race in the United States, 1880–1917*. Chicago: University of Chicago Press, 1995.

Beinart, William. *The Political Economy of Pondoland, 1890–1930*. New York: Cambridge University Press, 1982.

Beinart, William, and Colin Bundy. *Hidden Struggles in Rural South Africa: Politics and Popular Movements in the Transkei and Eastern Cape, 1890–1930*. Johannesburg: Ravan Press, 1987.

Beinart, William, and Saul Dubow, eds. *Segregation and Apartheid in Twentieth-Century South Africa*. New York: Routledge, 1995.

Bennett, Paula, ed. *Nineteenth-Century American Women Poets: An Anthology*. Malden, MA: Blackwell, 1998.

Benson, Mary. *The African Patriots: The Story of the African National Congress of South Africa*. London: Faber and Faber, 1963.

Bernardi, Daniel, ed. *The Birth of Whiteness: Race and the Emergence of U.S. Cinema*. New Brunswick, NJ: Rutgers University Press, 1996.

Bolster, W. Jeffrey. *Black Jacks: African American Seamen in the Age of Sail*. Cambridge, MA: Harvard University Press, 1997.

Bond, Horace. *Education for Freedom: A History of Lincoln University, Pennsylvania*. Princeton, NJ: Princeton University Press, 1976.

Booth, Alan. *The United States Experience in South Africa, 1784–1870*. Cape Town: A. A. Balkema, 1976.

Booth, Joseph. *Africa for the African*. 1896. Reprint, Lilongwe, Malawi: Kachere Press, 1996.

Boyd, Charles, ed. *Mr. Chamberlain's Speeches*. 2 vols. London: Constable, 1914.

Bradford, Helen. *A Taste of Freedom: The ICU in Rural South Africa, 1924–1930*. Johannesburg: Ravan Press, 1987.

Branford, Jean. *A Dictionary of South African English*. Cape Town: Oxford University Press, 1980.

Brownlee, W. T. *Reminiscences of a Transkeian*. Pietermaritzburg: Shuter and Shooter, 1975.

Buell, Raymond. *The Native Problem in Africa*. 2 vols. New York: Macmillan, 1928.

Bundy, Colin. *The Rise and Fall of the South African Peasantry*. Berkeley: University of California Press, 1979.

Bunting, Brian. *Moses Kotane: A South African Political Revolutionary*. London: Inkululeko, 1975.

Burkett, Randall. *Black Redemption: Churchmen Speak for the Garvey Movement*. Philadelphia: Temple University Press, 1978.

——. *Garveyism as a Religious Movement: The Institutionalization of a Black Civil Religion*. Metuchen, NJ: Scarecrow Press, 1978.

Callahan, Allen Dwight. *The Talking Book: African Americans and the Bible*. New Haven, CT: Yale University Press, 2008.

Campbell, James. *Middle Passages: African American Journeys to Africa, 1787–2005*. New York: Penguin, 2006.

——. *Songs of Zion: The African Methodist Episcopal Church in the United States and South Africa*. New York: Oxford University Press, 1995.

Carton, Benedict. *Blood from Your Children: The Colonial Origins of Generational Conflict in South Africa*. Pietermaritzburg: University of Natal Press, 2000.

Carton, Benedict, John Laband, and Jabulani Sithole, eds. *Being Zulu, Past and Present*. New York: Columbia University Press, 2010.

Cell, John. *The Highest Stage of White Supremacy: The Origins of Segregation in South Africa and the American South*. Cambridge: Cambridge University Press, 1982.

Chanock, Martin. *Unconsummated Union: Britain, Rhodesia, and South Africa, 1900–1945.* Manchester, UK: Manchester University Press, 1977.

Chenu, Bruno. *The Trouble I've Seen: The Big Book of Negro Spirituals.* Valley Forge, PA: Judson Press, 2003.

Chirenje, J. Mutero. *Ethiopianism and Afro-Americans in Southern Africa, 1883–1916.* Baton Rouge: Louisiana State University Press, 1987.

Clarke, John H., ed. *Marcus Garvey and the Vision of Africa.* New York: Vintage Books, 1974.

Clay, Gervas. *Your Friend Lewanika: The Life and Times of Lubosi Lewanika, Litunga of Barotseland, 1842–1916.* London: Chatto and Windus, 1968.

Clothier, Norman. *Black Valour: The South African Native Labour Contingent, 1916–18, and the Sinking of the Mendi.* Pietermaritzburg: University of Natal Press, 1987.

Cobley, Alan G. *Class and Consciousness: The Black Petty Bourgeoisie in South Africa, 1924 to 1950.* New York: Greenwood Press, 1990.

Comoroff, J., and J. Comoroff. *Of Revelation and Revolution: Christianity, Colonialism and Consciousness in South Africa.* Chicago: University of Chicago Press, 1991.

Conrad, Joseph. *Heart of Darkness.* Peterborough, Ontario, Canada: Broadview Press, 1999.

Cooney, Patrick L., and Henry W. Powell. *The Life and Times of the Prophet Vernon Johns.* Online publication: Vernon Johns Society, 1998, www.vernonjohns.org.

Cope, Nicholas. *To Bind the Nation: Solomon kaDinizulu and Zulu Nationalism, 1913–1933.* Pietermaritzburg: University of Natal Press, 1993.

Coplan, David B. *In Township Tonight! South Africa's Black City Music and Theatre.* 2nd ed. Chicago: University of Chicago Press, 2008.

Coppin, Levi. *Observations of Persons and Things in South Africa, 1900–1904.* Philadelphia: A.M.E. Book Concern, n.d.

Crais, Clifton. *The Politics of Evil: Magic, State Power, and the Political Imagination in South Africa.* Cambridge: Cambridge University Press, 2002.

Cronon, Edmund David. *Black Moses: The Story of Marcus Garvey and the Universal Negro Improvement Association.* Madison: University of Wisconsin Press, 1955.

Culverson, Donald. *Contesting Apartheid: U.S. Activism, 1960–1987.* Boulder, CO: Westview Press, 1999.

Davis, Peter. *In Darkest Hollywood: Exploring the Jungles of South African Cinema.* Athens: Ohio University Press, 1996.

Dean, Harry. *The Pedro Gorino.* New York: Houghton Mifflin, 1929.

Dean, Harry, and Sterling North. *Umbala: The Adventures of a Negro Sea Captain in Africa and on the Seven Seas in His Attempts to Found an Ethiopian Empire.* London: Harrap, 1929.

De Coy, Robert H. *Jack Johnson: The Big Black Fire.* Los Angeles: Holloway House, 1991.

Denoon, Donald. *A Grand Illusion: The Failure of Imperial Policy in the Transvaal Colony during the Period of Reconstruction, 1900–1905.* London: Longmans, 1973.

Drake, St. Clair. *The Redemption of Africa and Black Religion.* Chicago: Third World Press, 1970.

Dube, John. *A Familiar Talk upon My Native Land and Some Things Found There.* Rochester, NY: R.M. Swinburne and Co., 1892.

———. *The Zulu's Appeal for Light and England's Duty.* London: Evans Bros., 1910.

Duberman, Martin. *Paul Robeson: A Biography.* New York: New Press, 1995.

Du Bois, W. E. B. *Darkwater: Voices from within the Veil.* New York: Harcourt, Brace and Howe, 1920.

———. *Souls of Black Folk.* 1903. Reprint, New York: Vintage, New American Library, 1990.

———. *The World and Africa.* 1946. Reprint, New York: International Publishers, 1975.

Dubow, Saul. *Racial Segregation and the Origins of Apartheid in South Africa, 1919–1936.* New York: Palgrave Macmillan, 1989.

———. *Scientific Racism in Modern South Africa.* Cambridge: Cambridge University Press, 1995.

East, James. *Outline for Mission Study Classes.* Nashville, TN: National Baptist Convention, n.d.

Edgar, Robert R., ed. *An African American in South Africa: The Travel Notes of Ralph J. Bunche.* Athens: Ohio University Press, 1992.

———. *Because They Chose the Plan of God: The Story of the Bulhoek Massacre.* Johannesburg: Ravan Press, 1988.

Edgar, Robert R., and Hilary Sapire. *African Apocalypse: The Story of Nontetha Nkwenkwe, a Twentieth-Century South African Prophet.* Athens: Ohio University Press, 2000.

Edwards, Brent. *The Practice of Diaspora: Literature, Translation and the Rise of Black Internationalism.* Cambridge, MA: Harvard University Press, 2003.

Emmett, Tony. *Popular Resistance and the Roots of Nationalism in Namibia, 1915–1966.* Basel, Switzerland: P. Schlettwein Publishing, 1999.

Erlmann, Veit. *African Stars: Studies in Black South African Performance.* Chicago: University of Chicago Press, 1991.

———. *Music, Modernity and the Global Imagination.* New York: Oxford University Press, 1999.

Etherington, Norman. *Preachers, Peasants and Politics in Southeast Africa, 1835–1880.* London: Royal Historical Society, 1978.

Evans, Ivan. *Bureaucracy and Race: Native Administration in South Africa.* Berkeley: University of California Press, 1997.

Eze, Emmanuel Chukwudi. *Race and the Enlightenment.* Oxford: Blackwell Publishers, 1997.

Falola, Toyin, Niyi Afolabi, and Aderonke Adesola Adesanuya, eds. *Migrations and Creative Expressions in Africa and the African Diaspora.* Durham, NC: Carolina Academic Press, 2008.

Fatton, Robert. *Black Consciousness in South Africa: The Dialectics of Ideological Resistance to White Supremacy.* Albany: State University of New York Press, 1986.

Fields, Karen. *Revival and Rebellion in Colonial Central Africa*. Princeton, NJ: Princeton University Press, 1985.

Foucault, Michel. *The Archaeology of Knowledge*. New York: Pantheon Books, 1972.

——. *Discipline and Punish: The Birth of the Prison*. New York: Vintage Books, 1995.

Fredrickson, George. *Black Liberation: A Comparative History of Black Ideologies in the United States and South Africa*. New York: Oxford University Press, 1995.

——. *White Supremacy: A Comparative Study in American and South African History*. New York: Oxford University Press, 1981.

Garvey, Amy Jacques. *Garvey and Garveyism*. New York: Atheneum, 1969.

——, ed. *The Philosophy and Opinions of Marcus Garvey*. 2 vols. New York: Atheneum, 1992.

Gewald, Jan-Bart. *Herero Heroes: A Socio-political History of the Herero of Namibia, 1890–1923*. Athens: Ohio University Press, 1999.

Giliomee, Hermann. *The Afrikaners: Biography of a People*. Charlottesville: University of Virginia Press, 2003.

Gilroy, Paul. *The Black Atlantic: Modernity and Double Consciousness*. Cambridge, MA: Harvard University Press, 1993.

Gish, Steven D. *Alfred B. Xuma: African, American, South African*. New York: New York University Press, 2000.

Glaude, Eddie S., Jr. *Exodus! Religion, Race, and Nation in Early Nineteenth-Century Black America*. Chicago: University of Chicago Press, 2000.

Grant, Colin. *Negro with a Hat: The Rise and Fall of Marcus Garvey*. New York: Oxford University Press, 2008.

Grundlingh, Albert. *Fighting Their Own War: South African Blacks and the First World War*. Johannesburg: Ravan Press, 1987.

Gundar, J. S., and Ian Duffield, eds. *Essays on the History of Blacks in Britain*. Brookfield, VT: Ashgate Publishing, 1992.

Hahn, Steven. *A Nation under Our Feet: Black Political Struggles in the Rural South from Slavery to the Great Migration*. Boston: Belknap Press, 2005.

Hamilton, Carolyn, and John Wright, eds. *The Mfecane Aftermath: Reconstructive Debates in Southern African History*. Pietermaritzburg: University of Natal Press, 1995.

Hammond-Tooke, David. *Rituals and Medicines: Indigenous Healing in South Africa*. Johannesburg: A. D. Donker, 1989.

Hancock, W. Keith. *Smuts*. 2 vols. Cambridge: Cambridge University Press, 1962–68.

Harlan, Louis. *Booker T. Washington: The Making of a Black Leader, 1856–1901*. New York: Oxford University Press, 1975.

——. *The Wizard of Tuskegee, 1901–1915*. New York: Oxford University Press, 1983.

Harlan, Louis, and Raymond Smock, eds. *The Booker T. Washington Papers*. Champaign: University of Illinois Press, 1972–89.

Harold, Claudrena. *The Rise and Fall of Garveyism in the Urban South*. New York: Routledge, 2007.

Harris, Joseph E. *African-American Reactions to War in Ethiopia, 1936–1941*. Baton Rouge: Louisiana State University Press, 1994.

Harrison, Hubert. *When Africa Awakes*. Baltimore, MD: Black Classic Press, 1997.

Headlam, Cecil, ed. *The Milner Papers: South Africa, 1899–1905*. London: Cassell Press, 1933.

Hellman, Ellen. *Handbook on Race Relations in South Africa*. South African Institute of Race Relations. Cape Town: Oxford University Press, 1949.

Higgs, Catherine. *Ghost of Equality: The Lives of D. D. T. Jabavu*. Athens: Ohio University Press, 1997.

Hill, Robert A. "The Black Man": A Monthly Magazine of Negro Thought and Opinion. Millwood, NY: Kraus-Thompson, 1975.

———, ed. *The Marcus Garvey and Universal Negro Improvement Association Papers*. Berkeley: University of California Press, 1983–.

———, ed. *Pan-African Biography*. Berkeley: University of California Press, 1987.

Hill, Robert A., and Barbara Bair, eds. *Marcus Garvey: Life and Lessons*. Berkeley: University of California Press, 1987.

Hooker, James. *Henry Sylvester Williams, Imperial Pan-Africanist*. London: Collings, 1975.

Hostetter, David. *Movement Matters: American Antiapartheid Activism and the Rise of Multicultural Politics*. New York: Routledge, 2006.

Houser, George. *No One Can Stop the Rain: Glimpses of Africa's Liberation Struggle*. New York: Pilgrim Press, 1989.

Hunt, Nancy Rose, Tessie P. Liu, and Jean Quataert, eds. *Gendered Colonialisms in African History*. Oxford: Blackwell Publishers, 1997.

Hyman, Richard. *Strikes*. London: Fontana Press, 1972.

Jabavu, D. D. T. *The Black Problem: Papers and Addresses on Various Native Problems*. 1920. Reprint, New York: Negro Universities Press, 1969.

James, C. L. R. *The Black Jacobins*. New York: Random House, 1963.

———. *Spheres of Existence: Selected Writings*. London: Allison and Busby, 1980.

James, Winston. *Holding Aloft the Banner of Ethiopia: Caribbean Radicalism in Early Twentieth-Century America*. New York: Verso Press, 1998.

Johns, S., III, ed. *Protest and Hope, 1882–1934*. Vol. 1 of *From Protest to Challenge: A Documentary History of African Politics in South Africa*, edited by Thomas Karis and Gwendolen M. Carter. Stanford, CA: Hoover Institution Press, 1972.

Johnson, James Weldon. *Black Manhattan*. New York: Arno Press, 1968.

Johnson, James W., and J. Rosamond Johnson. *The Books of American Negro Spirituals*. 1925. Reprint, New York: Da Capo, 2002.

Johnson, Morris. *Archbishop Daniel William Alexander and the African Orthodox Church*. San Francisco: International Scholars Press, 1999.

Johnson, Walton. *Worship and Freedom: A Black American Church in Zambia*. New York: Africana Publishing, 1977.

Johnstone, Frederick. *Class, Race and Gold: A Study of Class Relations and Racial Discrimination in South Africa*. Halifax, Nova Scotia: Centre for African Studies, Dalhousie University, 1987.

Jordan, L. G. *Negro Baptist History, U.S.A.* Nashville, TN: National Baptist Convention, 1930.

Kadalie, Clements. *My Life and the I.C.U.: The Autobiography of a Black Trade Unionist in South Africa.* New York: Humanities Press, 1970.

Karis, Thomas, and Gwendolen M. Carter, eds. *From Protest to Challenge: A Documentary History of African Politics in South Africa.* Stanford, CA: Hoover Institution Press, 1972–.

Katz, Elaine. *The White Death: Silicosis on the Witwatersrand Gold Mines, 1886–1910.* Johannesburg: Witwatersrand University Press, 1994.

Keegan, Timothy. *Colonial South Africa and the Origins of the Racial Order.* Charlottesville: University of Virginia Press, 1996.

——. *Facing the Storm: Portraits of Black Lives in Rural South Africa.* Athens: Ohio University Press, 1988.

——. *Rural Transformations in Industrializing Southern Africa: The Southern Highveld to 1914.* New York: Macmillan, 1987.

Kelley, Robin D. G. *Race Rebels: Culture, Politics and the Black Working Class.* New York: Free Press, 1994.

Kerr, Alexander. *Fort Hare, 1915–48: The Evolution of an African College.* New York: Humanities Press, 1968.

Kirk, Joyce. *Making a Voice: African Resistance to Segregation in South Africa.* Boulder, CO: Westview Press, 1998.

Kornweibel, Theodore. *No Crystal Stair: Black Life and the Messenger, 1917–1923.* Westport, CT: Greenwood Press, 1976.

——. *"Seeing Red": Federal Campaigns against Black Militancy, 1919–1925.* Bloomington: Indiana University Press, 1998.

Krasner, David. *A Beautiful Pageant: African American Theatre, Drama, and Performance in the Harlem Renaissance, 1910–1927.* New York: Palgrave Macmillan, 2002.

Lacy, Marian. *Working for Boroko: The Origins of a Coercive Labor System in South Africa.* Johannesburg: Ravan Press, 1981.

La Hausse de Lalouviere, Paul. *Restless Identities: Signatures of Nationalism, Zulu Ethnicity and History in the Lives of Petros Lamula and Lymon Maling.* Pietermaritzburg: University of Natal Press, 2000.

Langworthy, Harry. *Africa for the African: The Life of Joseph Booth.* Blantyre: Christian Literature Association in Malawi, 1996.

Levine, Barry, ed. *The Caribbean Exodus.* New York: Praeger Books, 1987.

Lewis, Gavin. *Between the Wire and the Wall: A History of South African Coloured Politics.* Cape Town: David Philip, 1987.

Lewis, Rupert. *Marcus Garvey: Anti-colonial Champion.* London: Karia Press, 1987.

Lewis, Rupert, and Patrick Bryan, eds. *Garvey: His Work and Impact.* Trenton, NJ: Africa World Press, 1991.

Lewis, Rupert, and Maureen Warner-Lewis, eds. *Garvey, Africa, Europe and the Americas.* Mona, Jamaica: Institute of Social and Economic Research, 1986.

Litwack, Leon. *Trouble in Mind: Black Southerners in the Age of Jim Crow*. New York: Vintage Press, 1999.

Lott, Eric. *Love and Theft: Blackface Minstrelsy and the American Working Class*. Oxford: Oxford University Press, 1993.

MacMillan, William. *Complex South Africa: An Economic Footnote in History*. London: Faber and Faber, 1930.

Magubane, Zine. *Bringing the Empire Home: Race, Class, and Gender in Britain and Colonial South Africa*. Chicago: University of Chicago Press, 2004.

Mamdani, Mahmood. *Citizen and Subject: Contemporary Africa and the Legacy of Late Colonialism*. Princeton, NJ: Princeton University Press, 1996.

Mancoe, John. *First Edition of the Bloemfontein Bantu and Coloured People's Directory*. Bloemfontein: A. C.White, 1934.

Mandela, Nelson. *Long Walk to Freedom: The Autobiography of Nelson Mandela*. Boston: Little, Brown, 1995.

Marable, Manning. *Malcolm X: A Life of Reinvention*. New York: Viking Press, 2011.

Marks, Shula. *The Ambiguities of Dependence: Class, Nationalism, and the State in Twentieth-Century Natal*. Johannesburg: Ravan Press, 1986.

———. *Not Either an Experimental Doll: The Separate Worlds of Three South African Women*. Bloomington: Indiana University Press, 2001.

———. *Reluctant Rebellion: The 1906–8 Disturbances in Natal*. New York: Oxford University Press, 1970.

Marks, Shula, and Dagmar Engels. *Contesting Colonial Hegemony: State and Society in Africa and India*. New York: St. Martin's Press, 1994.

Marks, Shula, and Richard Rathbone, eds. *Industrialisation and Social Change in South Africa: African Class Formation, Culture, and Consciousness, 1870–1930*. London: Longman, 1982.

Marks, Shula, and Stanley Trapido, eds. *The Politics of Race, Class and Nationalism in Twentieth-Century South Africa*. New York: Longman, 1987.

Marsh, J. B. T. *The Story of the Fisk Jubilee Singers, with Their Songs*. 1881. Reprint, New York: Negro Universities Press, 1969.

Martin, Tony. *The Pan-African Connection*. Cambridge, MA: Schenken Press, 1983.

———. *Race First: The Organizational and Ideological Struggles of Marcus Garvey and the Universal Negro Improvement Association*. Dover, MA: Majority Press, 1976.

Masilela, Ntongela, ed. *Black Modernity: Twentieth-Century Discourses between the United States and South Africa*. Trenton, NJ: Africa World Press, 2001.

———. *The Cultural Modernity of H. I. E. Dhlomo*. Trenton, NJ: Africa World Press, 2007.

Massie, Robert. *Loosing the Bonds: The United States and South Africa during the Apartheid Years*. New York: Nan A. Talese, 1997.

Mathurin, Owen. *Henry Sylvester Williams and the Origins of the Pan-African Movement, 1869–1911*. Westport, CT: Greenwood Press, 1976.

Matthews, Z. K. *Freedom for My People: The Autobiography of Z. K. Matthews, Southern Africa, 1901–1968.* London: Collings, 1981.

Mbeki, Govan. *The Peasant's Revolt.* London: Harmondsworth, 1964.

McGuire, George Alexander. *The Universal Negro Catechism.* New York: Universal Negro Improvement Association, 1921.

———. *The Universal Negro Ritual, Containing Forms, Prayers, and Offices for Use in the UNIA.* N.p., 1921.

Meriwether, James. *Proudly We Can Be Africans: Black Americans and Africa, 1935–1961.* Chapel Hill: University of North Carolina Press, 2002.

Milner, Alfred. *The Nation and the Empire: A Collection of Speeches and Addresses.* London: Constable Press, 1913.

Minter, William, Gail Hovey, and Charles E. Cobb Jr. *No Easy Victories: African Liberation and American Activists over a Half Century, 1950–2000.* Trenton, NJ: Africa World Press, 2008.

Molema, Silas. *The Bantu Past and Present: An Ethnographical and Historical Study of the Native Races of South Africa.* Edinburgh: W. Green and Son, 1920.

Mudimbe, Valentin. *The Invention of Africa: Gnosis, Philosophy, and the Order of Knowledge.* Bloomington: Indiana University Press, 1998.

Mulzac, Hugh. *A Star to Steer By.* New York: International Publishers, 1972.

Musson, Doreen. *Johnny Gomas: Voice of the Working Class.* Cape Town: Buchu Books, 1989.

Nalty, Bernard. *Strength for the Fight: A History of Black Americans in the Military.* New York: Free Press, 1986.

Nesbitt, Francis Njubi. *Race for Sanctions: African Americans against Apartheid, 1946–1994.* Bloomington: Indiana University Press, 2004.

Newman, Richard, ed. *Black Power and Black Religion: Essays and Reviews.* West Cornwall, CT: Locust Hill Press, 1987.

Noer, Thomas J. *Briton, Boer, and Yankee: The United States and South Africa, 1870–1914.* Kent, OH: Kent State University Press, 1978.

Norrell, Robert J. *Up from History: The Life of Booker T. Washington.* Cambridge, MA: Harvard University Press, 2009.

Odendaal, Andre. *Vukani Bantu! The Beginnings of Black Protest Politics in South Africa to 1912.* Cape Town: David Philip, 1984.

Olaniyan, Tejumola, and James H. Sweet, eds. *The African Diaspora and the Disciplines.* Bloomington: Indiana University Press, 2010.

Opland, Jeff. *Xhosa Poets and Poetry.* Cape Town: David Philip, 1998.

Packard, Randall. *Chiefship and Cosmology: An Historical Study of Political Competition.* Bloomington: Indiana University Press, 1981.

———. *White Plague, Black Labour: Tuberculosis and the Political Economy of Health and Disease in South Africa.* Berkeley: University of California Press, 1989.

Perham, Margery, ed. *Ten Africans.* London: Faber and Faber, 1936.

Peires, Jeff. *The Dead Shall Arise: Nongqawuse and the Great Cattle Killing Movement.* Johannesburg: Ravan Press, 1989.

Perry, Jeffrey B., ed. *A Hubert Harrison Reader*. Middletown, CT: Wesleyan Press, 2001.

Perry, Jeffrey B. *Hubert Harrison: The Voice of Harlem Radicalism, 1883–1918*. New York: Columbia University Press, 2009.

Pirow, Oswald. *James Barry Munnik Hertzog*. Cape Town: Howard Timmins, 1957.

Plaatje, Sol. *Native Life in South Africa*. New York: Negro Universities Press, 1969.

Plummer, Brenda Gayle. *Rising Wind: Black Americans and U.S. Foreign Affairs, 1935–1960*. Chapel Hill: University of North Carolina Press, 1996.

Porter, Dorothy, ed. *Early Negro Writing, 1760–1837*. Boston: Beacon Press, 1971.

Pyrah, G. B. *Imperial Policy and South Africa, 1902–1910*. Oxford: Clarendon Press, 1955.

Redding, Sean. *Sorcery and Sovereignty: Taxation, Power and Rebellion in South Africa, 1880–1963*. Athens: Ohio University Press, 2006.

Rediker, Marcus, and Peter Linebaugh. *The Many-Headed Hydra: Sailors, Slaves, Commoners, and the Hidden History of the Revolutionary Atlantic*. Boston: Beacon Press, 2000.

Redkey, Edwin. *Respect Black: The Writings and Speeches of Henry McNeal Turner*. New York: Arno Press, 1971.

Rich, Paul. *State Power and Black Politics in South Africa, 1912–1951*. New York: St. Martin's Press, 1996.

Robinson, Randall. *Defending the Spirit: A Black Life in America*. New York: Dutton, 1998.

Rogers, Howard. *Native Administration in the Union of South Africa*. Johannesburg: University of Witwatersrand, 1933.

Rogers, Richard A. *Holy Piby: The Black Man's Bible*. Kingston: Research Associates School Times Publications, 2000.

Rolinson, Mary G. *Grassroots Garveyism: The Universal Negro Improvement Association in the Rural South, 1920–1927*. Chapel Hill: University of North Carolina Press, 2007.

Roll, Jarod. *Spirit of Rebellion: Labor and Religion in the New Cotton South*. Champaign: University of Illinois Press, 2010.

Rosenthal, Eric. *The Stars and Stripes in Africa*. Cape Town: National Books, 1968.

Roux, Edward. *Time Longer Than Rope: A History of the Black Man's Struggle in South Africa*. Madison: University of Wisconsin Press, 1964.

Sansone, Livio, Elisee Soumonni, and Boubacar Barry. *Africa, Brazil and the Construction of Trans Atlantic Black Identities*. Trenton, NJ: Africa World Press, 2008.

Saunders, Christopher, ed. *Studies in the History of Cape Town*. Vols. 1–3. Cape Town: David Philip, 1979–.

Shepherd, R. H. W. *Lovedale, South Africa 1824–1955*. Lovedale, South Africa: Lovedale University Press, 1971.

Shepperson, George, and Thomas Price. *Independent African: John Chilembwe and the Nyasaland Rising of 1915*. Edinburgh: Edinburgh Press, 1958.

Simons, H. J. *African Women: Their Legal Status in South Africa.* Chicago: Northwestern University Press, 1968.

Simons, Jack, and Ray Simons. *Class and Colour in South Africa, 1850–1950.* London: International Defence and Aid Fund, 1983.

Skota, T. D. *The African Yearly Register.* Johannesburg: Orange Press, 1930.

Smuts, Jan. *Africa and Some World Problems.* Oxford: Clarendon Press, 1929.

Soga, James H. *The South-Eastern Bantu.* Johannesburg: University of Witswatersrand Press, 1930.

South African Native Affairs Commission. *Minutes of Evidence and Reports.* 5 vols. Cape Town: Cape Times, 1905.

Southern, Eileen. *The Music of Black Americans.* 3rd ed. New York: Norton Press, 1997.

Spooner, Kenneth. *Sketches of the Life of K. E. M. Spooner: Missionary, South Africa.* N.p., n.d.

Stein, Judith. *The World of Marcus Garvey: Race and Class in Modern Society.* Baton Rouge: Louisiana State University, 1986.

Stewart, James. *Dawn in the Dark Continent.* Edinburgh: Oliphant Anderson and Ferrier, 1903.

———. *Lovedale, South Africa.* Edinburgh: David Bryce and Son, 1894.

Stoddard, Lothrop. *The Rising Tide of Color against White World Supremacy.* New York: Charles Scribner, 1920.

Sundiata, Ibrahim. *Brothers and Strangers: Black Zion, Black Slavery, 1914–1940.* Durham, NC: Duke University Press, 2003.

Sundkler, Bengt. *Bantu Prophets in South Africa.* 2nd ed. London: Oxford University Press, 1961.

———. *Zulu, Zion and Some Swazi Zionists.* New York: Oxford University Press, 1976.

Switzer, Les, ed. *South Africa's Alternative Press: Voices of Protest and Resistance, 1880s–1960s.* New York: Cambridge University Press, 1997.

Thomas-Hope, Elizabeth. *Explanation in Caribbean Migration: Perception and Image—Jamaica, Barbados, St. Vincent.* London: Macmillan, 1992.

Thompson, A. C. Terry. *The History of the African Orthodox Church.* New York, 1956.

Tolbert, Emory. *The U.N.I.A. and Black Los Angeles: Ideology and Community in the American Garvey Movement.* Los Angeles: Center for Afro-American Studies, University of California, 1980.

Turrell, Robert. *Capital and Labour on the Kimberley Diamond Fields, 1871–1890.* New York: Cambridge University Press, 1987.

Tyler, Josiah. *Forty Years among the Zulus.* Boston: Congregational Sunday-School and Publishing Society, 1891.

Van Onselen, Charles. *The Seed Is Mine: The Life of Kas Maine, a South African Sharecropper, 1894–1985.* New York: Hill and Wang, 1999.

Vincent, Theodore. *Black Power and the Garvey Movement.* Berkeley: University of California Press, 1972.

Von Eschen, Penny. *Race against Empire: African Americans and Anti-colonialism, 1937–57.* New York: Oxford University Press, 1998.

Walker, Cherryl, ed. *Women and Gender in Southern Africa to 1945.* Cape Town: David Philip, 1990.

Walshe, Peter. *The Rise of African Nationalism in South Africa: The African National Congress, 1912–1952.* Berkeley: University of California Press, 1971.

Washington, Booker T. *The Story of the Negro: The Rise of the Race from Slavery.* 1909. Reprint, New York: Negro Universities Press, 1969.

———. *Up from Slavery.* Garden City, NY: Doubleday, 1963.

Ward, Geoffrey C. *Unforgivable Blackness: The Rise and Fall of Jack Johnson.* New York: Alfred A. Knopf, 2004.

Watkins-Owens, Irma. *Blood Relations: Carribean Immigrants and the Harlem Community, 1900–1930.* Bloomington: Indiana University Press, 1996.

Webb, Colin de B., and John Wright, eds. *The James Stuart Archive.* 5 vols. Pietermaritzburg: University of Natal Press, 1979–2001.

Wells, Ida B. *Crusade for Justice: The Autobiography of Ida B. Wells.* Chicago: University of Chicago Press, 1991.

Wells, Julia. *We Now Demand! The History of Women's Resistance to Pass Laws in South Africa.* Johannesburg: University of Witswatersrand, 1993.

Western, John. *Outcast Cape Town.* Minneapolis: University of Minnesota Press, 1981.

Wickins, Peter. *The Industrial and Commercial Workers Union of South Africa.* Cape Town: David Philip, 1978.

Willan, Brian. *Sol Plaatje: A Biography.* Johannesburg: Ravan Press, 1984.

———, ed. *Sol Plaatje: Selected Writings.* Athens: Ohio University Press, 1996.

———. *Sol Plaatje: South African Nationalist, 1876–1932.* Berkeley: University of California Press, 1984.

Wilson, Monica. *Reaction to Conquest: Effects of Contact with Europeans on the Pondo of South Africa.* London: Oxford University Press, 1961.

Wilson, Monica, and A. Majefe. *Langa: A Study of Social Groups in an African Township.* Cape Town: Oxford University Press, 1963.

Worger, William. *South Africa's City of Diamonds: Mine Workers and Monopoly Capitalism in Kimberley, 1867–1895.* New Haven, CT: Yale University Press, 1987.

Wright, John, and Andrew Manson. *The Hlubi Chiefdom in Zululand-Natal: A History.* Ladysmith, South Africa: Ladysmith Historical Society, 1983.

Zimmerman, Andrew. *Alabama in Africa: Booker T. Washington, the German Empire, and the Globalization of the New South.* Princeton, NJ: Princeton University Press, 2009.

ARTICLES

Adhikari, Mohamed. "Voice of the Coloured Elite: APO, 1909–1923." In *South Africa's Alternative Press: Voices of Protest and Resistance, 1880s–1960s,* edited by Les Switzer, 127–46. Cambridge: Cambridge University Press, 1999.

Ashley, Michael. "Features of Modernity: Missionaries and Education in South

Africa, 1850–1900." *Journal of Theology for Southern Africa* 38 (March 1982): 123–45.

Atkins, Keletso. "The Black Atlantic Communication Network: African American Sailors and the Cape of Good Hope Connection." *Issue: Journal of Opinion* 24, no. 2 (1996): 6–11.

Bagnall, Robert. "The Madness of Marcus Garvey." *Messenger* 5 (March 1923): 638–64.

Beinart, William. "Chieftancy and the Concept of Articulation: South Africa ca. 1900–1950." In *Segregation and Apartheid in Twentieth-Century South Africa*, edited by William Beinart and Saul Dubow, 176–88. New York: Routledge, 1995.

Berger, Iris. "An African American 'Mother of the Nation': Madie Hall Xuma in South Africa, 1940–1963." *Journal of Southern African Studies* 27, no. 3 (September 2001): 547–66.

Bonner, Philip. "The Transvaal Native Congress, 1917–1920: The Radicalisation of the Black Petty Bourgeoisie on the Rand." In *Industrialisation and Social Change in South Africa: African Class Formation, Culture, and Consciousness*, edited by Shula Marks and Richard Rathbone, 270–313. London: Longman, 1982.

Bozzoli, Belinda. "Marxism, Feminism and Southern African Studies." *Journal of South African Studies* 9 (1983): 139–71.

Bradford, Helen. "Women, Gender and Colonialism: Rethinking the History of the British Cape Colony and Its Frontier Zones, c. 1806–1970." *Journal of African History* 37 (1996): 351–70.

Bridgman, Frederick. "American Negroes Making Mischief in South Africa." *Missionary Review of the World* (May 1903): 396–97.

Butler, Kim. "Defining Diaspora, Refining a Discourse." *Diaspora* 10, no. 2 (Summer 2002): 189–219.

Campbell, James. "Models and Metaphors: Industrial Education in the United States and South Africa." In *Comparative Perspectives on South Africa*, edited by Ran Greenstein, 90–134. New York: St. Martin's Press, 1998.

Cobley, Alan G. "Far From Home: The Origins and Significance of the Afro-Caribbean Community in South Africa to 1930." *Journal of South African Studies* 18, no. 2 (June 1992): 349–70.

——. "Forgotten Connections, Unconsidered Parallels: A New Agenda for Comparative Research in Southern Africa and the Caribbean." *African Studies* 58, no. 2 (1999): 133–56.

Costa, A. A. "Chieftaincy and Civilisation: African Structures of Government and Colonial Administration in South Africa." *African Studies* 59, no. 1 (2000): 13–43.

Davey, Alan. "Kroomen: Black Sailors at the Cape." Undated research paper, Simon's Town Museum, Simon's Town, South Africa.

——. "Tindals, Seedies and Kroomen." *Simon's Town Historical Society Bulletin* 17 (1993): 150–59.

Davis, R. Hunt, Jr. "The Black American Education Component in African Responses to Colonialism in South Africa (ca. 1890–1914)." *Journal of Southern African Studies* 3 (1978): 65–83.

———. "John L. Dube: A South African Exponent of Booker T. Washington." *Journal of African Studies* 1, no. 2 (1975): 497–528.

De Waal, E. "American Black Residents and Visitors in the South African Republic before 1899." *South African Historical Journal* 6 (1974): 52–55.

Digby, Anne. "Early Black Doctors in South Africa." *Journal of African History* 46 (2005): 427–54.

Dube, John. "Are Negroes Better Off in Africa? Conditions and Opportunities of Negroes in America and Africa Compared." *Missionary Review of the World* 27 (August 1904): 583–88.

———. "Need of Industrial Education in Africa." *Southern Workman* 27 (July 1897): 141–42. Available in Hampton University Archives, Hampton, VA.

Du Bois, W. E. B. "The African Roots of War." *Atlantic Monthly* 115 (May 1915): 707–14.

———. "Back to Africa." *Century Magazine* 105 (February 1923): 539–48.

———. "Close Ranks." *Crisis* 16 (July 1918): 111.

———. "Marcus Garvey." *Crisis* 21, no. 2 (December 1920): 57–60, and no. 3 (January 1921): 112–15.

Dubow, Saul. "The Elaboration of Segregation Discourse in the Inter-war Years." In *Segregation and Apartheid in Twentieth-Century South Africa*, edited by William Beinart and Saul Dubow, 145–75. London: Routledge, 1995.

———. "Race, Civilization, and Culture: The Elaboration of the Segregationist Discourse in the Inter-war Years." In *The Politics of Race, Class and Nationalism in Twentieth-Century South Africa*, edited by Shula Marks and Stanley Trapido, 71–94. London: Longman, 1987.

Duffield, Ian. "Pan-Africanism, Rational and Irrational." *Journal of African History* 18, no.4 (1977): 597–620.

———. "Some American Influences on Duse' Mohamed Ali." In *Pan-African Biography*, edited by Robert A. Hill, 11–56. Los Angeles: African Studies Association, 1987.

Dugmore, Harry. "Becoming a Somebody." *African Studies* 51, no. 1 (1992): 9–45.

Edgar, Robert R. "African Educational Protest in South Africa: The American School Movement in the Transkei in the 1920s." In *Apartheid and Education: The Education of Black South Africans*, edited by Peter Kallaway, 184–91. Johannesburg: Ravan Press, 1984.

———. "Garveyism in Africa: Dr. Wellington and the American Movement in the Transkei." *Ufahamu* 6, no. 1 (1976): 31–57.

———. "New Religious Movements." In *Missions and Empire*, edited by Norman Etherington. Oxford: Oxford University Press, 2005.

———. "The Prophet Motive: Enoch Mgijima, the Israelites and the Background to the Bulhoek Massacre." *International Journal of African Historical Studies* 15, no. 3 (1982): 401–22.

——. "The Strange Career of Dr. Wellington—An African Garvey." In *The Societies of Southern Africa in the 19th and 20th Centuries*. Postgraduate seminar, Institute of Commonwealth Studies, 1982, University of London, London, UK.

Edgar, Robert R., and Christopher Saunders. "A. A. S. Le Fleur and the Griqua Trek of 1917: Segregation, Self-Help, and Ethnic Identity." *International Journal of African Historical Studies* 15 (1982): 201–20.

Edwards, Brent Hayes. "The Uses of Diaspora." *Social Text* 19, no. 1 (Spring 2001): 45–73.

Elkins, W. F. "Marcus Garvey, the Negro World and the British West Indies: 1919–1920." *Science and Society* 36, no. 1 (Spring 1972): 63–75.

——. "Suppression of the Negro World in the British West Indies." *Science and Society* (Fall 1971): 344–47.

Elphick, Richard. "Evangelical Missions and Racial Equalization in South Africa, 1890–1914." In *Converting Colonialism: Visions and Realities in Mission History, 1706–1914*, edited by Dana L. Robert, 112–33. Cambridge, UK: William Eermans, 2008.

Erlmann, Veit. "'A Feeling of Prejudice': Orpheus McAdoo and the Virginia Jubilee Singers in South Africa, 1890–1898." *Journal of Southern African Studies* 14, no. 3 (1988): 331–50.

Etherington, Norman. "Mission Station Melting Pots as a Factor in the Rise of South African Black Nationalism." *International Journal of African Historical Studies* 9, no. 4 (1976): 592–605.

Faris, John T. "James Stewart, of Lovedale." *Missionary Review of the World* 33 (January 1910): 46–49.

Fitzgerald, Michael W. "'We Have Found a Moses': Theodore Bilbo, Black Nationalism, and the Greater Liberia Bill of 1939." *Journal of Southern History* 63, no. 2 (May 1997): 293–320.

Fyfe, Christopher. "Race, Empire and the Historians." *Race and Class* 33, no. 4 (1992): 123–45.

Gaitskell, Deborah. "Devout Domesticity? A Century of African Women's Christianity in South Africa." In *Women and Gender in Southern Africa to 1945*, edited by Cherryl Walker, 251–72. Cape Town: David Philip, 1990.

——. "Housewives, Maids, or Mothers: Some Contradictions of Domesticity for Christian Women in Johannesburg, 1903–1939." *Journal of African History* 24 (1983): 241–56.

Gatewood, Willard. "Black Americans and the Boer War, 1899–1902." *South Atlantic Quarterly* 75 (1976): 226–44.

Glotzer, Richard. "The Career of Mabel Carney: The Study of Race and Rural Development in the United States and South Africa." *International Journal of African Historical Studies* 29, no. 2 (1996): 309–36.

Halliday, Richard. "Social Darwinism: A Definition." *Victorian Studies* 14 (1971): 389–404.

Harrison, Hubert "The Negro and the War." In Harrison, *When Africa Awakes*, 25–38. Baltimore, MD: Black Classic Press, 1997.

Higginson, John. "Liberating the Captives: Independent Watchtower as an Avatar of Colonial Revolt in Southern Africa and Katanga, 1908–1941." *Journal of Social History* 26, no. 1 (Fall 1992): 55–80.

Hill, Robert A. "Dread History: Leonard P. Howell and Millenarian Visions in Early Rastafari Religions in Jamaica." *Epoche: Journal of the History of Religions* 9 (1981): 30–71.

———. "The First England Years and Africa, 1912–1916." In *Marcus Garvey and the Vision of Africa*, edited by John H. Clarke, 38–76. New York: Vintage Books, 1974.

Hill, Robert A., and Gregory A. Pirio. "Africa for the Africans: The Garvey Movement in South Africa, 1920–1940." In *The Politics of Race, Class and Nationalism in Twentieth-Century South Africa*, edited by Shula Marks and Stanley Trapido, 209–53. New York: Oxford University Press, 1987.

Houle, Robert J. "The American Mission Revivals and the Birth of Modern Zulu Evangelism." In *Zulu Identities: Being Zulu, Past and Present*, edited by Benedict Carton, John Laband, and Jabulani Sithole, 222–39. Pietermaritzburg: Gardners Books, 2008.

Hughes, Arnold. "Garveyism in Africa." In *Garvey, Africa, Europe and the Americas*, edited by Rupert Lewis and Maureen Warner-Lewis, 99–120. Mona, Jamaica: Institute of Social and Economic Research, 1986.

Hughes, Heather. "Doubly Elite: Exploring the Life of John Langalibalele Dube." *Journal of Southern African Studies* 27, no. 3 (September 2001): 445–58.

Jones, Absalom. "A Thanksgiving Sermon, Preached January 1, 1808, in St. Thomas's, or the African Episcopal Church, Philadelphia: On Account of the Abolition of the African Slave Trade." In *Early Negro Writing, 1760–1837*, edited by Dorothy Porter, 335–42. Boston: Beacon Press, 1971.

Jones, Absalom, and Richard Allen. "A Narrative of the Proceedings of the Black People, during the Late Awful Calamity in Philadelphia, in the Year, 1793." In *Negro Protest Pamphlets*, edited by Dorothy Porter Wesley, 19–30. New York: Arno Press and New York Times, 1969.

Jones, Roderick. "The Black Peril in South Africa." *Nineteenth Century and After* 55 (May 1904): 712–23.

———. "The Black Problem in South Africa." *Nineteenth Century and After* 56 (May 1905): 770–76.

Keegan, Timothy. "Gender, Degeneration and Sexual Danger: Imagining Race and Class in South Africa ca. 1912." *Journal of Southern African Studies* 27, no. 3 (September 2001): 455–77.

Kelley, Robin D. G. "The Religious Odyssey of African Radicals." *Radical History Review* 51, no. 3 (Fall 1991): 5–26.

Kemp, Amanda, and Robert Trent Vinson. "Poking Holes in the Sky: Professor James Thaele, American Negroes and Modernity in Segregationist South Africa." *African Studies Review* 43, no. 1 (April 2000): 141–59.

Keto, Clement. "Black Americans and South Africa, 1890–1910." *Current Bibliography of African Affairs* 5 (1972): 383–406.

Khan, Farieda. "Rewriting South Africa's Conservation History—The Role of the Native Farmers Association." *Journal of Southern African Studies* 20, no. 4 (December 1994): 499–515.

Lahouel, Badra. "Ethiopianism and African Nationalism in South Africa before 1937." *Cahiers d'Etudes Africaines* 104, no. 4 (1986): 321–33.

Lerer, Leonard B. "The Kimberley Board of Health." *South African Medical Journal* 86, no. 4 (1996): 369–70.

Levine, Lawrence. "Marcus Garvey and the Politics of Revitalization." In *Black Leaders of the Twentieth Century*, edited by John Hope Franklin and August Meier, 105–37. Champaign: University of Illinois Press, 1982.

Linebaugh, Peter. "All the Atlantic Mountains Shook." *Labour/LeTravailleur* 10 (1982): 213–31.

Manicom, Linzi. "Ruling Relations: Rethinking State and Gender in South African History." *Journal of African History* 33 (1992): 441–65.

Manning, Patrick. "Africa and the African Diaspora: New Directions of Study." *Journal of African History* 44, no. 3 (November 2003): 487–506.

Marable, W. Manning. "Booker T. Washington and African Nationalism." *Phylon* 35, no. 4 (1974): 398–406.

Marks, Shula. "Natal, the Zulu Royal Family and the Ideology of Segregation." In *Segregation and Apartheid in Twentieth-Century South Africa*, edited by William Beinart and Saul Dubow, 91–117. New York: Routledge, 1995.

———. "White Masculinity: Jan Smuts, Race and the South African War." *Proceedings of the British Academy* 111 (2001): 199–223.

Masilela, Ntongela. "The Black Atlantic and African Modernity in South Africa." *Research in African Literatures* 27, no. 4 (Winter 1997): 88–95.

McFadden, Grace Jordan. "Septima P. Clark and the Struggle for Human Rights." In *Women in the Civil Rights Movement: Trailblazers and Torchbearers, 1941–1965*, edited by Vicki L. Crawford and Jacqueline A. Rouse, 85–97. Bloomington: Indiana University Press, 1993.

McLaughlin, Malcolm. "Reconsidering the East St. Louis Race Riot of 1917." *International Review of Social History* 47, no. 2 (August 2002): 187–212.

Meintjes, Sheila. "Family and Gender in the Christian Community at Edendale, Natal, in Colonial Times." In *Women and Gender in Southern Africa to 1945*, edited by Cherryl Walker, 124–45. Cape Town: David Philip, 1990.

Mills, Wallace G. "Millennial Christianity, British Imperialism, and African Nationalism." In *Christianity in South Africa: A Political, Social, and Cultural History*, edited by Richard Elphick and T. R. Davenport, 337–47. Berkeley: University of California Press, 1997.

Morris, Charles S. "A Work for American Negroes." In *Ecumenical Missionary Conference*, 1:469–71. New York: American Tract Society, 1900.

Nakasa, Nat. "Mr. Nakasa Goes to Harlem." In *To Kill a Man's Pride and Other Short Stories from South Africa*, edited by Marcus Ramogale, 85–98. 2nd ed. Johannesburg: Ravan Press, 1996.

Nasson, Bill. "'She preferred living in a cave with Harry the snake catcher': Towards an Oral History of Popular Leisure and Class Expression in District Six, Cape Town c. 1920s–1950s." Witwatersrand History Workshop, Johannesburg, South Africa, 9–14 February 1987.

Natsoulas, Theodore. "Patriarch McGuire and the Spread of the African Orthodox Church to Africa." *Journal of Religion in Africa* 12, no. 2 (1981): 81–104.

Nembula, John Mavuma. "Sermon on the Necessity of Religious Faith, Co-operation and Moral and Social Problems." (Chicago, 1887).

Newman, Richard. "Daniel William Alexander and the African Orthodox Church." *International Journal of African Historical Studies* 16, no. 4 (1983): 615–30.

Okwonkwo, Rina. "Garveyism in West Africa." *Journal of African History* 13 (1980): 105–17.

Page, Carol. "Conrad Rideout, Afro-American Advisor to the Chiefs of Lesotho and Pondoland, 1899–1903." In *Pan-African Biography*, edited by Robert A. Hill, 1–10. Los Angeles: African Studies Association, 1987.

Parry, R. "In a Sense Citizens, but Not Altogether Citizens . . . : Rhodes, Race and the Ideology of Segregation at the Cape in the Late Nineteenth Century." *Canadian Journal of African Studies* 17 (1983): 384–91.

Platt, Warren. "The African Orthodox Church: An Analysis of Its First Decade." *Church History* 58, no. 4 (1989): 474–88.

Ranger, Terence. "The Myth of the Afro-American Liberator." Seminar paper, UCLA, 1971.

Redding, Sean. "A Blood Stained Tax: Poll Tax and the Bambatha Rebellion in South Africa." *African Studies Review* 43, no. 2 (December 2000): 212–34.

———. "Government Witchcraft: Taxation, the Supernatural, and the Mpondo Revolt in the Transkei, South Africa, 1955–1963." *African Affairs* 95, no. 381 (1996): 555–80.

"A Review of the World." *Current Literature* 48 (June 1910): 606.

Rich, Paul. "The Appeals of Tuskegee: James Henderson, Lovedale and the Fortunes of South African Liberalism, 1906–1930." *International Journal of African Historical Studies* 20, 2 (1987): 271–91.

Saunders, Christopher. "Henry Sylvester Williams in South Africa." *Quarterly Bulletin of the National Library of South Africa* 55, no. 4 (2001): 145–55.

———. "Tile and the Thembu Church: Politics and Independence on the Cape Eastern Frontier in the Late Nineteenth Century." *Journal of African History* 11, no. 4 (1970): 553–70.

Shepperson, George. "Ethiopianism and African Nationalism." *Phylon* 14, no. 1 (1953): 12–26.

———. "Ethiopianism: Past and Present." In *Christianity in Tropical Africa*, edited by C. G. Beata, 249–68. London: Oxford University Press, 1968.

———. "Notes on Negro American Influences on the Emergence of African Nationalism." *Journal of African History* 1, no. 2 (1960): 24–44.

Shiels, Ross. "John Mavuma Nembula, 1860–1897: First Black Physician in Southern Africa." *Journal of the National Medical Association* 80, no. 11 (1988): 1255–58.

Simkins, C. "Agricultural Production in the African Reserves of South Africa, 1918–69." *Journal of Southern African Studies* 7 (1981): 256–83.

Stewart, James. "What Is Education?" In *Outlook on a Century*, edited by Francis Wilson and Dominique Perrot, 65–76. Lovedale: Lovedale Press, 1973.

Stoler, Ann. "Making Empire Respectable: The Politics of Race and Sexual Morality in Twentieth Century Colonial Culture." *American Ethnologist* 16 (1989): 634–60.

Streible, Dan. "Jack Johnson Fight Films." In *The Birth of Whiteness: Race and Emergence of U.S. Cinema*, edited by Daniel Bernardi, 170–200. New Brunswick, NJ: Rutgers University Press, 1996.

Swanson, Maynard. "The Sanitation Syndrome: Bubonic Plague and Urban Native Policy in the Cape Colony, 1900–1909." *Journal of African History* 18, no. 3 (1977): 212–37.

Trapido, Stanley. "The Friends of the Natives: Merchants, Peasants and Ideological Structure of Liberalism in the Cape, 1854–1910." In *Economy and Society in Pre-industrial South Africa*, edited by Shula Marks and Anthony Atmore, 247–74. London: Harmondsworth, 1980.

Turner, Henry M. "My Trip to South Africa." In *Respect Black: The Writings and Speeches of Henry McNeal Turner*, edited by Edwin Redkey, 178–81. New York: Arno Press, 1971.

Vinson, Robert Trent. "Citizenship over Race? African Americans in American–South African Diplomacy, 1890–1925." *Safundi: The Journal of South African and American Comparative Studies* 15 (April 2004): 13–32.

——. "'Sea Kaffirs': American Negroes and the Gospel of Garveyism in Segregationist South Africa." *Journal of African History* 47, no. 2 (July 2006): 281–303.

West, Michael O. "Seeds Are Sown: The Garvey Movement in Zimbabwe in the Interwar Years." *International Journal of African Historical Studies* 35, no. 2–3 (2003): 335–62.

White, Gavin. "Patriarch McGuire and the Episcopal Church." *Historical Magazine of the Protestant Episcopal Church* 38 (1969): 112–33.

Wickins, Peter. "General Labour Unions in Cape Town, 1918–1920." *South African Journal of Economics* 40 (1976): 275–301.

Wilcox, William. "The Booker Washington of South Africa." *Oberlin Alumni Magazine* (March 1927). Available in Wilcox Papers, Oberlin College Archives, Oberlin, OH.

Willan, Brian. "DeBeers, Sol Plaatje and an Old Tram Shed: Class Relations in a South African Town, 1918–19." *Journal of South African Studies* 4 (1978): 78–91.

Wright, Josephine. "Orpheus Myron McAdoo." *Black Perspectives in Music* 4, no. 3 (Fall 1976): 55–66.

DISSERTATIONS AND THESES

Bethel, Leonard. "The Role of Lincoln University in the Education of African Leadership: 1854–1970." PhD diss., Rutgers University, 1975.

Brock, Sheila. "James Stewart and Lovedale: A Reappraisal of Missionary Attitudes on African Responses in the Eastern Cape, South Africa." PhD diss., University of Edinburgh, 1974.

Budlender, Deborah. "A History of Stevedores in Cape Town Docks." Bachelor's thesis, University of Cape Town, 1976.

Dinnerstein, Myra. "The American Board Mission to the Zulu, 1835–1910." PhD diss., Columbia University, 1971.

Edgar, Robert R. "In the Name of God: Enoch Mgijima and the Bulhoek Massacre." PhD diss., University of California, Los Angeles, 1977.

Gordon, David. "The Cape Town Renaissance and the Genesis of African Nationalism, 1918–1926." Bachelor's thesis, University of Cape Town, 1993.

Hofmeyr, Willie. "Agricultural Crisis and Rural Organisation in the Cape: 1929–1933." Master's thesis, University of Cape Town, 1985.

Hughes, H. "Politics and Society in Inanda, Natal: The Qadi under Chief Mqhawe, c. 1840–1896." PhD diss., University of London, 1996.

Huyser, J. D. "Die Naturelle-Politiek van die Suid-Afrikaanse Republiek." PhD diss., University of Pretoria, 1936.

Kemp, Amanda. "'Up from Slavery' and Other Narratives: Black South African Performances of the American Negro (1920–1943)." PhD diss., Northwestern University, 1997.

Kingwill, Rosalie. "The African National Congress in the Western Cape: A Preliminary Study." Bachelor's thesis, University of Cape Town, 1977.

Leanne, Shelley. "African-American Initiatives against Minority Rule in South Africa: A Politicized Diaspora in World Politics." PhD diss., Oxford University, 1994.

Lewis, Gavin. "The Bondelswaarts Rebellion of 1922." Master's thesis, Rhodes University, 1977.

Marable, W. Manning. "African Nationalist: The Life of John Langalibalele Dube." PhD diss., University of Michigan, 1976.

Mears, W. J. G. "A Study in Native Administration in the Transkeian Territories, 1894–1943." PhD diss., University of South Africa, 1947.

Moeti, Moitsadi. "Ethiopianism: Separatist Roots of African Nationalism in South Africa." PhD diss., Syracuse University, 1981.

Page, Carol. "Black America in White South Africa: Church and State Reaction to the A.M.E. Church in Cape Colony and Transvaal, 1896–1910." PhD diss., University of Edinburgh, 1978.

Scott, Julius. "The Common Wind: Currents of Afro-American Communication in the Era of the Haitian Revolution." PhD diss., Duke University, 1986.

Vinson, Robert Trent. "In the Time of the Americans: Garveyism in Segregationist South Africa, 1920–1940." PhD diss., Howard University, 2001.

SOUTH AFRICAN AND AMERICAN NEWSPAPERS AND PERIODICALS

Abantu-Batho
African World
Afro-American Ledger

AME Church Review
APO
Associated Negro Press
Bantu World
Black Man
Bloemfontein Friend
Bloemfontein Post
Cape Argus
Cape Standard
Cape Sun
Cape Times
Century Magazine
Chicago Tribune
Cleveland Gazette
Crisis
Crusader
Current Literature
Daily Negro Times
Diamond Fields Advertiser
East London Daily Dispatch
Government Gazette
Guardian
Ilanga lase Natal
Imvo Neliso Lomzi
Imvo Zabantsundu
Indianapolis Freeman
Izwi Lama Afrika
Kaffrarian Watchman
Kansas City Call
Kokstad Advertiser
Lagos Weekly Record
Liberator
Literary Digest
Los Angeles Times
Messenger
Missionary Reports, S.P.G.
Missionary Review of the World
Mission Herald
Natal Advertiser
Natal Witness
Nation
Negro Churchman
Negro World
New York Age

New York Times
New York Tribune
New York World
Philadelphia Tribune
Richmond Planet
South African Outlook
South African Worker/Umsebenzi
Southern Workman
Standard and Mail
Times of Natal
Transvaal Advertiser
Umtata Territorial News, Ltd.
Umteteli wa Bantu
Voice of Missions
Washington Bee
Washington Post
Worcester Herald
Workers Herald

ARCHIVAL SOURCES

Anti-slavery International, London, and Rhodes House, Oxford, England
Aborigines Protection Society Papers

Emory University, Atlanta, Georgia, Pitts Theology Library, Archives and Manuscripts
African Orthodox Church Records

Emory University, Atlanta, Georgia, Robert W. Woodruff Library, Manuscript, Archives, and Rare Book Library
Universal Negro Improvement Association Records
Theodore Draper Papers

Hampton University Archives, Hampton, Virginia

Library of Congress, Washington, D.C.
Booker T. Washington Papers

National Archives of Namibia, Windhoek, Namibia

National Archives of South Africa (NASA), Cape Town, Pietermaritzburg, and Pretoria, South Africa

Cape Town

Records of the Chief Native Commissioner, Natal (CNC) 348
Records of the Chief Magistrate of the Transkeian Territories (CMT)
Records of Resident Magistrates of Transkeian Districts:
Cape Peninsula (2/OBS)
East London (1/ELN)
Engcobo (1/ECO)
Kentani (1/KNT)
Mount Fletcher (1/MTF)
Nqamakwe (1/NKE)
Qumbu (1/QBU)
Sterkspruit (2/SPT)
Tsolo (1/TSO)
Records of the Secretary of Native Affairs (NTS) 1455, 1681, 7602, 7603, 7606
South African Police files (SAP) 41

Pietermaritzburg
Minister of Justice and Public Works Records
Records of the Chief Native Commissioner, Natal (CNC)

Pretoria
Annual Report of the Commissioner of Police
Criminal Investigation Division
Department of Justice
Department of the Interior
Governor-General Department
Records of the Governor-General
Records of the Secretary of Native Affairs

Oberlin College Archives, Oberlin, Ohio

Oberlin College Library Special Collections, Oberlin, Ohio

Public Record Office, London, England
Public Records, London, England

Schomburg Center for Research in Black Culture, New York Public Library
John Bruce Papers
Phelps-Stokes Papers
UNIA Central Division Records

United States National Archives and Records Administration (NARA), College Park, Maryland
Cape Town General Records of the Department of State

Department of State Records of British Africa
Johannesburg General Records of the Department of State
Pretoria General Records of the Department of State

University of Cape Town, Manuscript Division

Ray and Jack Simons Papers

University of the Witwatersrand

A. L. Saffery Papers
Alfred Xuma Papers

INTERVIEWS AND PERSONAL COMMUNICATIONS

Alexander, Ray. Personal communication with author. 2 July 1998. Cape Town.
Brooks, Weah. Interviews by author. Tape recordings. 20 and 22 June and 8 July 1998. Cape Town.
East, Gladys. Interview by author. 26 December 1995. Philadelphia.
Kolbe, Vincent. Conversation with author. 27 April 1998. Cape Town.
Lyner, Dorothy. Interviews by author. Tape recordings. 27 June and 10 July 1998. Cape Town.
Mathebe, C. P., Aliwal North. Interview with Bob Edgar. 3 July 1974.
Noble, Alice. Interview by author. Tape recording. 10 July 1998. Cape Town.
Older Garveyite. Interview in Stanley Nelson, *Look for Me in the Whirlwind* (film). PBS, 2001.
Peires, Jeff. Personal communication with author. 3 August 2000.
Sisulu, Walter. Interview by author. Tape recording. 26 April 1998. Cape Town.
Timm, Joan. Interview by author. Tape recording. 20 June 1998. Cape Town.
Watlington, E. Personal communication with author. 12 April 1998.

Index

227

Athlicanity doctrine, 94
Atlanta Federal Penitentiary, 88
Atlanta University, 15, 134
Atlantic Charter, 139, 141
Australia, 15, 19, 24–25, 32, 36, 39, 71
Azikiwe, Nnamdi, 145, 178n91

Babylon. *See* Biblical imagery: Babylon
Bagnall, Robert, 85–86
Bam, Edward Chalmers, 111
Bantu Men's Social Center, 139
Bantu Purity League, 132
Bantu World (newspaper), 140, 143–44, 198n98
Bantu Youth League, 135–36
Barbados, 74
Barnard, "Jolly" Jack, 58
Barnett, Claude, 135
Basutoland, 45, 72, 105, 109, 115, 120, 122, 140, 163n43
Bechuanaland, 45, 140, 163n43
Belgium Congo, 79, 106
Bethune, Mary McLeod, 135
Biblical imagery, 15–16, 20, 75, 77–78, 88, 91–94, 97, 105–7, 109, 138–39, 144, 172n84; Acts, 70; Babylon, 15, 21, 68, 169n42; Egypt, 3, 7, 15, 20–21, 44–45, 70, 77, 106, 109, 182n24; Elijah, 16, 181n13; Ethiopia, 20, 35, 45, 70, 77, 93–94, 105; Ezekiel, 88; Israelites, 1, 7, 15, 21, 77, 88, 92, 109, 138; Jesus Christ, 21, 39, 70, 81–82, 86–88, 106, 126, 181n13; Moses, 1, 3, 16, 21, 38, 70–71, 77, 88, 90, 92–93, 139, 144; Nehemiah, 21; Psalms, 20–21, 70, 77
Biko, Steve, 59
Bilbo, Theodore, 85, 128
Birth of a Nation (film), 69, 174n5
black and white minstrels. *See* minstrelsy
Blackburn, Katherine, 41
Black Consciousness Movement, 145
Black Cross Navigation and Trading Company, 87–88, 93, 126
Black Cross Nurses, 69, 80
black liberation movement, 4, 15, 32, 63–66, 94, 99, 119, 142, 145
Black Man (newspaper), 78, 91, 98, 127, 147
black nationalism, 45, 63–64, 84
Black Peril, 4–5, 8, 22, 24, 27, 124, 155n44
black people (South Africa), 4–10, 38, 42, 65, 112–13; as British subjects, 32, 43; 46–48, 71; disenfranchisement, 4, 8, 36, 43, 114, 116, 124, 160n11, 163n54, 170n59; education, 7–8, 10, 17, 19, 29–30, 34–35, 40–41, 43–45, 47–49, 63, 67, 74–76, 100–101, 104, 110, 132–33, 135–36, 138, 140, 162n35 (*see also* education, industrial); land, 4, 8, 22, 25, 31, 41–44, 46–49, 94, 98–99, 105, 108, 112–13, 116, 122, 134, 140; liberation (*see* black liberation

movement); rights, 17–19, 21, 42–43, 46–48, 65, 71, 98–99, 112–13; schools, 36, 109–11 (*see also* Universal Negro Improvement Association [UNIA], schools); taxation, 113
black people (South West Africa), 79–81
Black Star Line, 55, 63, 67–69, 72–73, 76, 79, 83–85, 87–90, 93, 95, 126, 168n31, 173n3
Bloemfontein Post (newspaper), 26–27
Boas, Franz, 136
Bondelswaarts, 98
Booker T. Washington (ship), 87–88
Booth, Joseph, 39–40, 162nn31–32
Boston Chronicle (newspaper), 135
Boston Guardian (newspaper), 38
Botha, Louis, 28, 143
Botswana. *See* Bechuanaland
Boulin, Herbert, 84
boxing, 10, 24–27, 32, 136–37
Briggs, Cyril, 75, 84, 89
British Colonial Office, 28
British Empire, 20, 41, 43, 47, 64–65, 81, 100
British Guyana, 74
British Home Office, 28
"British West Indies in the Mirror of Civilization, The" (essay) (Garvey), 65
Brotherhood of Sleeping Car Porters, 85
Brown, James, 23
Brown, Thomas, 23
Bruce, John, 69
Bryan, William Jennings, 26
Buchanan Institute, 29–31
Bull, Oswin, 133
Bunche, Ralph, 137–38
Bunga. *See* Transkeian General Council (Bunga)
Bureau of Investigation. *See* Federal Bureau of Investigation
Burns, Tommy, 24–26
Burrowes, Alfred, 64
Butelezi, Wellington Elias, 9–10, 58, 102–18, 120–25, 129–31, 180nn3–4, 181n11, 187n88, 189n4

Caluza, Reuben, 40, 135–36
Canada, 15, 32, 35, 143
Cape Argus (newspaper), 72
Cape Colony, 14, 18, 35, 41–42, 45, 73, 114, 116, 134, 160nn11–12
Cape franchise, 43
Cape Indian Council, 97
Cape Times (newspaper), 20
Cape Town, 13–4, 16, 28–29, 31, 39, 51, 55–57, 59, 72–80, 91, 95–97, 144–45, 165n1, 171n70
Caribbean, 15, 56, 63, 65, 69, 73, 81, 83, 147–48
Carnegie, Andrew, 37
Carnegie Foundation, 133, 135

Frazier, E. Franklin, 135
Frederick Douglass (ship), 69, 72, 83, 168n31
Freedman's Bureau, 14, 37
Friends of Negro Freedom, 85

Gandhi, Mohandas, 68, 97
Gane, P. C., 131–2, 144
Garvey, Amy Ashwood (1st wife), 65, 143
Garvey, Amy Jacques (2nd wife), 84, 127, 143
Garvey, Malchus (father), 64
Garvey, Marcus, 1–4, 9–10, 32, 40, 49, 54, 57–
    59, 63–95, 97, 99–101, 103–4, 106–7, 109,
    115, 118–20, 124–32, 140, 143–45, 166n4;
    death, 143; family, 64–65, 84, 127, 143;
    political marginalization, 126–28; trial
    and incarceration, 87–8, 92, 97, 120
Garveyism, 1–4, 9–10, 30, 32–33, 47–48, 63–64,
    70–72, 75–77, 80, 83, 85–86, 104, 143–45;
    Africa, 4, 10; South Africa, 2–4, 9, 33,
    49, 64, 71–72, 75–77, 81–82, 88–91, 93,
    95–97, 102, 105, 107–9, 118–19, 124, 143,
    145; South West Africa, 79–80; Transkei,
    105, 107–11, 120–22, 124
Garvey's Watchman (newspaper), 64
George V, King of England, 46, 103
George, David Lloyd, 47
German colonies. *See* colonies, Africa
Ghazu, James, 75, 92, 129–32
Gibson, Ewart, 28
Glen Grey Act of 1894, 17
global color line, 2, 5–8, 13, 20, 24, 27, 32,
    40–41, 82, 142, 145
Goethels (ship). *See Booker T. Washington*
    (ship)
gold, 8, 17, 48, 74, 95
Gold Coast, 74
Goncalves, Robert, 56
Gow, Francis, 91, 136
Grant, Madison, 101
Gulwa, Paul, 58, 124, 129, 144, 180n3
Gumbs, James, 78–9
Gumede, Josiah, 95

Haitian Revolution, 1791–1803, 64
Hall-Xuma, Madie, 138
Hampton Institute, Virginia, 7, 13–17, 35–37,
    40–42, 96, 133, 135–36
Hampton-Tuskegee model, 8, 82, 133, 142,
    161n20. *See also* Tuskegee Institute
Harden, Bessie Mae. *See* Payne, Bessie Mae
Harding, Warren, 85, 87
Harlem, New York, 63, 66–67, 69–71, 85, 87,
    135
Harris, Lionel, 111
Harrison, Hubert, 66–69, 85, 167n14
Hartmann, D. F., 122
Harvard University, 37–38
Haynes, Samuel, 92
Headly, Fitzherbert, 79–80, 91

Henry Highland Garnet Literary Society, 96
Herschel and Transkei Trading Company, 116
Hertzog, James, 1, 68, 98–99, 103, 114, 116,
    124–26, 140, 143
Hill, Joseph, 96
Hill, Robert A., 4
Hills, Harold, 114
Hitler, Adolf, 117, 128, 142–43
Holy Piby (Rogers), 94, 145, 177n73
Hoover, J. Edgar, 86–87
Hope, Hamilton, 122, 192–93n28
Houghton, Alfred, 135
House of Athlyi, 92–94, 144
Hughes, Charles, 71
Humble, J. C., 91
Hunter, David, 22
Hunton, Alpheus, 59

Ilanga lase Natal (newspaper), 27, 42–43, 48,
    115
Immigration Restriction Act of 1896 (U.S.),
    36, 160n11
Immigration Restriction Act of 1913 (S.A.),
    28, 43
Imvo Zabantsundu (newspaper), 16–17, 30, 38,
    42, 90, 115, 126, 144
Inanda Mission, 36, 160n12, 160–61n13
Inanda Seminary, 35, 132, 134
Independent ICU (IICU), 116, 187n89
India, 6, 15, 68, 97
Indianapolis Freeman (newspaper), 21
Indians, 36, 74, 95, 97, 101, 160n11. *See also*
    West Indians
Industrial and Commercial Workers Union
    (ICU), 9, 57, 75, 78–79, 97–99, 112
Ipepa lo Hlanga (newspaper), 42
Ireland, 6, 68, 97
Israelites. *See* Biblical imagery: Israelites
Israelites (religious group), 72, 98, 106
Italy, 80, 94, 117, 128
Izwi Labantu (newspaper), 38, 42
Izwi lama Afrika (newspaper), 122

Jabavu, D. D. T., 30–31, 89
Jabavu, John Tengu, 16, 30, 38
Jackson, William, 77, 79
Jacques, Amy. *See* Garvey, Amy Jacques
Jamaica, 49, 63–66, 71, 84, 94–95, 126–27,
    143, 145
Jamaican Advocate (journal), 64
James, C. L. R., 128
Japan, 6, 25, 32, 71, 97, 130
jazz, 135, 200n133
Jeffries, Jim, 26–27, 52
Jim Crowism, 5–6, 13, 23, 29, 32, 36–38, 64,
    67, 79, 84–85, 119, 133, 142. *See also*
    Crow, Jim
Johnson, Andrew, 14
Johnson, Jack, 8, 24–27, 32, 52, 136–37

Powell, Adam Clayton, 128
Powell, John, 85
Proffit, Joseph, 23–24

Qadi people, 35–36, 160–61nn12–13
Queenstown, 98, 106, 115

racial equality, 6, 9–10, 17, 20, 25, 32, 65, 71, 81,
    136, 139, 141
racial separatism, 63, 68, 83–85, 98, 124, 143
racism, 3–9, 13–15, 19, 22–24, 26–27, 43, 64–65,
    90, 125, 128, 137, 141–42
Radebe, Mark, 48
Ramus, Esau, 86
Randolph, A. Philip, 63, 66, 68, 75, 85–86
Rastafarian movement, 60, 94, 145, 177n73
"Regeneration of Africa, The" (essay) (Seme),
    44, 164n57
religious imagery. See Biblical imagery
reserves, 35, 42, 124, 133–34, 173n100
Rhodes, Cecil John, 43
Rhodesia, 106
Richards, Sarah Jane, 64
Richmond Planet (newspaper), 26, 39
Rising Tide of Color against White World
    Supremacy, The (Stoddard), 101
Robertson, Timothy, 55, 76–77
Robeson, Eslanda, 138
Robeson, Paul, 10, 138, 140–41
Rockefeller, John, 37
Rogers, Richard Athlyi, 93–94, 177n73
Roosevelt, Franklin, 136, 139
Roosevelt, Theodore, 25, 38
Rose, Rudolph, 39
Ross, John, 18–19
Rubusana, Walter, 53
Rumsey, F. J., 123
Russia, 25, 32

Sampson, William Henry, 23
Schauffler Missionary School, 135
Schmeling, Max, 136
Schuyler, George, 86
Scott, Horatio, 21
Scott, Reynolds, 41
segregation, 4, 23, 74; South Africa, 1–2, 4–6,
    8–9, 17–20, 23–24, 27, 32–34, 42–44, 46–
    49, 65, 74, 83, 90, 93, 97–102, 116, 124–25,
    132, 137–39, 141–43, 160n12; South West
    Africa, 79–80, 173n100. See also apartheid
Selassie, Haile, 128
Seme, Pixley, 8, 44–45, 48–49, 164n56
Semekazi, Lutoli, 129–32
Semouse, Josiah, 17
separatism. See racial separatism
Shadyside (yacht), 83, 168n31
Sherman, William T., 14
Sierra Leone, 74
Sigidi, chief of the Mpondo, 123

silicosis. See phthisis
Sinn Fein, 68
Sisulu, Walter, 109–10, 139, 142, 149
Skota, T. D. Mweli, 92
slavery, 1–2, 8, 20, 71; abolition, 14, 65;
    America, 3, 7, 13–14, 16, 80, 92, 100, 136,
    138. See also up from slavery narrative
Smuts, Jan, 5, 41–42, 44, 46–47, 68, 71–72, 98,
    103, 112, 124–26, 139, 141, 143
Soga, Allen K., 38
Sonjca, John, 31
Souls of Black Folk (Du Bois), 13, 90
Souls of White Folk (Du Bois), 71, 142
South Africa, 4–6, 8, 42–47, 96, 124–25, 140;
    African Association, 74; Department
    of Agriculture, 30; Department of the
    Interior, 28–29, 105; election, 1929, 4,
    116, 124, 140; immigration policy, 28–29;
    relationship with the United States, 13, 29
South Africa Act of 1909, 43
South African Citizens Defense Committee
    of West Indians, Coloureds, Africans and
    Indians, 74
South African Native Affairs Commission
    (SANAC), 1903, 21; final report, 1905, 22
South African Native College, 30
South African Native Convention (SANC), 43
South African Native Labour Contingent,
    46, 120
South African Native National Congress
    (SANNC), 16, 44–49, 53. See also
    African National Congress (ANC)
South African Party, 98
South African Police (SAP), 111
South African Spectator (newspaper), 38, 42
South African War, 1899–1902, 1, 4, 8, 16, 20,
    41–43, 74, 143
South African Worker (newspaper). See
    Umsebenzi (newspaper)
South America, 38, 56, 81
South West Africa, 9, 46, 59, 79–81, 84, 98,
    106, 127, 141
Southern Letter (journal), 42
Southern Workman (journal), 18, 42
Spanish-American War, 3, 25
Spooner, Kenneth, 72
St. Booker Washington Liberty Industrial
    College, 109, 116
St. Welford Universal Industrial College, 109,
    120–21
Stewart, James, 6, 95–96
Stoddard, Lothrop, 6, 101
Swaart Gevaar. See Black Peril
Swaziland, 45, 140
Swazi royal family, 44–45

Tambo, Oliver, 139, 142
taxation, 22, 108–9, 111, 120, 131, 134; without
    representation, 43, 48

Thaele, James, 9, 57, 75–76, 82–3, 95–102,
    104–5
Thema, R. V. Selope, 48
Thompson, James, 23
Thompson, Will, 19
Times of Natal (newspaper), 18, 26–27
Transkei, 103, 105, 107–18, 120–24, 129, 144
Transkeian General Council (Bunga), 113–14,
    124, 186n68
transnational black liberation movement, 13,
    32, 119, 142, 145
Transvaal, 16, 18–19, 23, 44; relationship with
    the United States, 20, 23–24
Trinidad, 74
Trotter, Monroe, 38
Turner, Henry McNeal, 19, 64
Tuskegee Institute, 26, 30, 36–38, 40, 48–50,
    52, 63, 66, 90, 95–96, 133–34, 137–38,
    140; agricultural methods, 30–31, 44;
    industrial education model, 6, 8, 30–31,
    38. *See also* Hampton-Tuskegee model
Tuskegee Student (journal), 42, 66
Tyamzashe, H. D., 78–79

Umanyano Church, 58, 129, 144
Umsebenzi (South African Worker)
    (newspaper), 101
Umteteli wa Bantu (Mouthpiece of the
    People) (newspaper), 89–91, 105, 137
Union Missionary Training Institute, 36
United Nations, 5, 41, 141–42
United Nations Universal Declaration of
    Human Rights, 67, 142
United States, 4–5, 10, 14–15, 22, 24, 27–28, 81;
    Jim Crow legislation (*see* Jim Crowism);
    laws, 19; relations with South Africa,
    13, 29; relations with the Orange Free
    State, 20
United States Department of Justice, 82–84,
    87
United States Department of State, 19, 23, 29,
    31, 83, 86, 127
United States Supreme Court, 23
Universal Negro Alliance, 86
Universal Negro Catechism (McGuire), 1, 70,
    77, 172n84
Universal Negro Improvement Association
    (UNIA), 1–2, 4, 9–10, 55, 58, 63,
    68–73, 81–88, 90, 93, 95–96, 99–100,
    115, 118, 120, 126–29, 131, 143–44;
    African Christian Church, 109, 120–21;
    churches, 109–10, 113, 120, 122, 129;
    conventions, 125–26, 130; Declaration
    of Rights of the Negro Peoples of the
    World, 67; foundation, 65–66; Liberia,
    87, 90; membership certificate, 56;
    School of African Philosophy, 144;
    schools, 109–11, 113–14, 120–23, 129–30,
    193n32; South Africa, 63, 72, 75–79,

82, 89–93, 95–97, 102, 106, 108, 114,
    129, 144–45, 165–66n1, 171n70, 188n96;
    South West Africa, 79–81; Transkei,
    110–11, 113–14, 120–24, 129–31; Wellington
    movement (*see* Wellington movement)
Universal Negro Ritual (McGuire), 1, 70
Universal Restaurant, 69
University of Alabama and Auburn, 37
University of Cape Town, 59
University of Edinburgh, 137
University of Michigan, 34, 37
Up from Slavery (Washington), 13, 38, 49, 78,
    133
up from slavery narrative, 2, 7, 13–14, 16, 19,
    24, 32, 66, 78, 81, 102, 104, 119, 138–40.
    See also slavery

Van Ness, William, 19
Van Rensselaer, Courtlandt, 96
Vereeniging, Treaty of, 42–43
Vernon, William T., 72, 89, 107–8
Versailles Peace Conference, 1919, 79, 85
Victoria, Queen of England, 46, 74, 92, 100
Vilakazi, B. W., 40
Virginia Jubilee Singers, 7, 13–19, 21, 24, 32,
    39, 51, 81, 119, 138, 145
Virginia Theological Seminary and College,
    28–29
Voice (journal), 67
Voice of Missions (newspaper), 19, 21–22
Voice of the Negro (journal), 21
Voortrekker, The (film), 25

Wallace-Johnson, I. T. A., 128
Waller, Fats, 139, 200n133
Ware, William, 127
Washington, Booker T., 2, 8, 10, 13, 16, 24, 26,
    30–34, 36–38, 40, 44–45, 48–50, 52, 57,
    63, 74, 76, 78, 81, 84–85, 90, 101, 132–34,
    138, 140; death, 66
Watt, Thomas, 28, 89
Wattlington, Emile, 79
Wellington, Butler Hansford. *See* Butelezi,
    Wellington
Wellington movement, 103–11, 113–16, 121–22
Wells, Ida B., 66, 68, 83
Welsh, Robert, 114, 121
Welsh, W. T., 122
West Indian Protective Society, 73
West Indian-American Association, 56, 78–79
West Indians, 2, 5, 7, 65–66, 129; South Africa,
    73–76, 78–79, 89; South West Africa,
    79–80. *See also* Indians
White, George, 39
White America Society, 85
White Star Line, 69
white supremacy, 4–7, 13, 27, 32, 42, 49, 71,
    74–75, 77, 81–82, 86, 96–99, 101–2,
    106–7, 109, 140, 142

Wickins, Peter, 78
Wilberforce Institute in South Africa, 136, 138
Wilberforce University, 41, 126, 136
Wilcox, William Cullen, 35
Wilkins, Roy, 138
Williams, Henry Sylvester, 54, 64, 73–75, 81, 170n64
Wilson, Woodrow, 47, 71, 143
Winfrey, Richard, 47
Wooding School, 74
Workers Herald (newspaper), 97
World (newspaper), 89
World War I, 3, 8–9, 46–47, 78, 103, 106, 120
World War II, 10, 32, 117, 142

Xaba, Jacobus, 21
Xhosa people, 90, 106, 163n43, 176n43
Xuma, Alfred B., 10, 59, 137–42
Xuma, Madie Hall. *See* Hall-Xuma, Madie

Yergan, Max, 10, 59, 138, 140
YMCA, 133, 138, 140

Zibi, Anne, 122, 124
Zibi, Edward, 120–21, 124, 189n2, 190n10
Zibi, Johannes, amaHlubi chief, 120, 190n10
Zulu people, 34, 36, 115, 126, 136
"Zulu's Message to Afro-Americans, A" (essay) (Dube), 38–39